WHEN LATINS FIGHT

WHY IS THERE
NO UNITED STATES
OF SOUTH AMERICA?

WHEN LATINS FIGHT

WHY IS THERE
NO UNITED STATES
OF SOUTH AMERICA?

WALTER THOMAS MOLANO

Graphic Design: Juan Cruz Nanclares - Rosario Salinas

Images used for cover and back cover illustration:
Batalla de Potrero Sauce (fragment), Bates y Cia.
Public domain.
Super Etenard and Sea Harrier, source: US Department of Defense
Public domain.
Batalla de Juncal (fragment), José Murature. Public domain

Images used for chapter cover page illustrations, chapters 1 and 2:
Archivo General de la Nación Dpto. Doc. Fotográficos.
Buenos Aires. Argentina.

Images used for chapter cover page illustrations, chapters 3 - 8:
Ataque a Pan de Azúcar, Carlos Wood. Public domain.
Modus-Vivendi con el Perú, Francisco Javier Vergara y Velasco.
Public domain.
Batalla de Juncal (fragment), José Murature. Public domain
Brazilian artillery, Bates y Cia. Public domain.
Paraguayan troops in Fort Alihuata, photo-reportage
Dr. Carlos De Sanctis. Public domain.

To Mary Beth

CHAPTERS

PROLOGUE.. 9

1 | COLONIAL LEGACIES 17

2 | THE CISPLATINE AND PLATINE WARS (1820–1852)..................... 27

3 | THE WAR OF THE CONFEDERATION (1836–1839)........................ 45

4 | THE WAR OF THE TRIPLE ALLIANCE (1864–1870)...................... 65

5 | THE WAR OF THE PACIFIC (1879–1884)............................. 93

6 | THE RUBBER CONFLICTS (1890–1995)............................... 121

7 | THE CHACO WAR (1932–1935)...................................... 141

8 | THE MALVINAS (1982).. 159

UNFINISHED BUSINESS... 177

PROLOGUE

The dawn of the nineteenth century was a watershed moment in history. Europe was in the midst of a revolutionary upheaval that would mark the end of autocratic monarchies. The Industrial Revolution was harnessing new economic forces that would transform technology, the productive process, and the distribution of power. At the same time, the new nations in the Americas that were sprouting from the collapse of the European monarchial system had the resources, scale, and scope to become global superpowers. The former colonies in North America were able to coalesce through a combination of vision, aggression, and assimilation—despite being of English, French, and Spanish origins—to become a leviathan that would reign beyond the end of the nineteenth century. Yet, despite its close social ties, South America crumbled into a kaleidoscope of fractious, small nations, irrelevant on the international stage and afflicted with poverty and social unrest. Yet it could have been very different. South America could have united into a single entity that would have rivaled the North American giant. Indeed, South America could still become a superpower. Therefore, this book examines this pressing question: "Why is there no United States of South America?"

From abroad, South America appears homogeneous, with similar cultural roots, a common language, and a collective colonial identity. The region's economic and political structures were comparably arranged to maximize an extractive process, with colonial institutions using coerced labor to support large mining ventures. Small groups of Europeans and their descendants controlled large slave- and indentured-labor populations by discouraging unity and promoting conflict, isolating groups by race, caste, and religion.[1] The region prospered economically until the start of the nineteenth century, when it found itself adrift after Napoleon's forces invaded the Iberian Peninsula. The South American colonists broke away in fear of being forced out of their homes by their new French overlords as had happened in other colonies, such as Quebec, Dutch Pernambuco, and various Caribbean islands.[2] With the exception of Brazil, which was converted into the seat of the Portuguese Empire—after the Braganza family, along with fifteen thousand

---

[1] Christin Cleaton, *Spaniards, Caciques, and Indians: Spanish Imperial Policy and the Construction of Caste in New Spain, 1521–1570* (Saarbrücken, Germany: VDM Verlag, 2008).

[2] John Mack Faragher, *A Great and Noble Scheme: The Tragic Story of the Expulsion of the French Acadians from their American Homeland* (New York: W.W. Norton, 2005).

members of the royal court, fled Lisbon—the colonies were suddenly forced to establish independent national frameworks, thus leading to a sudden divergence in trajectories.

Today, each South American country is very different, with specific traditions, dialects, and histories. Social identities vary greatly, appearing as diverse as the nationalities that color the European continent. Not surprisingly, the region has had its share of bloody conflicts over the centuries. All of the wars were territorial in nature, wherein ill-defined colonial demarcations were often settled militarily, but they were generally abetted by the commercial interests of external powers—particularly the United Kingdom and the United States.

Although the major South American wars are not within the everyday lexicon of Western military history, they were extremely violent affairs—with a total of six hundred thousand casualties—and critical in shaping the course of regional development. Several excellent works have examined these conflicts, including Robert Scheina's *Latin America's Wars (Volumes I and II)*.[3] Scheina presents, in great depth, the conflicts that punctuated the region, outlining the tactics, strategies, and heroism displayed. René de La Pedraja's *Wars of Latin America* series provides an exhaustive examination of the battles that raged throughout South and Central America.[4] Additionally, Miguel Angel Centeno's work *Blood and Debt* takes a deep look at the internal capacities of Latin American countries to engage in war.[5] Centano finds that the lack of many of the traditional domestic institutions found in bellicose societies, such as strong militaristic traditions or fiscal resources, did not impede Latin American states from coming to blows.

It is important to note that there have been countless books that have delved deeply into individual conflicts, providing crucial insights into the political, economic, and social forces that led to the outbreak of hostilities, as well as the conduct of the war and the outcomes. However, this work takes a step back from the myopia of the battlefield to examine the international context, as well as how each conflict shaped the region's map in many ways: by establishing important precedents that have impeded regional integration; by sowing the seeds of the deep distrust that flourishes in the region; by affecting trade and investment flows, as well as the distribution of power; and, finally, by cementing South America's perception

[3]   Robert L. Scheina, *Latin America's Wars, Volume I: The Age of the Caudillo, 1791–1899* (Washington, DC: Brassey's Incorporated, 2003); Robert L. Scheina, *Latin America's Wars, Volume II: The Age of the Professional Soldier, 1900–2001* (Washington, DC: Brassey's Incorporated, 2003).

[4]   René De La Pedraja, *Wars of Latin America: 1899–1941* (Jefferson, NC: McFarland & Company, Inc., 2006); René De La Pedraja, *Wars of Latin America, 1948–1982: The Rise of the Guerrillas* (Jefferson, NC: McFarland & Company, Inc., 2013); René De La Pedraja, *Wars of Latin America, 1982–2012: The Path to Peace* (Jefferson, NC: McFarland & Company, Inc., 2013).

[5]   Miguel Angel Centeno, *Blood and Debt: War and the Nation-State in Latin America* (University Park, PA: Pennsylvania State University Press, 2002).

of and relationship with the rest of the world. Not only is it important to establish the forces that led to each conflict but also critical to identify the common denominators in order to tease out the causal factors. In this way, we can address these problems and set the stage for further political and economic cooperation.

War is the ultimate form of political violence. Ideally, it is the instrument resorted to only after diplomatic means are exhausted—the use of raw power to protect national interests. There is a rich and extensive literature on war. A very interesting perspective is the concept of *enduring rivalries*. Scholars such as Paul F. Diehl and Gary Goertz model the competition between biological species to study the rivalry between states.[6] Stuart Bremer develops the concept of *dangerous dyads*, neighboring states whose characteristics lead to a greater propensity to engage in military conflicts, including stunted economic developed and weak democracies.[7] The problem is exacerbated if they are part of an empire that abruptly disappears.[8] In the case of South America, the viceroyalties were the administrative units used by the Spanish colonial system. The collapse of the empire at the start of the nineteenth century unexpectedly converted these units into a handful of large states, with similar sizes, and with very fragile economies and democracies. The boundaries between these dyads were poorly defined, due to the nature of the colonial system. Although most of the disputes were resolved peacefully, several of them erupted in bloody conflicts.

Indeed, all of the South American disputes had common elements, which centered on territorial issues. This allows us to establish a hypothetical question: What led to the wars? I found that there were three necessary conditions. The first was uncertainty about the lines of demarcation. The second was the presence of strategic natural resources in the disputed region, either in the form of a commodity or geographical location; strategic locations, such as the mouth of an important waterway or a deepwater port, can be as valuable as an abundant natural resource. The third was the presence of an external instigator. None of these factors alone guaranteed a war, but when combined together, the three conditions typically ignited an armed conflict. By using this conceptual framework, we can examine the forces that led to the wars, the conduct of the war, and the outcomes.

The interregional wars had major implications for individual countries. They established a clear list of winners and losers. The fate of Bolivia, for example, was sealed during the War of the Confederation and the War of the Pacific. The aspirations of Paraguay were permanently crushed during the War of the Triple Alliance.

---

[6]   Paul F. Diehl and Gary Goertz, *War and Peace in International Rivalry* (Ann Arbor, MI: University of Michigan Press, 2000).

[7]   Stuart Bremer, "Dangerous Dyads: Conditions Affecting the Likelihood of Interstate War, 1816–1965," *Journal of Conflict Resolution* 36, no. 2 (1992): 309–341.

[8]   Niall Ferguson, "Complexity and Collapse: Empires on the Edge of Chaos," *Foreign Affairs*, March/April 2010.

In these three engagements, Bolivia and Paraguay lost their access to the sea, a condition that sentences them to grievous impoverishment. The Cisplatine and Platine conflicts defined the border between Brazil and Argentina, and led to the birth of Uruguay. Likewise, the various Rubber Wars transformed the Amazon into one of the most prized possessions of the southern continent—and triggered a series of confrontations that allowed Colombia, Peru, Brazil, Ecuador, and Bolivia to come to blows and exchange territories. All of these engagements implanted the traces of hatred, jealousy, and rivalry that permeate the continent to this day. They are one of the most important reasons why South American governments are so distrustful of each other and why most attempts at regional integration fail, despite the countries' enormous similarities, proximities, and opportunities for cooperation.

This work examines the interregional conflicts that had the most important impact on shaping the region. It purposely skips the wars of liberation, which were campaigns against a common enemy. This book also avoids the civil wars that roiled almost all of the countries. Civil wars are internal affairs influenced by domestic issues, although it is also true that almost all external conflicts have an internal component as well. The War of the Confederation, for example, was as much a civil war between northern and southern Peru as it was a struggle between Chile and the Peruvian-Bolivian Confederation. Yet, in order to allow for a more parsimonious analysis, I narrowed the list to six general engagements.[9] This allowed me to employ a more comparative, in-depth approach to understand how each conflict started and how each affected interregional relations, development, and cooperation.

A comparative framework can go a long way toward relating and differentiating among countries and events, making it possible to tease out the most important variables and how they interact. This methodology has been used successfully by such scholars as Wim Klooster, who employed it in *Revolutions in the Atlantic World*.[10] The approach allows scholars to dissect the legacies and international factors of each case, and to study how each war changed the balance of power in the region and affected the scope for future cooperation.

The book begins with the Cisplatine and Platine Wars between Argentina and Brazil. Not only did this conflict lead to the birth of Uruguay, it cemented the schism that would darken relations between these two regional giants. This is followed by an examination of the War of the Confederation, which was an attempt by Peru and Bolivia to come together into a single state, an effort thwarted by Chile. Not only did that war hamstring the Bolivian economy by forcing it to rely

9   The chapter on the rubber wars is the compilation of three separate conflicts. I also add a seventh conflict, the Malvinas; it is not a purely interregional war, but it is an important campaign for the region.

10 Wim Klooster, *Revolutions in the Atlantic World: A Comparative History* (New York: New York University Press, 2009).

on a series of small ports along the Atacama Desert for its principle access to the outside world, but it also demonstrated Chile's dark side. Chile is very small geographically, but its proclivity for aggression has always made it a contender well above its weight class.

The third conflict, the War of the Triple Alliance, introduced an important twist in regional confrontations. While the early conflicts revolved around territorial disputes, subsequent ones had more geopolitical elements. In the case of the War of the Confederation, Chile fought desperately to avert the unification of Peru and Bolivia because it feared that the creation of a larger state would dwarf its own capabilities. Brazil, Uruguay, and Argentina used the War of the Triple Alliance as a means to subvert the hopes of Paraguay to use the superior technology and organization that would allow it to emerge as a regional powerhouse.

By the end of the nineteenth century, the nature of the interregional wars had shifted once more. Although there were still territorial and geopolitical elements to all the conflicts, they were incited by external powers seeking access to rare industrial natural resources, such as nitrates, rubber, and oil. Not surprisingly, these proxy wars took form as Europe and North America moved headlong into the Industrial Revolution, increasing their demand for raw materials.

The first of these new engagements was the War of the Pacific, where Chile, once again, took on Peru and Bolivia. This time it was at the behest of British interests. Well armed and trained, Chile was able to lay waste to the two countries, permanently reducing Bolivia to a landlocked status and occupying the Peruvian capital for four years. The next chapter is an amalgamation of the various Rubber Wars that were fought in the Amazon. As in the War of the Pacific, external forces were also at work. In this case, the Americans and British led the way. Oil played a central role in the sixth conflict, the Chaco War, when Bolivia and Paraguay battled over a hydrocarbon field that never existed. The chapter on the Malvinas is not a war between Latins, although Chile did play an important role in aiding and abetting Britain; still, it was territorial in nature, and it highlighted the high level of military sophistication that can be displayed by South American military forces.

The chapters highlight the vast differences that mark the region. They stress the reasons why the desire for regional integration remains low, despite the benefits that would be gained from greater cooperation, trade, and investment. Shared values, religion, and cultural elements are characteristics that that are rare across other large regions of the planet, but they are not enough to overcome South America's internal and external grudges. Of course, the continent's reluctance for greater integration is a boon for Europe, North America, and Asia. The unification of South America could transform it into a superpower. Although keeping South America divided is hardly an acknowledged policy objective in Washington, Brussels, or Tokyo, the continent's lack of integration serves other power brokers well. Indeed, one of the motivations behind Simón Bolívar's ("The Liberator") attempt to permanently establish Gran Colombia was to produce a state that could rival the large states emerging in Europe and North America. Such a dream must have raised many eyebrows in the fine salons of Paris, London, and Washington. It might also have been the root cause of the diplomatic intrigues used to sow mistrust and dissent among the nascent republics.

It is important to note that many Latin American engagements have not been addressed in this book. In addition to the wars of liberation and civil wars, I did not include some of the smaller conflicts, particularly those in Central America and the Caribbean. The Gran Colombia–Peru War of 1828 is mentioned in the chapter on the War of the Confederation, but it was a short conflict with only two major battles. Some of the Central American wars bordered on the ridiculous, such as the Football War, when El Salvador and Honduras fought over a football grudge on the eve of the 1970 World Cup. Tensions between the two countries had been on the rise for several years. While Honduras was five times the physical size of El Salvador, the latter had twice the population. A large influx of Salvadorian immigrants had been causing social problems in both countries, to the extent that any spark could have lit the powder keg. In this case, it was a football match. The skirmish itself was no laughing matter, however—three thousand people died in the "100-Hour War"—but I chose to exclude it here because it was more of a footnote in Latin American military lore than a turning point in regional development. A similar conflict was the Coto War between Panama and Costa Rica in 1921, which was fought over a small border village.

This work does not examine the various incursions made by external powers into Latin America, such as blockades and invasions. Despite the tenets of the Monroe Doctrine, which warned European countries to keep out of Latin American politics, foreign forces constantly intervened in the continent's affairs. Sometimes, it was to gain access to markets. Other times, it was to recoup defaulted loans. Often, interventions were intended to redirect political trends, and some employed military force, while others were effected through proxies, particularly mercenaries, who were ready and able to sail into action for the right price.

Last of all, this book does not study the countless buildups that *almost* resulted in wars. There were many incidents that almost erupted into open hostilities: the Beagle conflict between Argentina and Chile in 1978; Colombia's incursion into Ecuadorian airspace to kill FARC leader Raul Reyes in 2008; the Colombian-Venezuelan tensions in 2009 and 2010. However, full-blown crises were averted by cooler minds or external intervention. Nevertheless, these incidents resonate within the context of the conflicts that are examined in these pages. They are part of the historical fabric and collective memory that makes up the geopolitical and sociological maps of Latin America.

Examining these differences, similarities, and events leads to a more robust understanding of the region—an appreciation of both the forces that ripped the countries apart and the impediments that they must overcome if they desire greater cooperation and economic integration. These legacies constitute the undercurrents that shape regional discussions involving trade, cross-border investment, and political cooperation. Last of all, they facilitate a multidimensional understanding of Latin America that transcends the typical two-dimensional presentation.

1 COLONIAL LEGACIES

COLONIAL LEGACIES

The study of South America always begins with an examination of the colonial legacies left by Spain. Fifteenth-century Spain was savage. Eight centuries of unending wars had molded the Spanish who arrived on the shores of the Americas into conquerors, not explorers. The Iberian Peninsula has always differed from its European neighbors. Although an integral part of the continental landmass, the barrier formed by the Pyrenees and its proximity to Africa allowed the people of the peninsula to maintain a closer affinity with the Maghreb than with the rest of Europe. Indeed, the southern part of the peninsula became an essential part of the Carthaginian Empire in 575 BCE, transforming it into one of the most prosperous provinces of the Mediterranean. In 206 BCE, Carthage ceded the Iberian Peninsula to Rome as part of the peace treaty that ended the Second Punic War. Known for its rich mines, olive oil, and wool, Hispania became an affluent part of the Roman Empire. The Romans constructed large cities with impressive public works in Mérida, Segovia, and Alentejo. However, the decline of the empire eventually allowed the Vandals and Visigoths to pour across the mountains and overrun the Roman garrisons.

By the fifth century CE, Carthage had fallen, eliminating one of the last remaining pillars of stability in the Western Mediterranean. The ensuing anarchy produced a vacuum across the North Africa plain that was soon filled by the Islamic hordes spilling in from the east. Less than a century after the Prophet Muhammad's death, Moorish armies stood poised on the straits of Gibraltar. They made the crossing at the turn of the eighth century, and over the next four years, they swept through the entire peninsula, defeating the Iberian tribes. They called it Al-Andalus, or the Land of the Vandals. Under the command of the Umayyads, who had fled a power struggle in Damascus, the Moors brought order and civilization to a place that had been wrecked by several centuries of pillaging and chaos. Over the next eight hundred years, Al-Andalus flowered into a beacon of science, art, philosophy, medicine, architecture, and mathematics. It became an oasis of tolerance that allowed a kaleidoscope of beliefs and cultures to coexist.

Nevertheless, age-old tribal rivalries and disputes among the ruling caliphates in the surrounding regions eventually poisoned Al-Andalus. Although most of the indigenous tribes were subdued in the resulting battles, a small band of Visigoths held out in the rugged mountains of the Cantabric coast. Over the course of time, those tribes had converted to Christianity, and now they were pursuing a crusade to regain their lost lands. In 718 CE, the Visigoth King Pelayo scored the first victory against the Moors at the Battle of Alcama. The incident was nothing more than a skirmish for the Moorish forces, but it marked an important psychological turning point. Slowly, the Christians began to beat back the Islamic invaders. For the next eight centuries, they drove farther south. Facing superior numbers, technology, and firepower, they were forced to rely on deceit and guile to divide and conquer the enemy.

The major milestone in the struggle occurred in 1009, when the Hammudids, led by a Berber army, sacked Medina Azahara, the royal palace of the Umayyads' caliph, Hisham III, in a bloody confrontation. The defeat marked the end of the Umayyad Caliphate. The Kingdom of Cordoba fragmented into almost two dozen *taifas*, or Muslim-ruled kingdoms or principalities. Heartened by the crumbling of the Moorish juggernaut, the Christians quickly provided military support to the sparring states. By exploiting differences among the Moors, the Christians picked off the weaker states and advanced farther south. In reality, the reconquest of Spain was the self-immolation of the Moorish empire.

Unfortunately, a pall of intellectual darkness fell over the Iberian Peninsula as the Christian forces marched closer to the Mediterranean. As each city fell, it was sacked, with libraries burned and madrasas (schools) torched. The region was slowly infected by the same lack of intellectual curiosity characteristic of Christian Europe during the Dark Ages. The Christian conquerors went to great pains to suppress many of the great advances in arts and sciences that had been achieved by the polytheist Roman and Greek civilizations, so convinced were they of the supremacy of their own monotheistic beliefs.

In 1492, Granada, the last bastion of Moorish power, fell. Flush with the booty that had been looted from the rich citadel, the Spanish monarchs decided to invest in a Genoese-led expedition to find a new trade route to Asia. Although he never admitted it, the itinerant Christopher Columbus never made it to his intended destination. Instead, he found two continents, brimming with unfamiliar agricultural products and precious metals. First, however, the Europeans had to deal with the Aztecs and Incas. Faced with the proposition of taking on two daunting adversaries, the Spanish immediately reverted to the tactics that they had used against the Moors. Like the Moors, the Aztec and Inca civilizations were technologically and numerically superior, but they were also badly divided—and they had plenty of resentful neighbors that were more than willing to settle old scores by allying themselves with the invaders.

To that end, the Spanish unfurled three tactics to gain control. Continuing their tradition of deeply mistrusting all alien technology and culture, they employed brute force to eradicate existing social, cultural, religious, and leadership organizations and traditions. The Aztecs and Incas had made great strides in medicine, astronomy, and architecture; unfortunately, the Spaniards' destruction of records, structures, and property set the region's knowledge capital back by hundred of years. Second, they resorted to treachery as an essential element of their military campaigns, forging temporary alliances with smaller tribes to move aggressively against powerful adversaries, and then betraying their allies after winning the battles. Third, they used their age-old "divide and conquer" tactics, imposing a caste system based on religious, ethnic, and tribal differences, dominating large groups by disenfranchising them; this was the main reason why the Spanish eradicated all existing organizations and institutions. Through the imposition of a new religious and social order, the colonists were able to gain control over a large segment of the population.

Unfortunately, the various mechanisms the Spanish used to gain and maintain control became permanent features of Latin America, and serious impediments to its economic development.[11] The three tactics evolved into the central tenets of Spanish colonial administration, and they became even more effective when mining became the main objective of the enterprise. Mining is labor intensive, requiring a massive work force. To maintain control over such a large population, the Spanish divided the population into categories and castes, and each group had defined rights, benefits, and obligations; this fomented competition rather than cooperation, effectively keeping the groups from forming alliances and rebelling. At the bottom of the social pyramid were the slaves and indigenous people; above them were the mestizos (part Spanish) and freed slaves; above them were the *criollos*, or creoles, the second-generation Europeans of Latin American birth; and at the very top of the pyramid were the *peninsulares*, the Spaniards who were born in Europe. Spaniards born in Latin America were treated differently from those born in Europe to ensure that no one with mixed blood could occupy senior positions of authority. Of course, that practice infuriated the creoles, and it became one of the drivers behind the independence movement.

The emphasis on social order and European-controlled stability gave Latin America its conservative tilt. The countries with greater social mobility, such as Argentina and Uruguay, were those with smaller indigenous populations. Given that these were not mining regions, their native populations were pushed into the hinterlands—or exterminated through military campaigns similar to those employed in North America. However, the countries with large mineral deposits, such as the Andean nations of Peru, Bolivia, and Colombia, required a large labor force. Instead of eradicating the native population, the Spanish harnessed it by establishing their rigid social systems.

These legacies are still shared throughout the region, and the concept of social control is emblazed on several flags. Both Colombia and Brazil have the word "order" sewn on their national standards. Unfortunately, the emphasis on social control later worked against these countries during times of war. Uneducated and

[11]   Misha Kokotovic, *The Colonial Divide in Peruvian Narrative: Social Conflict and Transculturation* (East Sussex, England: Sussex Academic Press, 2007); Murdo J. MacLeod and Robert Wasserstrom (Eds.), *Spaniards and Indians in Southeastern Mesoamerica: Essays on the History of Ethnic Relations* (Lincoln, NE: University of Nebraska Press, 1983).

unmotivated troops make poor soldiers. Often, the lack of allegiance and motivation among the troops to fight prolonged the conflicts and inflated costs in terms of resources and soldiers. It also affected the organization of the countries' defensive forces. Most of the militaries in Latin America were focused on suppressing insurrections and rebellions to maintain internal order. They were often unprepared for cross-border campaigns. Troops and equipment were usually deployed in large urban areas, not along the borders.

The emphasis on social control also politicized the military; used to put down uprisings or repress political adversaries, they were imbued with the high commands' overt political agendas.[12] Nevertheless, some of the militaries were more offensive in nature. This was particularly the case in Chile, a country whose territory encompasses a narrow strip of land that hugs the western littoral of the continent. Like a porcupine with prickly bristles, Chile always displayed its impressive military preparedness to dissuade invaders and, meanwhile, impose its will on its neighbors.

Besides the legacies of imposed religion and social order, the Spanish institutionalized their form of colonial organization. In the same way that the social system was structured to dominate a large population, the colonial regions were organized to maximize control over the exploitation of precious metals. Colonists could own land, but the subsoil and mineral rights were property of the crown, and they were administered through Seville. The monarch appointed viceroys as the direct representatives. These individuals were assisted by *audiencias*, or royal courts, which mainly consisted of judges who listened to complaints, adjudicated disputes, and implemented royal decrees. Initially, the Spanish American colonies were divided into two viceroyalties, but they were eventually reorganized into four, of which New Spain was the most important. It centered on the immense silver operations in México, and included Central America, the Caribbean, and the Philippines. The second-most important was Peru, which included the huge indigenous population that survived the decimation of the Inca Empire, as well as the immense mining operations of Alto Perú. The third viceroyalty was Nueva Grenada, which covered the small mining operations throughout present-day Colombia, Ecuador, and Venezuela. The last viceroyalty to be created was Río de la Plata in 1776. Although this fourth region did not have any major mining operations, it was organized as a means to stem the contraband activity that was siphoning off a significant portion of the silver produced in Potosí. The viceroyalties were subdivided into smaller units called captaincies. They usually represented nonstrategic, non-mining regions, such as present-day Chile and Central America.

---

[12] The Bourbon Reforms of 1776, which allowed creoles to become officers in the colonial military, converted the military into a vehicle for social mobility. As a result, the most ambitious individuals enrolled in an attempt to realize their aspirations. The politicization of the military eventually led to a tradition of coups and dictatorships that can be traced back to the first days of the republics.

Although the viceroyalties and captaincies were rooted in Spanish traditions, they also developed their own cultural identities, and these persist to this day. South American accents and dialects are largely grouped around the original vice-royalties.[13] For example, Ríoplatense Spanish is the dialect spoken in the Greater Buenos Aires area, Uruguay, Mesopotamia, and Paraguay. Not surprisingly, this was the center of the viceroyalty of Río de la Plata. Farther south and west, the dialect changes dramatically in the regions that were under the command of the captaincy of Chile. Likewise, the regions that comprised the viceroyalty of Peru, which consist of modern-day Peru and Bolivia, share similar linguistic traits. Last of all, the territories of the viceroyalty of Nueva Granada, which evolved into Colombia, Venezuela, and Ecuador, speak with similar intonations and vocabulary.[14]

The same was true with respect to basic diets. South American national cuisines developed along European and local traditions. Nevertheless, the identities were delineated by viceroyalty.[15] The heavy use of beans and rice runs deep across the nations that emerged from Nueva Granada. Meanwhile, the prevalent use of grilled meats is characteristic of the countries that were part of the viceroyalty of Río de la Plata. The use of maize-type of grains, such as choclo and corn, are part of the basic diet in the nations that were once part of the viceroyalty of Peru. The same can be said for liquor. Sugarcane-based aguardiente is typical of the Nueva Granadian countries of Colombia, Venezuela, and Ecuador. Chileans and Peruvians both claim to have invented pisco, a fruit brandy, and argue over who makes the best variation. Even the Ecuadorians get into the tussle. Such trivial-seeming competitions are ingrained characteristics of the viceroyalty system, which was often in flux. Changes in Spanish monarchs, palace intrigues, or competitions among viceroys led to reforms that reconstituted territorial responsibilities or even created new viceroyalties. For example, the viceroyalties of Río de la Plata and Nueva Granada were carved out of the viceroyalty of Peru.

Given that the region was part of a larger empire, the boundaries were not designed to sustain individual states. That became a problem after independence from Spain. The colonial lines of demarcation became the legal basis for the formation of new, independent countries. At the 1826 Panama Congress, Simón Bolívar cited the principle of *uti possidetis juris,* a roman legal term that postulates that the territory and property of a conquered land remains with the victorious party, define the independent nations. In other words, the territories and assets of the viceroyalties and captaincies remained with the forces that liberated them. Un-

---

13 Manuel Alvar López, *Manual de Dialectología Hispánica: El Español de América* (Barcelona: Ariel, 1996).

14 Luis Flórez, *El Español Hablado en Colombia y su Atlas Lingüístico: Presente y Futuro de la Lengua Española* (Madrid: OFINES, 1964).

15 Kenneth F. Kiple, *A Movable Feast: Ten Millennia of Food Globalization* (Cambridge: Cambridge University Press, 2007).

fortunately, this later led to tensions within the newly established countries.[16] It is important to reiterate that the Spanish colonial authorities organized the territory to maximize the efficiency and defense of mining operations, not to optimize the political and economic functionality of sovereign nations. One of the places where the new demarcations created enormous problems was in Alto Perú, which was spun off into Bolivia. It became the center of two of the bloodiest regional conflicts of the nineteenth century, the War of the Confederation and the War of the Pacific. The outcome was to cut the country off from the rest of the world and allow it to wither into one of the poorest nations on the planet.

Another important legacy of Spanish colonialism was the mercantilist commercial system. The colonies were captive markets for Spanish merchants and brokers. The colonies were not allowed to industrialize or trade with any other nations, which meant that they had to import most of their manufactured goods from authorized agents. This allowed Spain to maximize profits from every part of the mining operations, right down to trading in supplies. Not only did this create huge inefficiencies and stunt economic development, but it also stymied interregional trade, communication, and trust. All commercial activities were bilateral, with Spain. As a result, there was almost no interconnection among the various colonies. The lack of interaction fueled mistrust, manifesting as jealousies, rivalries, and even war. Unfortunately, the legacy still survives. The connections among Latin American countries are extremely limited. There are often just a few border crossings. As recently as two decades ago, most telephone calls and flights between South American countries had to go through the United States or Europe. Sadly, there remains a great deal of deep animosity between the South American states.

Obviously, these colonial legacies left indelible marks on the South American psyche. Not only do they explain some of the inherent social and economic problems that led to chronic underdevelopment, but they also established the basis for future conflicts. Moreover, the lack of integration and the emphasis on bilateral trade help scholars understand why regional commerce and investments remain so low. In 2010, for example, inter-Latin American trade was $133 billion, representing only 6.5 percent of total exports and imports.[17] Meanwhile, intraregional trade in Europe accounted for almost a third of all external commercial activity. The situation was even more acute in cross-border foreign direct and portfolio investment. That same year, less than 4 percent of the region's foreign direct investment was directed at other Latin American countries. Portfolio investments were even less. Latin America has enormous potential for expanding trade and investment.

[16]   Paul R. Hensel and Michael E. Allison, "The Colonial Legacy and Border Stability: *Uti Possidetis* and Territorial Claims in the Americas" (paper presented at the International Studies Association Meeting, Montreal, 2004).

[17]   2011. "Latin America Inter-Region Trade Soared 24.6% in 2010." *MercoPress*, February 2. Retrieved from http://en.mercopress.com/2011/02/02/latin-america-inter-region-trade-soared-24.6-in-2010

With a combined GDP that rivals those of Europe, the United States, and China, a population of more than half a billion people—not to mention a very young society, overall—Latin America could become an engine of global economic growth. Yet, it is not. The following chapters will delve deeper into the conflicts that deepened the schisms among these countries in order to establish a better understanding of the factors that have impeded regional cooperation and economic integration.

2 THE CISPLATINE AND PLATINE WARS: THIS SIDE AND THAT

THE CISPLATINE AND PLATINE WARS:
THIS SIDE AND THAT

On December 1, 1807, a regiment commanded by General Jean-Andoche Junot marched into Lisbon. Junot was under strict orders to arrest Prince Regent Dom João VI, along with other members of the royal family, for their refusal to adhere to Napoleon's Continental System. When he arrived, however, he found the capital deserted. Two days earlier, on November 29, the Braganza family, along with fifteen thousand citizens and members of the royal court, had decamped for Brazil, conveyed by and under the protection of fifty-eight British warships. This relocation of the monarchy marked the start of an era that imbued the Portuguese colony with territorial ambitions that would reshape the boundaries of South America.

Portugal's presence in South America commenced six years after the 1494 signing Treaty of Tordesillas, when Pedro Álvares Cabral debarked in present-day Bahia, Brazil. The accord had been a diplomatic solution to a conflict that appeared after Columbus returned from his voyage of discovery. The Kingdom of Portugal claimed Africa, but it wanted to make sure that the new discoveries did not encroach on its domain. Therefore, the two sides decided to divide the globe along a line of demarcation that was 370 leagues, roughly two thousand kilometers, west of Cape Verde Islands. Spain was granted exclusive rights over any undiscovered lands west of the line, while Portugal controlled everything to the east. Unbeknownst to the two kingdoms, the eastern rump of South America juts into Portugal's realm. Thus, Cabral's landfall in 1500 allowed Portugal to legally claim part of South America, even though the New World had previously been considered as solely under Spanish domain. This brought two of Europe's most powerful kingdoms in direct contact, and it would be the genesis of future conflicts.

The new Portuguese colony prospered, thanks to its lucrative timber and sugar industries, but it lacked the precious metals that abounded in the Spanish colonies. Therefore, Brazil did not play such an important role in the Portuguese imperial system. It was a chess piece on a vast board that included colonies in Africa and Asia.

Most of the Brazilian settlements were scattered along the Atlantic coast. Hence, the administration of the colony was relatively simple, with maritime transportation being the main form of communication. This allowed the Portuguese to use Salvador, the capital of Bahia, as its base, thus avoiding the segmentation of the colony into separate viceroyalties, as the Spanish had done with their territories.

The discovery of gold and precious stones at the very end of the seventeenth century, deep in the hinterlands of Río de Janeiro, elevated the importance of the colony. Almost overnight, the hamlet of Vila Rica became the center of a gold rush. In 1720, the region was separated from the captaincy of São Paulo and renamed Minas Gerais. For the next century, the mines produced twelve hundred tons of gold, accounting for 80 percent of global production. Not surprisingly, the nexus of colonial power shifted south, with the viceroy moving to Río de Janeiro in order to exert tighter control over the lucrative operations. The gold boom brought new life to the Portuguese empire. Taxing 20 percent of the gold that was produced allowed the empire to modernize its military and deepen its global trade operations. Therefore, by the time Dom João was escaping Napoleonic invasion, Brazil had already become the crown jewel of the Portuguese empire; that was the very reason why he had chosen it for his self-imposed exile.

On January 22, 1808, the British fleet arrived in Salvador, allowing the weary passengers to disembark. The crossing had been hard on the royal court. Two of the ships suffered massive infestations of lice; their passengers, ladies of the court, had been forced to shave off their hair and wrap their bald heads in turbans. When the turbaned ladies arrived, the people of Bahia thought that this was the latest European fashion and rushed to do the same. The entourage rested for several weeks before continuing onto Río de Janeiro, where they arrived on March 7. Not only was the escape from Lisbon a historic feat, but it also marked the only relocation of a European imperial court to the New World. This was a momentous event for South America, particularly for Brazil. Although the region was prosperous thanks to its lucrative mining operations, it had remained a backwater. There were oases of education and culture, but local elites lacked sophistication. Fortunately, things were about to change.

The House of Braganza was an important European dynasty, commanding one of the largest empires on the planet. Its diplomatic corps was talented, and well versed in geopolitical maneuvering, international law, and strategic thinking. The military high command was trained in the latest technologies and tactics. The Kingdom of Portugal's fleet of heavily armed frigates, or men-of-war, was considered to be among the deadliest warships on the high seas, with crews who were extremely well disciplined. Despite the small size of the country, the regime's institutions had given Portugal the ways and means to compete against larger European rivals, and the transfer of these resources to Brazil energized the colony. Soon, the ambitions and maneuverings that were typical of European courts were at work in the sweltering tropics of South America.

While unpacking their baggage, the Portuguese fugitives knew that their world was crumbling. Spain was in turmoil. Years of war had wrecked the economy. General disaffection with the political and economic uncertainty turned into bloody riots. Within days of Dom João VI's arrival in Río de Janeiro, the Spanish monarch, Charles IV, was forced to abdicate. His son, Ferdinand VII, who clung to power for just six weeks, replaced him. Then Napoleon, smelling weakness, installed his older brother, Joseph Bonaparte, on the throne. This raised consternation in the colonies, as they watched their homeland disintegrate into a series of juntas that continued to fight. One by one, the juntas fell to the French onslaught, leaving the colonies isolated and vulnerable.

Even before the start of the Napoleonic invasion, major European powers had been trying to pick off the most valuable colonies. In 1806 and 1808, British forces tried to invade the rich port of Buenos Aires, only to be defeated and repelled by local militias. The colonists believed that it was only a matter of time until the new French overlords arrived to end their prosperous way of life. It had happened many times in the past, including their expulsion of the Moors from the Iberian Peninsula at the start of the sixteenth century. That is why in 1810, after the collapse of the Junta of Seville, most of the Spanish colonies declared independence. However, not all of the colonies broke away. Cities with large royal garrisons, such as Lima and Montevideo, remained loyal to Spain for far longer. They became the bastions for the bloody counterattacks that would embroil the region in flames for more than a decade. It was within this mayhem that the newly arrived Portuguese court decided to put its skills to work by making a land grab for the remnants of Spanish empire, a conflict that evolved into the Cisplatine and Platine Wars.

Dom João VI was a corpulent man, and he was never supposed to become king. Second in the line of succession, he was thrust into the role when his older brother, Dom José, died of smallpox in 1788. There had been great hopes for Dom José. He was intelligent, and he embraced the ideals of the Enlightenment. There had been optimism that he would modernize the country and pull Portugal out of its feudal condition. Unfortunately, his younger brother was his exact opposite. Dom João was conservative, blindly espousing the tenets of absolutism. To complicate matters, his mother, Maria I, had been declared mad in 1792; Dom João had been named prince regent, empowered to reign until she died and he could be named king. His accession to power coincided with the French Revolution, and the turmoil that spread throughout the rest of the continent.[18] Therefore, he ruled with an iron grip, and introduced an authoritarian atmosphere to his new seat of government.

Under Dom João, Brazil was transformed into the embodiment of the Portuguese sovereign state. It was no longer a colony. It was the "new" Portugal, and Río de Janeiro was its capital. For the next years, the royal entourage focused on fitting out the city, constructing palaces, organizing institutions, and building infrastructure. The government established universities, imported printing presses, and formed banks. The monarch laid the groundwork for great public works, including the construction of the botanical gardens in Río de Janeiro and the mint.[19]

---

[18] Oliveira Lima, *Dom João VI No Brazil: 1808–1821* (Río de Janeiro: De Rodrigues & Co., 1908).

[19] Anyda Marchant, "Dom João's Botanical Garden," *Hispanic American Historical Review* 41, no. 2 (1961), 259–274.

Yet, there were problems in the private quarters of the royal family. Despite Dom João's authoritarian demeanor, he was weak—and he was married to a strong-willed Spanish woman, Doña Carlota Joaquína. She was the daughter of the abdicated Spanish king, Charles IV, and the sister of the deposed sovereign, Ferdinand VII. Wildly ambitious, she schemed to carve a new monarchy on the western shores of the Atlantic—with herself as the queen of the River Plate. Using political connections in Spain and the Americas, she hatched a plot to take control of the former Spanish colonies, claiming that her royal lineage made her the rightful successor. The enterprise became known as Carlotism.[20]

Portugal always sought control of the River Plate. The rivers that flowed into the estuary provided fluvial access to the southwestern fringes of Brazil, particularly the states of Río Grande do Sul, Mato Grosso, and Santa Catarina. The administrative seat of one of the most powerful Spanish colonies, Buenos Aires, was on the western shore, but the eastern side was relatively empty. The Eastern Band, as it was known at the time, was bereft of natural resources. It was also inhabited by roaming bands of mestizos called gauchos, who focused most of their activities on herding cattle through the vast grasslands that extended through parts of modern-day Argentina, Uruguay, and southern Brazil.[21] To impose a more notable presence, the Portuguese established the military fort of Colónia do Sacramento directly across the river from Buenos Aires, but it never achieved the presence that they were seeking. That opportunity would come after the Napoleonic wars.

Doña Carlota's plan was to begin with the territories on the near side of the River Plate, and then advance on the other colonies. Thus, the Portuguese court set in motion a series of events that culminated in the Cisplatine and Platine Wars. *Cis* is a Latin word meaning "the near side of something." *Plata* is the Spanish word for silver, making the Río de la Plata the "River of Silver." In English, Platine means "near the River Plate." Therefore, Cisplatine means "this side of the river of silver." The annexation of the closest bank of the river would provide the royal military with a base from which it could to launch a campaign to take over the other side, which was one of the richest colonies of the Spanish empire.

The wheels swirled into motion after Napoleon's defeat in 1815. With the French despot defeated, the court could safely return home. However, Dom João wanted to stay; he was happy in his tropical capital, as was his queen, who was scheming to stitch together her own kingdom from the debris of the Spanish empire. As a result, the government decided to elevate the colonial outpost to the same status as Portugal by creating the United Kingdom of Portugal, Brazil, and the Algarves.

As mentioned earlier, the end of the Napoleonic wars also sparked the former Spanish colonists into action. Believing that it was only a matter of time until

[20] Thomas E. Skidmore, *Brazil: Five Centuries of Change*, 2nd ed. (Oxford: Oxford University Press, 2010).

[21] Walter Rela, *Colonia del Sacramento: Historia Política, Militar, Diplomática 1678–1778* (Montevideo, Uruguay: Academia Uruguaya de Historia, 2006).

their former colonial masters would disembark on their shores to reclaim what had been theirs. The smaller territories were especially anxious to carve out their own sovereign states while the boundaries were still in flux. The Eastern Band was such an area, squeezed by two hostile forces. To the north, the Portuguese queen harbored a not-so-hidden desire to annex it. Royal troops invaded in 1811 at the behest of the Spanish governor of Montevideo; rebel forces besieged the port. The royal troops left after the rebels were routed, but many thought that it was only a matter of time until they would return. To the west, the monopolizing might of Buenos Aires wanted to reunite the former viceroyalty under its iron grip.

Desperate to remain independent, the Eastern Band turned to José Gervasio Artigas, the free-spirited leader of the rebel militia. Artigas was working on a coalition to break the hegemonic grip of Buenos Aires and Brazil. The confederation became known as the Federal League, and it consisted of the provinces that bordered the major rivers that flowed into the River Plate, principally Santa Fe, Entre Ríos, Cordoba, and the Eastern Band.[22] These four provinces wanted to open their ports to international trade, but Buenos Aires would not allow them to do so; this would break its monopoly over all external commercial activities. Hence, Artigas's movement became a serious threat for Buenos Aires. Concerned about the rebel leader, the creoles looked the other way when Portugal launched another invasion of Uruguay in January 1817. At last, Doña Carlota's ambitions were being realized. However, Portugal's position was tenuous. Artigas remained on the run, and his gauchos were constantly harassing Portuguese garrisons and supply convoys. In January 1820, Royalist forces finally defeated the rebel leader at the Battle of Tacuarembó, putting an end to his subversive activities. One year later, the Eastern Band was formally annexed by the Kingdom of Brazil, and renamed the Cisplatina Province.

Fortunately, Brazil could afford expensive military expeditions because its economy was doing well. The gold boom had faded toward the latter half of the eighteenth century, but it was replaced by the rise of cotton, coffee, and cacao exports. The dawn of the Industrial Revolution had increased the demand for commodities. As a result, export tariffs were filling the royal coffers. Most of the taxes that were once slated for Portugal were staying in Brazil, allowing the former colonial government to invest in new public works and spread the wealth among loyal subjects. Under the terms of his rescue by the British, Dom João agreed to open Brazil's ports, allowing a wide range of European luxury goods to arrive.

Unfortunately, things were not so rosy back home. The country was in ruins. Bereft of its colonial income, the Portuguese economy struggled to remain afloat. By 1820, insurrections were breaking out. There was a great deal of frustration among those elites who had stayed behind in Europe to fight Napoleon. Porto, the

---

[22] Carlos María Ramírez, *Artigas: Debate Entre "El Sud-América" de Buenos Aires y "La Razón" de Montevideo* (Montevideo: A. Barreiro y Ramos, 1884).

country's second-largest city, was the first to revolt. Its leaders called for the formation of a new government, and they demanded the return of the king so he could
repatriate his enormous colonial wealth. Ever since the royal court had left for Río
de Janeiro, Portugal had been reduced to second-class status. Its army had been
placed under the command of William Carr Beresford, one of the British generals
who had been defeated by the Buenos Aires militia in 1806. British imports were
given preferential status, further weakening Portuguese industries. There was also
a sense of shame that Lisbon was taking orders from a colonial outpost, but Dom
João did not want to leave his lush paradise for the dank cold of Lisbon. The creoles also begged him to stay. They realized that the king's departure would reduce
the colony to its previous status—and a return to the previous practice sending all
of its taxes abroad. The infrastructure would crumble and their lavish lifestyles
would evaporate.

Nevertheless, Dom João had no choice. By that time, he was no longer prince
regent; he was the king. His mother, Maria I, had died in 1816, passing the crown
to her son. If he did not return home, the country would secede and his monarchy
would collapse. That was why, after thirteen years in Río de Janeiro, Dom João,
along with four thousand members of the royal court, boarded vessels to return to
Lisbon. Tears streaked down the king's face as the verdant hills of Río de Janeiro
drifted below the horizon. He left his son, Pedro I, to govern the realm.[23]

Dom João's return to Lisbon did not go well. He was forced to swear allegiance
to the new constitution, and was reduced to titular head. The colony was also subdued. By the end of the year, the Kingdom of Brazil was abolished, and all of the colonial territories were once again made subordinate to Lisbon. Portuguese officers
were dispatched to take command of the Brazilian military units, and Dom Pedro
was ordered back home.

He refused. Instead, Dom Pedro declared independence. He formed the Empire of Brazil at the end of 1822, and he was crowned emperor.[24] For the next two
years, the new government fought a series of skirmishes with the royal garrisons
that remained behind, but they were no match for the powerful colony. The two
sides finally arrived at an amicable resolution in 1825. Brazil became a sovereign
state; in return, it agreed to assume all of Portugal's war debt—the price it had to
pay for liberty.

Unfortunately, the political unrest allowed the unsettled matters in the Cisplatina Province to resurface. The queen's depredation of the Eastern Band, and her
ambitions to carve out a new kingdom, had been the original motive behind the annexation of the province, but now she was on the other side of the Atlantic. Therefore, it was no longer clear how the newly independent country would proceed.

[23] João Paulo Guerra, *Descolonização Portuguesa: O Regresso das Caravelas*, 1st ed. (Alfragide, Portugal: Oficina do Livro, 2012).

[24] Marcus D. Góes, *João: O Trópico Coroado* (Río de Janeiro: Biblioteca do Exército Editora, 2008).

Buenos Aires's initial reaction to the Portuguese invasion of the Eastern Band was muted. In fact, it was complicit in the invasion, since it was glad to be rid of Artigas. However, the rebel's defeat did not dismantle the Federal League. On the contrary, a month after the Battle of Tacuarembó, the Federal League vanquished Buenos Aires at the 1820 Battle of Cepeda. This allowed the provinces to coalesce and finish the war against Spain. Yet, the inclusion of the Cisplatina Province into the new Empire of Brazil was too much for the creoles to accept. They pleaded with the emperor to transfer control to the Spanish-speaking population. When that did not occur, an independence movement began to grow. Led by the Thirty-Three Orientals (or Thirty-Three Easterners), an assembly of young exiles from the Eastern Band, a group of Uruguayans prepared a small invasion force, determined to retake the country. They disembarked on Playa de la Agraciada on April 19, 1825, and advanced on Montevideo.

At first, the government in Río de Janeiro dismissed the events as a minor uprising. However, Dom Pedro was under a great deal of pressure to act decisively. He had arrived in Brazil at the age of six, and spent most of his life in the Americas. Although he had been well educated by tutors, he was not as polished as many of his European peers. He also had a liberal streak that put him under suspicion. With the rebels gaining ground, it was clear that the young monarch needed to demonstrate resolve. It was his first test as sovereign, and everyone was watching. However, his military resources had thinned with the departure of the royal forces. A large part of the remaining army was deployed in Pernambuco to quell a rebellion. Dom Pedro also realized that Buenos Aires was instigating the Cisplatine uprising. Therefore, he decided to hit back the best way he could: he ordered his imperial fleet to blockade the River Plate, thus severing the main artery to the city's economic heart.[25] One of the legacies of the Portuguese was their deep commitment to a strong navy, which allowed the small country to wield enormous influence. This was a lesson that became embedded in the Brazilian psyche, and it would become an important factor in determining future military outcomes.

The blockade proved effective from an economic perspective, but the Argentines would not capitulate. Dom Pedro knew he needed an army to impose his will, but he had very few soldiers. Most of the professional army had returned to Europe, leaving behind only a few garrisons of poorly trained militias. Therefore, he started an extensive rearmament program. In the meantime, he procured the services of Irish and German mercenaries, veterans of the other Latin American wars of liberation, to launch an offensive against Buenos Aires. The rearmament program, blockade operations, and mercenaries, as well as the assumption of Portugal's war debt, drained his financial resources. Furthermore, Brazil was now facing a different adversary from its earlier Cisplatine encounter. It was no longer coming up against a ragtag group of gauchos. It was facing the immense might of Buenos Aires.

---

[25] Leslie Bethell (Ed.), *Colonial Brazil* (Cambridge: Cambridge University Press, 1987).

The Argentines, however, lacked the naval strength of the Brazilian Imperial Navy. They had fourteen brigantines against Brazil's eighty warships. Fortunately, they had a secret weapon, of sorts, in the form of the small fleet's commander, Irish-born Argentine William (Guillermo) Brown. A merchant seaman by training, Brown had been pressed into service by Britain's Royal Navy. He had eventually made his way to Argentina, where he entered service during the Argentine War of Independence and founded the Argentine Navy.

Brown was a tenacious fighter, known for taking difficult odds. Despite facing a much larger force, he delivered a powerful blow at the Battle of Juncal in February 1827. The audacious Brown used a combination of amphibious and maritime forces to ambush the Imperial Navy and temporarily break the blockade. With the river crossing cleared, Buenos Aires moved to reinforce its military forces on the Eastern Band. Later that month, the Argentines used the momentum to rout the Brazilian Imperial Army at the Battle of Ituzaingó, thus winning control of the Cisplatina Province. Still, the conflict was far from resolved. The Brazilian Imperial Navy regrouped and renewed the blockade, but the Argentines would not surrender. The problem for Brazil was that with the costs of the military and naval operations becoming such an economic drain, Río de Janeiro was under pressure to end the war.

This was when John Ponsonby entered the scene. London ordered the British diplomat to broker a solution to the Cisplatine conflict—in a way that was favorable to Britain, of course; this meant granting them free navigation of the River Plate, for the British, too, recognized the strategic importance of the estuary. Ever since the collapse of the Spanish, Portuguese, and French empires, Britain had promoted itself as the world's principal powerhouse by developing extensive trade links and foreign colonies. Ponsonby arrived with two propositions. The first was the reincorporation of the Eastern Band into Argentina, in return for a heavy compensation for Brazil, which he knew would never be accepted. The second was independence for the province by creating a new sovereign state.[26] The Eastern Band already had a powerful independence movement, and the creation of Uruguay served as a buffer between Brazil and Argentina. This was the period when diplomats resorted to the use of buffer states like Belgium and Luxemburg to separate bitter rivals.

At first, Dom Pedro and Argentine President Bernardino Rivadavia rejected the proposals. However, the economic damage produced by the blockade led to their acquiescence. The decision sparked a popular backlash in both Argentina and Brazil. It led to the collapse of Rivadavia's government and that of his successor, Manuel Dorrego. The latter tried to restart the war, but the economic privations forced him to accept Uruguay's independence. In the end, Rivadavia escaped to Spain, where he remained for the rest of his life. Dorrego was not as fortunate; he was executed for treason.

....

[26] David F. Marley, *Wars of the Americas: A Chronology of Armed Conflict in the New World, 1492 to the Present* (Santa Barbara, CA: ABC-CLIO, 1998).

Brazil's dissatisfaction with Dom Pedro was equally harsh. Involved in a series of personal scandals with a female courtier, the monarch's reputation was reduced to tatters. Not only had he been forced to hand over a hard-fought part of his country, but also he surrendered Brazil's access to the Paraná and Uruguay Rivers. This would have dire economic consequences for the southwestern states. Within three years, Dom Pedro would be forced to abdicate; he passed the reins to his son six-year-old son, Pedro II, and returned to Europe.

The transformation of Uruguay into a sovereign state meant that the River Plate had become an international waterway, thus allowing free navigation. It also created a buffer between the two largest nations in South America. Along with Paraguay, it would limit the direct contact between them. Nevertheless, the creation of the buffer state did not prevent the start of another Argentine-Brazilian conflict. Less than two decades later, the two sides would come to blows again. This time it would be called the Platine War.

After the Cisplatine War, Argentina and Uruguay entered a prolonged period of political instability. Buenos Aires came under the influence of Juan Manuel de Rosas, a rich plantation owner who governed according to his commercial interests, many of which were at odds with the preferences of the other provinces. This resulted in a constant internal struggle.

Buenos Aires owes its immense power to its dominant geographical position at the source of the River Plate. Given its location, it had long served as the back door to the giant silver mines of Potosí. The city initially thrived as a center of contraband, importing cheap luxury goods to resell them at much higher prices to the miners. So much of the precious metal flowed down the river that the estuary became known as the River Plate, or the river of silver, and the region became known as Argentina, or the land of silver.[27]

In 1776, the Spanish monarchy introduced a set of changes known as the Bourbon Reforms. Among many other modifications, it recognized the importance of Buenos Aires by designating it a viceroyalty and transferring to it control of Potosí. As a result, the customs house of Buenos Aires became one of the most important sources of revenues for Spain. After independence, the city retained its economic hegemony by becoming the only portal for the provinces.[28] This put it at loggerheads with the rest of the rest of the country. Covetous of the revenue produced by the customs house and the immense commercial operations of the port, they were anxious to share the spoils.

No one burned with more desire than Justo José de Urquiza, a rich rancher from the neighboring province of Entre Ríos. Urquiza stood at the head of a vast commercial empire that spanned agriculture, transportation, and banking. He

[27] Walter Thomas Molano, *In the Land of Silver: 200 Years of Argentine Political-Economic Development* (North Charleston, SC: CreateSpace, 2012).

[28] Roberto P. Payró, *El Río de la Plata: De Colonias a Naciones Independientes: De Solís a Rosas, 1516–1852* (Buenos Aires: Alianza Editorial, 2006).

was also a military leader, fielding a powerful private army that he used to defend his economic and political interests. Urquiza and Rosas were initially allies, but the rivalry between the two turned acrimonious when the latter tried to depose Urquiza.

Rosas's properties and assets spanned across the province of Buenos Aires, and he used the port of Buenos Aires as the embarkation point for the products that he sold abroad. Urquiza's properties, which were in the fertile delta of Entre Ríos, were equally prosperous. As his holdings expanded, Urquiza tried to dispatch his exports from his own docks and warehouses, particularly in the port of Paraná. This would allow him to collect the tariffs and service fees associated with international trade, but Rosas refused. Rosas rejected similar proposals from the other ports, such as Rosario and Cordoba, which were scattered along the Paraná River; he clearly understood that Buenos Aires's power was derived over its monopoly over international trade, and he refused to surrender it. This led to the bitter rivalry between the two men and the constant tug of war between Buenos Aires and the provinces.

On the other side of the river, the political environment was equally tumultuous. Soon after independence, Uruguay descended into civil war. The country was divided into two camps—the commercial interests of Montevideo versus the rest of the country. The reason for the schism was geographical. Uruguay has an immense coastline, but it has just one major port. This allowed Montevideo, like Buenos Aires, to exert a monopolizing control over the country's external commerce.

Montevideo's harbor is deep, with easy access to the Atlantic and the River Plate estuary. It is a much better port than Buenos Aires, which is shallow and needs to be constantly dredged. This was the reason why the Spanish fleet used Montevideo as its headquarters, and why the city remained loyal to the crown long after most of the region declared independence. It was often said that Rosas understood that Montevideo could eventually become the region's gateway if it was part of the same country, thus undermining his immense commercial interests. Perhaps that was why he allowed Uruguay to remain independent.

Uruguay's political factions coalesced in two major parties. The Colorados represented Montevideo, and the Blancos represented everyone else. Given Buenos Aires's rivalry with Montevideo, Rosas naturally supported the Blancos, since they were opposed to Montevideo. The difference in constituencies prescribed their policies. Montevideo was a melting pot of nationalities and ideas, and the Colorados were liberal; the Blancos represented rural landowners, and they were conservative, which suited Rosas. This led to a great deal of cooperation between Rosas and the Blancos and reached a point where the Blancos became an appendage of Rosas's political apparatus. With his support, the Blancos defeated the Colorados, thus ending the Uruguayan civil war.

Between 1838 and 1840, Buenos Aires came under a new blockade, this time by the French, in response to the country's role in the War of the Confederation, the subject of a subsequent chapter. Uruguay was under the control of President Man-uel Oribe, an ally of Rosas. Seeing an opportunity to seize power, the leader of the Colorados, Fructuoso Rivera, appealed to the French for help in overthrowing the government. The French agreed. They figured that it would sever the link between the two countries and undermine Buenos Aires's influence. As a result, Oribe fled to Argentina.

Uruguay plunged into a period of civil unrest that became known as the Great War. For thirteen years, it was rocked by incessant fighting. With Argentina's support, the Blancos defeated the Colorados in a series of battles. The survivors retreated to Montevideo, which was their last bastion of political support. The Blancos responded by laying siege. In 1840, the French Navy lifted the blockade of Buenos Aires after the end of the War of the Confederation, but the siege of Montevideo remained in place. The city's large port allowed it to be resupplied by sea, but living conditions were onerous. Many of the immigrants who lived in the city formed foreign legions to help with the defense. The two largest legions were the French and Italians. The latter came under the command of an itinerant math teacher, Giuseppe Garibaldi, who used his experience to become a central figure in the Italian Risorgimento.

Sympathy for the beleaguered port caught the world's imagination. In 1845, Britain and France announced another blockade of Buenos Aires, this time to counter the help it was providing the Blancos in besieging Montevideo. The block-ade lasted five years and savaged the already-weakened Argentine economy. In addition to breaking the siege of Montevideo, Britain sought better access to Par-aguay, which had the potential of becoming an important source of cotton.[29] An exponential demand for cotton from its textile mills had forced British merchants to scour the planet for alternate sources. The only route to Paraguay, however, was via the Paraná River, which crossed through Argentine territory. Therefore, Britain wanted to force the Argentines to allow its vessels free access, but they refused. The blockade was finally lifted in 1850, when the two countries realized that the cost of the operation was too high, and very little progress was being made.

While Argentina and Uruguay were convulsed by their internal disputes, the situation in Brazil was not much better. Pedro II, too young to govern after his father abdicated, was assisted by a small group of regents, but constant infighting among them created an unstable environment that soon erupted into open rebel-lions. The first insurrection occurred in 1835, when Pará revolted. The state sits at the entrance to the Amazon River. More than three thousand kilometers from Río de Janeiro, it was isolated from the decision-making that was taking place in the capital. It was also plagued by deep poverty, with most of its wealth controlled by a small group of creoles. The uprising was called the Cabanagem, named after the

---

[29] Andrew Graham-Yooll, *Imperial Skirmishes: War and Gunboat Diplomacy in Latin America* (New York: Interlink Books, 1983).

simple huts that were used by the poor. Río de Janeiro dispatched troops to arrest the leaders and quell the unrest, but the situation remained tense. That same year, Río Grande do Sul moved to secede. That rebellion was known as the Farroupilha Revolution, after the rags worn by the combatants, and it was part of a movement to create the Ríograndense Republic. The republic was intended to be a variation of the Federal League that had been promoted by Artigas. This time, the movement included Uruguay and Paraguay, with the followers connected largely by cultural commonality. Given the prevalence of the gaucho and Guaraní cultures throughout the southeastern plains, there was a strong sense of kinship among the neighboring communities.[30] Brazil and Argentina felt that the communities' solidarity posed an existential threat; this was the root cause of the War of the Triple Alliance a few decades later.

The imperial troops dispatched to Río Grande do Sul restored order, but there was a feeling that Brazil was coming apart. Part of the problem was the lack of defined leadership. Under the constitution, Pedro II could not be named monarch until he was eighteen years old. However, the government decided to accelerate the process and coronate him in 1841, when he was only fifteen. The coronation helped centralize power in the symbol of the monarchy, but did not mitigate the atmosphere of instability. In 1848, a revolt in the state of Pernambuco marked the third insurrection since Pedro II assumed power. Known as the Praieira revolt, it was a reaction to the rebellions that were rocking Europe. The rebels called for the introduction of democracy and civil liberties.

Not surprisingly, the government became desperate to stabilize the political atmosphere. The situation in Río Grande do Sul remained shaky; the government refused to allow the state to break away. The loss of the Cisplatina Province had produced so much social unrest that Dom Pedro I had been forced to abdicate. The breakaway of such an integral part of Brazil would produce a far greater political backlash and endanger the monarchy's future.

The government in Río de Janeiro concluded that the civil war in Uruguay needed to be stopped in order to extinguish similar movements that were sprouting across the land. The only way that could be done was by end Argentina's involvement in Uruguay, but that meant declaring war against Juan Manuel de Rosas. Left with no other choice, the government moved to ally itself with Rosas's enemies.

The Argentine tyrant had two main adversaries, Justo José de Urquiza and the Colorados of Montevideo. Therefore, Río de Janeiro dispatched diplomatic missions to these two groups to form a grand coalition. In 1849, the Brazilian government began openly assisting the besieged Colorados in Montevideo. This aid was also transformed into military support against the Blancos. Realizing what was taking place, Argentina knew that war with Brazil was on the horizon.

30 Antonio Augusto Fagundes, *Revolução Farroupilha: Cronologia do Decênio Heróico, 1835 à 1845*, 2nd ed. (Porto Alegre, Brasil: Martins Livrerio, 2003).

At the same time, the Brazilians convinced Urquiza to join their venture. The plan would consist of two parts. The first was an allied invasion of Uruguay, with Brazilian forces entering from the north and Urquiza's cohort invading from the west. The second would be the deployment of the Brazilian Navy to prevent any reinforcement from Buenos Aires. This would allow the allies to defeat the Blancos and break the siege of Montevideo.

At the end of May 1851, the alliance was formally announced, and imperial troops landed in Uruguay in August. This left Argentina no choice but to declare war on Brazil. The next month, an invasion force of sixteen thousand Brazilian soldiers entered from the north, while fifteen thousand gauchos from Entre Ríos entered from the west. The two groups converged on Montevideo. Realizing that they were surrounded and cut off from Argentina, the Blancos capitulated without firing a shot.[31] The Argentine members of the army were then incorporated into the Brazilian force, and they headed for Buenos Aires.

In early February 1852, the allies arrived on the outskirts of the capital, ready to take on Rosas. The Argentines were waiting, and the two sides met at the town of Caseros. The sides were numerically matched, but morale among Rosas's troops collapsed when they surveyed the immense coalition that was arrayed before them. They knew they had little chance of defeating the imperial might of Brazil and Urquiza's gauchos, thus it sapped their willingness to fight. The ensuing battle of Caseros lasted only three hours before Rosas's men began slipping away or switching sides. Realizing that all was lost, the Argentine leader fled. He tendered his resignation and boarded a British warship bound for England. This marked the end of the Platine War.

The Cisplatine and Platine Wars were born of a queen's ambition to establish a new empire, but her departure for Lisbon ended the enterprise. As a result, Brazil was left with an unstable territory that generated two serious political problems. The first was the inherent friction of sharing a border with a neighbor as powerful as Argentina, which was too dominant to acquiesce to Río de Janeiro's whims. Therefore, there would always be a potential for military confrontation. The second difficulty was the deep-seated gaucho and Guaraní culture that thrived in the southeastern plains of South America. Those people's yearning for independence manifested itself in the Farroupilha Rebellion, threatening the geographical integrity of Brazil. The excision of Uruguay into an independent country was a way to cure these two problems. As a buffer state, it separated Brazil from Argentina. The new border would also corral the influences that fueled the separatist fires in Río Grande do Sul.

Argentina was not as eager create an independent buffer state. Rosas may have initially permitted it as a way to remove a competitive threat to Buenos Aires, but

---

[31] Beatriz Bosch, *Urquiza: Gobernador de Entre Ríos, 1842–1852*, 2nd. ed. (Paraná, Argentina: Editorial de Entre Ríos, 2001).

his constant intervention kept Uruguay in a permanent state of subjugation. The ongoing instability finally convinced Río de Janeiro that it had no other choice but to organize an alliance to dispose of Rosas. Yet, the Guaraní culture would remain a thorn in Brazil's side, and the wound would soon fester into the War of the Triple Alliance.

3 THE WAR OF THE CONFEDERATION: UPPER PERU, LOWER PERU, AND CHILE

THE WAR OF THE CONFEDERATION:
UPPER PERU, LOWER PERU, AND CHILE

O n a frigid morning in 1837, the omnipotent Chilean minister Diego Portales was riding in his carriage when it jerked to a halt. His military escorts ordered him out and brutally murdered him. Although Portales was widely disliked, his violent death rallied the nation to support an unpopular war against Bolivia and Peru—the War of the Confederation—that further exacerbated the problems caused by the precipitous collapse of the Spanish monarchy and the subsequent fragmentation of the empire. The colonies had been relatively stable and prosperous, but the process of liberation unleashed a torrent of forces that led to a rash of civil wars and border conflicts.

In contrast to other revolutions, ideology was not a major driver in Latin America's quest for independence. The main objective was the preservation of the status quo. Creoles and Europeans, overwhelmingly outnumbered by slaves and natives, dared not promote the ideals of the Enlightenment, such as self-determination and liberty. The few printing presses were largely dedicated to religious issues and administrative affairs.[32] A few creoles, such as José Antonio de Rojas in Chile and Francisco de Miranda in Venezuela, who were wealthy enough to have been educated in Europe, and who thus sought a liberal form of government. Others, such as Simón Bolívar and Bernardo O'Higgins, said that they wanted to demolish the rigid social order by freeing slaves and destroying the caste system that kept the indigenous population in servitude...only to repeal many of these civil liberties soon after they were granted following the war. The liberals were the minority, and they were often at odds with the conservative majority that led the struggle. Hence, the essence of the revolution was for the upper classes to preserve their way of life.

Previous attempts to improve social conditions had sparked social unrest. In 1542, at the behest of the Jesuits, Charles I introduced the New Laws, a set of measures to eliminate the *encomienda* system, under which Spaniards were granted land in exchange for their promise to convert the indigenous slaves to Christianity. Blasco Núñez Vela, the first viceroy of Peru, was sent from Spain with strict orders to implement the New Laws. Realizing that ending slavery would destroy their lucrative mining operations, the colonists rose up in arms against the viceroy. An army led by Francisco Pizarro's brother, Gonzalo, defeated and murdered Núñez.

32 Eduardo Cavieres and Crístobal Aljovín de Losada, *Chile-Perú, Perú-Chile en el Siglo XIX: La Formación del Estado, la Economía y la Sociedad* (Valparaíso, Chile: Ediciones Universitarias de Valparaíso, Pontificia Universidad Católica de Valparaíso, 2005).

The uprising was quelled in 1548, and Pizarro was executed. Nevertheless, the Spanish monarch repealed the New Laws, fearing that ending slavery would lead to the secession of his most prosperous colony. The precedent was set, and it was no surprise that when the creole elites finally decided to strike out on their own, their inspiration was the need to preserve their socioeconomic system. Some fought for better business opportunities by breaking the Spanish yoke and opening their ports to free trade. Not only would this allow them to gain access to more goods, but also the tariffs would become an important source of government revenue. Others were driven by political ambition, unwilling to limit their upward ascendance because they had not been born in Europe. Therefore, the principles of the Enlightenment were never a meaningful part of the independence struggle.[33]

The egalitarian concepts of the Enlightenment undermined the rigid social hierarchy, and embracing them would have destroyed the colonial labor system. The deep sense of conservatism was particularly strong in Lima, which was the bastion of Spanish authority, and one of the last colonies to fall. After independence, the Peruvians dedicated themselves to recreating the wealth, power, and glory of the former viceroyalty.

As was mentioned earlier, the Spanish colonies were initially organized in two large governing units, each centered on the administration of a major civilization, the Aztecs and the Incas, along with the supervision of the mining operations in Zacatecas and Potosí. As the colonies prospered, Spain carved out smaller viceroyalties, shrinking the territories and resources of the original ones. The previous chapter discussed how the Bourbon Reforms of 1776 marked an important watershed for the viceroyalty of Peru because it transferred the Royal Audiencia of Charcas to the newly created viceroyalty of the River Plate. This reorganization stripped Peru of almost half its territory—and its main source of revenue—which is why the Peruvian elite became so obsessed with recovering the former possession after the war of independence.

Peruvians always considered Charcas to be an integral part of their territory, tracing their union back to the Inca Empire. The Royal Audiencia of Charcas was established in 1559 to give King Phillip II personal control over the lucrative mining area. The region became known as Alto (Upper) Peru since it was located in the altiplano or high plains. Meanwhile, the rest of the country was known as Bajo or Lower Peru, since it was located closer to sea level. Trade between Upper and Lower Peru declined after the territory was transferred to the viceroyalty of the

---

[33] The heavy presence of the Catholic clergy was another interesting aspect of the Latin American independence movement. The Catholic Church played an important role, with religious figures becoming integral members of the new provisional governments. This was partly due to residual animosity against the Spanish homeland for the expulsion from Latin America of the Jesuits in 1767 and partly due to the colonists' recognition that they could control the social order through religion.

River Plate, but cultural and social ties remained strong. There was a fluid movement of people, with families and businesses straddling both regions.

To keep control over so much territory, the Spanish governed with a firm hand. They enforced the social hierarchy through the rigid caste system and a heavy dose of religion.[34] However, the independence movement swept away the colonial institutions, resulting in chaos. Law and order broke down after the Royalist troops were routed and much of the clergy fled. The ruggedness of the land, poor channels of communication, and the heavy presence of indigenous and mixed populations heightened the sense of anarchy. Local strongmen reestablished order, in the process carving out fiefdoms that they attempted to transform into sovereign countries. As mentioned in the first chapter, Simón Bolívar applied the Roman precedent of *uti possidetis juris* to prevent the empire from crumbling into dozens of small states. Therefore, the new Latin American map would roughly mirror the original viceroyalties, captaincies, and audiencias.

Historians tend to use geopolitical terms to explain the decision to convert Charcas into an independent state. They argue that it was a move by Bolívar to limit the power of Peru and Argentina by creating a buffer state, similar to what had happened with the creation of Uruguay. There is much truth to that explanation, but the primary motivation was the need by Marshall Antonio José de Sucre to find revenues to pay his army.[35] Sucre was Bolívar's most trusted general.

On December 9, 1824, Sucre led an army of eighty-five hundred men against a slightly bigger contingent of Royalists at the Battle of Ayacucho. The engagement culminated in the defeat of the last remaining Spanish regiment and the capture of the viceroy, José de la Serna. As the cannon smoke cleared, however, Sucre faced a pressing problem: he was out of money, and he now had a huge contingent of soldiers and mercenaries demanding to be paid. Failure to do so could lead to mutiny. Moreover, under the terms of the Spanish surrender, the South American general agreed to continue paying the wages of the defeated officers and arrange for their safe-conduct to Spain.

Lower Peru was tapped out. Its economy had been annihilated, in large part thanks to the expropriation of property by San Martin's adjutant, Bernardo de Monteagudo. Commercial activity collapsed when most of the Spaniards and foreigners were expelled. Sucre knew that tax collection in Upper Peru was still strong, thanks to the silver mining operations. The battlefield in Ayacucho was at the foothills of the altiplano, so he quickly made his way to Charcas, with the intent of carving it into a sovereign state; in that way, he reasoned, he could appropriate the tax receipts for his men.

Upon hearing the news of Sucre's intentions, Bolívar flew into a rage. He did not consider Charcas viable as a sovereign state; since it lacked a deepwater port,

[34]   Leslie Bethell, *Colonial Spanish America* (Cambridge: Cambridge University Press, 1987).

[35]   José Luis Roca, *Ni con Lima ni con Buenos Aires: La Formación de un Estado Nacional en Charcas* (Lima: Instituto Francés de Estudios Andinos, 2007).

there was no way it could survive as a trading nation. Nevertheless, Bolívar also knew that assigning it to Argentina or Peru would destabilize the continent by creating a behemoth that would alter the balance of power. The Liberator oscillated for a long time, and even lived in Alto Perú for a period of five months—briefly serving as president. He grew fond of the people and finally gave in to the idea of its independence when the legislature decided to name the country Bolivia in his honor.

Bolívar's concerns about the economic viability of the country were valid. Technically, Bolivia had access to the Pacific through the department of Atacama, but most of its trade traditionally flowed through the port of Arica and, to a lesser extent, through Ilo, both of which are in southern Peru. Bolívar pleaded with the Peruvians to transfer the port of Arica to the new nation, but they refused—using the argument of *uti possidetis juris* as the reason why the territory could not be subdivided. As a result, he worked to establish the Bolivian port of Cobija, but its location was impractical. To reach it, merchants needed to cross the Atacama, one of the most inhospitable deserts in the world. Not only was it devoid of the people and infrastructure needed to operate a trade hub, Cobija was far from Bolivia's centers of economic activity. The travel time from the capital city of Santa Cruz was eighteen days by mule, a journey that meandered past snowy peaks and through the inhospitable desert. In contrast, the trip to Arica took only three days.

The decision to reroute Bolivia's trade to Cobija also produced a backlash in southern Peru. For centuries, the communities of Cuzco and Arequipa produced many of the products that were used in Potosí. As a result, commercial and social links were tight. However, the economy of southern Peru suffered after 1776, when Charcas was transferred to the viceroyalty of the River Plate. Under the new arrangement, much of the trade was redirected to Buenos Aires. Nevertheless, some commercial activity still survived, and all shipments of mercury arrived through Arica. Mercury was vital to the mining operations, as it was used in the amalgamation process that became imperative when the higher quality ore was depleted and the miners were forced to turn to lower grade materials. The main source of mercury was a set of mines in Huancavelica in central Peru. The liquid metal was carried by mule to the port of Pisco, and then barged to Arica, where it was transported to the silver operations.[36]

Trade between Charcas and Argentina came to a halt during the War of Independence after Buenos Aires rebelled. As a result, all commerce was rerouted to southern Peru, leading to a revival of old business ties. The Royalist presence in Charcas remained strong throughout the war, and the colony never seceded. It formed a junta to repel the repeated incursions by Argentine rebels. However, the rerouting of trade through Cobija after the country's independence depressed business ties with southern Peru once more.

---

[36] Nicholas A. Robins, *Mercury, Mining, and Empire: The Human and Ecological Cost of Colonial Silver Mining in the Andes* (Bloomington, IN: Indiana University Press, 2011).

While there was a natural affinity between southern Peru and Bolivia, not everyone liked the idea of cooperation. To the south, the newly established country of Chile was trying to find its footing. Like most of the other countries that were spun out of the Spanish empire, the Chileans were struggling with how to administer their nation. The country was divided into two camps. One side advocated the centralization of power in a strong authoritarian government, and the other pushed for a loose democratic arrangement of regional states.[37]

At first, the differences in opinions were discussed in pamphlets and weighed in public debates, but soon the disagreements decayed into a military confrontation between the leaders of the camps, Bernardo O'Higgins and Ramón Freire. O'Higgins was a larger-than-life character. He was the illegitimate son of Ambrosio O'Higgins, the former viceroy of Chile and Peru. Although an Irishman, the senior O'Higgins had attained his high rank because he had been born in Europe—an issue that rankled the creoles. The viceroy never met his son, but the boy was given the finest education abroad. Upon his return, the fledgling young man became one of the heroes of the independence movement, and in 1817, he became Supreme Director O'Higgins. Although he was a liberal at heart, he had developed a strong, authoritarian style. After some time, a rebellion, led by Freire, broke out in the south.

Unlike O'Higgins, Freire had not come from a wealthy family. An orphan who had grown up in a succession of homes and families in the southern city of Concepción, he joined the independence movement at an early age and rose through the ranks. After the war, he returned home to a ruined country. Farms and factories had been destroyed, and thousands were starving. Freire blamed the economic malaise on O'Higgins's failure to transfer the resources needed to stabilize the regions and communities. Newspapers took up the liberal cause and attacked the supreme director. Sensing that he was losing support, and refusing to plunge the country into a civil war, O'Higgins resigned in 1823, passing the baton to his opponent. As the new supreme director, Freire immediately began to decentralize Chile, rewriting the constitution and delegating more control to local governments.

Nevertheless, Freire faced a major economic obstacle that could only be resolved at the national level. During the war, the Chilean government had taken out a loan for one million pounds from a London countinghouse, Hullet & Co., to finance the campaign in Peru. Ever since independence, the suspension of trade with Lima had been devastating the economy. As long as Lima remained a Royalist stronghold, Peruvian merchants were prohibited from trading with rebel states. Chile lacked the abundance of precious metals that served as such a source of wealth in the other colonies. It had given up on mining during the latter half of the eighteenth century, when the Bourbon Reforms finally allowed the colonies to trade with each other, and almost overnight, Chilean wheat farmers began to

---

[37] Debates weighing these two approaches to government would be repeated throughout Latin American history. Unfortunately, the intense contest between Centralism and Federalism remains an impediment to the region's growth and development.

prosper as they exported grains to the arid cities of northern Peru. During the war, however, the loss of the Peruvian market was a heavy blow for Chile's merchants, farmers, and landowners, which was one reason they supported Peru's independence. To that end, in 1819, Chile appointed a battle-tested Argentine general, José de San Martín, to lead an expeditionary force to Lima. To secure the funds needed to buy warships, arms, and mercenaries, the newly independent Chilean government took out a loan. They succeeded in funding the expedition, but the loan left the new nation highly indebted.

To service the debt, the government turned to a politically connected entrepreneur, Diego Portales. Slight, with dark hair and piercing eyes, the misogynist and unsavory character had once aspired to join the clergy. Sensing a unique business opportunity, Portales agreed to service the country's debt if the government gave him a monopoly to import such socially proscribed goods as tobacco, liquor, and playing cards. The operation should have been lucrative, but it was not. Under Freire's decentralization initiative, the troops and officials that were used to patrol against contraband trade had been relaxed. As a result, merchants were able to circumvent the tariff controls, thus undermining Portales's monopoly. He soon fell into arrears with the London bankers, and Chile became the scorn of the international financial community. The country's economic elite was badly affected when other London financiers cut off credit lines, further dampening trade and commerce.[38]

It was within this context that Portales began to support a political upstart gaining popularity in the south. Like Freire, José Joaquín Prieto was a veteran of the war against Spain. He was an ally of O'Higgins, and supported a strong centralized government, fearing that decentralization would leave the country vulnerable to invasion and internal political instability—a view commonly shared by most creole elites. Tired of Freire's liberal policies, Prieto raised a force of a thousand men in 1829 and marched on Santiago.

Portales learned of the advancing army, and he saw an opportunity to establish an authoritarian regime that would improve his business operations. Prieto was low on munitions, arms, and funds and was therefore receptive to Portales's offer of financing. For the next six months, Chile was savaged by civil war. Finally, in April 1830, Prieto won a stunning victory at the Battle of Lircay, placing the country under his conservative yoke. The new government was led by José Tomás Ovalle, who rewarded Portales by naming him minister of Defense, Internal Affairs, and Foreign Relations.

As Chile's main power broker, Portales consolidated his position by sending Freire into exile and dismissing 136 senior officers who had fought against the conservatives. Since many of them were veterans of the war of independence, the

---

[38] Francisco Antonio Encina, *Portales: Introducción a la Historia de la Época de Diego Portales, 1830–1891* (Santiago, Chile: Nascimento, 1934).

action triggered a fierce public backlash. Nevertheless, Portales remained very popular among the country's commercial elites. He introduced measures to help business by conducting the first census, ordering a national survey to map out Chile's mineral deposits, and building infrastructure. Nevertheless, Portales's primary concern was the promotion of his own commercial interests.

In the meantime, things in Bolivia were going poorly. Once the crown jewel of the Spanish empire, it was falling apart. The mines of Potosí were abandoned after the war, allowing the shafts to flood. There was also widespread resistance to Sucre and his occupying force of Colombian soldiers, whose culture grated against the traditions of the altiplano. The Bolivian elites also protested their high level of taxation, and there were complaints that the defeat of the Spanish had only led to the imposition of new Colombian overlords. Neighboring countries were also maneuvering to destabilize Bolivia. Colombian officers and soldiers were repeatedly bribed by Peruvian and Argentine agents to revolt, and Sucre was forced to put down at least four mutinies.

Angered by Peru's attempts to undermine the stability of Bolivia and its refusal to transfer the port of Arica, Bolívar's Gran Colombia declared war on Peru in June 1828. The Liberator ordered Sucre's army to abandon the highlands to engage the enemy, but his departure from Bolivia only made matters worse. In his absence, the situation turned chaotic, allowing local caudillos to take over. Law and order was only restored when Andrés de Santa Cruz arrived from Peru.

Santa Cruz was a mestizo from a prosperous family in Charcas. The Bourbon Reforms had allowed young mestizos and creoles, previously restricted to the rank of foot soldier, to ascend socially by allowing them to become members of the officer corps. As a result, creole families were eager to enroll their sons, and the Santa Cruz family was no different. Andrés de Santa Cruz had enrolled in the Spanish Army as a military cadet, with a burning ambition to climb the social ladder.

Royal militias and military garrisons were scattered throughout the viceroyalties, but there was a massive concentration in Lima due to its importance. Baroque convents, monasteries, palaces, and cathedrals in center of Lima still serve as physical testaments to the wealth and power that abounded. Lima was the envy of South America, with the high societies of Santiago, Bogotá, and Buenos Aires aspiring to copy its style. Given its importance, Lima was also the center of the Spanish military high command, and every ambitious creole wanted to be stationed there. That was why few of them joined the rebel cause until the outcome was all but certain.

Like most of his peers, Santa Cruz fought valiantly alongside the Royalists until he was captured a month after the Battle of Pasco. At that point, the midranking officer was brought before San Martin, and he switched sides. Word had gotten out that an expeditionary force of twenty thousand recruits had revolted in Spain, sparking an uprising against the reactionary policies of Ferdinand VII. The Royalists realized that since the Spanish had more pressing problems at home, they were cut off, and it would be only a matter of time until they were defeated.

This gave the ever-ambitious Santa Cruz a new opportunity to move ahead by embracing the liberal cause. He rose through the ranks, gaining Bolívar's confidence, and was appointed chief of staff. The Liberator ordered him to remain in Peru while he returned to Colombia in 1826 to attend to the ongoing political intrigue. While Bolívar was away, Santa Cruz became involved in local politics, and even served as interim president. However, being of Bolivian birth, he was never fully accepted in Peruvian society, so he eventually retired to his homeland. Fortuitously, his country was in the midst of an upheaval; the population, desperate for a leader who would reestablish order, proclaimed him president after his arrival.[39]

Santa Cruz stabilized the country. He pacified the caudillos and reactivated the economy. Like many Bolivians, his personal connections with southern Peru were strong. His wife was from the region and he kept close commercial ties with his in-laws. He understood that Bolivia would benefit enormously from a union with its neighbor, but Lima and northern Peru were opposed to the notion. Greater cooperation with Bolivia would allow the south to prosper, and that would shift the nexus of power away from the north; therefore, Lima stubbornly refused to allow further integration. If Santa Cruz wanted to realize his dream, he would need to make it happen.

His opportunity arrived later that year when Peruvian President José de la Mar's government imploded. The war against Gran Colombia had gone sour. Although young, handsome, and ambitious, he was a poor tactician and suffered dramatic reversals at the Battles of Saraguro and Tarqui. He was overthrown by his former ally, General Agustín Gamarra, after he was defeated and lost popular support.

Like most of his Peruvian peers, Gamarra was a mestizo. He was born in Cuzco and joined the royal militia when he was twenty-four. In 1814, he saw action during the Argentine rebel incursions. Gamarra performed with distinction and attained the rank of colonel in 1820, but, like Santa Cruz, he switched sides when he realized that the war was lost. After the war, he accepted a commission in the Peruvian Army, but soon found himself at odds with the president. Tired of José de la Mar's bumbling in the war against Gran Colombia, Gamarra led a coup to oust him. He assumed the presidency and sued for peace in order to turn his full attention to stabilizing the internal chaos that was consuming the nation.

The abundance of unemployed and ambitious creole officers was a huge problem for all of the colonies, but especially in Peru due to its large garrisons. Most of the European officers and soldiers were repatriated after they surrendered, but the creoles had no future in Europe. They would be discriminated and unable to advance. Their roots were in the Americas. The incorporation of these officers into the rebel armies helped turn the tide against Spain, but they became a source of instability after war.

---

[39] Oscar de Santa Cruz, *El General Andrés de Santa Cruz, Gran Mariscal de Zepita y el Gran Perú: Documentos Históricos* (La Paz, Bolivia: Escuela Tipográfica Salesiana, 1924).

In 1833, Gamarra's term in office ended, and a national convention appointed General Luis José de Orbegoso to replace him. The two were bitter rivals, and Gamarra tried to topple the new supreme leader, but the citizens of Lima rose up and forced him to flee. In January 1834, he crossed into Bolivia and proposed to Santa Cruz that he would engineer the unification of Peru and Bolivia if Santa Cruz helped defeat Orbegoso. The Bolivian leader was elated at the thought that he might finally realize his dream, but he deeply distrusted Gamarra. The Peruvian general had been his second in command, and Santa Cruz knew how treacherous Gamarra could be. Moreover, he had just witnessed Gamarra's betrayal of José de la Mar. Therefore, Santa Cruz decided to accept a similar overture from Orbegoso.

Stunned by Santa Cruz's rejection, Gamarra returned to Lima, where he was captured and deported to Costa Rica. In the meantime, Felipe Santiago Salaverry, another military upstart, snatched the reins from Orbegoso, and sallied forth to engage Santa Cruz.[40] However, Salaverry's military skills were no match for the seasoned general. Salaverry lacked Santa Cruz's gravitas and acumen—and his forces. Bolivia, soon after independence, had one of the best armies in South America, with European drill sergeants and line officers. Among some of the more formidable mercenary leaders were General Otto Phillipp Braun, a nationalized Prussian officer, and Francisco Burdett O'Connor, from Ireland. These two officers were Santa Cruz's most trusted lieutenants—and the secret to many of his victories.

The Bolivians assembled a military force and marched to engage Salaverry's army, which had disembarked at Cobija. The Peruvian force turned inland toward the regional capital of Arequipa, hoping to find a warm reception from their fellow compatriots. Southern Peru, however, was more sympathetic to Santa Cruz than to Salaverry, and the population provided him with very little assistance. On the morning of February 7, 1836, his soldiers were ambushed at Socabaya. Although the two forces were similarly matched, Santa Cruz had a larger cavalry and was able to rout the enemy. The hapless Salaverry was captured, taken to Arequipa, and executed. With the army defeated, Santa Cruz marched into Lima and declared the creation of the Peru-Bolivian Confederation on October 28, 1836.[41]

The Confederation consisted of three equal parts: Bolivia, southern Peru, and northern Peru. General Ramón Herrera was appointed president of southern Peru, General José Miguel de Velasco was named president of Bolivia, and Orbegoso was given northern Peru. Santa Cruz took the title "Protector of the Confederacy," assigning himself the position for life. The Peruvians welcomed him because he was renowned for his strong leadership, but not everyone was enamored of the new or-

[40] David P. Werlich, *Peru: A Short History* (Carbondale: Southern Illinois University Press, 1978).

[41] Carlos Donoso Rojas and Jaime Rosenblitt Berdichesky, *Guerra, Región, y Nació: La Confederación Peru-Boliviana, 1836–1839* (Santiago de Chile: Ediciones de la Dirección de Bibliotecas, Archivos y Museos, 2009).

ganizational format. A prominent group of citizens from the north preferred the incorporation of Bolivia into Peru; they disliked the notion of a confederation of equals since such an arrangement diminished the importance of Lima. Armed with a new cause, the ever-ambitious Gamarra returned to Lima, ostensibly to assemble the Restoration Movement, which sought to return the two countries to their former conditions.

Chile was also opposed to the Confederation. During the colonial period, Chile had been subordinate to Lima, which gave Chileans a certain sense of inferiority. Santiago was considered to be a frontier garrison, but the transformation of Chile into a sovereign nation allowed it equal footing.[42] The Confederation appeared to be the reincarnation of the old viceroyalty of Peru, and many Chileans believed that it would become a new hegemonic power that would impose its will on its former vassal. Furthermore, Chile began to realize that its future rested in the empty stretches of the Atacama Desert. Just as the United States used the doctrine of Manifest Destiny as its justification for appropriating and annexing territories, Chile believed that its rightful claims to prosperity lay beyond its northern boundary. However, the union of Peru and Bolivia impeded such a scenario. Therefore, Chile decided to make a preemptive strike.

Geopolitical concerns were not the only factor behind Chile's animosity toward the Confederation. Portales's economic interests were also at stake. Although Chilean businesses were happy to finance the liberation of Peru, the end of the conflict introduced new commercial complications. The ports of Callao, Peru, and Valparaíso, Chile, are the best harbors on the South American Pacific Coast. As the new nations began to prosper, the two ports began to compete. Valparaíso, a deepwater port relatively close to Cape Horn and the Straits of Magellan, is defended by tall surrounding cliffs, but provides little shelter against ocean storms. Callao's harbor is enclosed by San Lorenzo Island, which offers protection against the elements, and it also has more potential for regional trade, given its central location on the Pacific coastline. As Valparaíso began to lose out to Callao, it cut into Portales's commercial activities. Other Chilean business owners shared similar sentiments, particularly after Lima raised tariffs on grain imports. In 1835, the two countries tried to calm the situation by signing a treaty to foster cooperation and trade. Nevertheless, it was not enough to temper the growing enmity against Peru.

Chile's economic elites wanted war, but the public was not interested. The embers of the revolution were still smoldering, and nationalism had not yet taken hold. Peruvians and Chileans were neighbors, and their populations saw each other as brethren, not enemies. Things changed in late 1836 when the former Chilean president, Ramón Freire, was discovered off the coast with two frigates and an

---

[42] Guillermo Feliú Cruz, *Historiografía Colonial de Chile* (Santiago de Chile: Fondo Histórico y Bibliográfico José Toribio Medina, 1958).

invasion force headed for the island of Chiloé in southern Chile. Along the way, the crew of one of the ships mutinied and captured the rebel leader. They tried him and forced him back into exile.

It was never clear whether Santa Cruz had anything to do with that failed campaign, but it was sufficient for Portales to blame the Confederation. He sent a diplomatic delegation to Lima with five demands. The first was that Peru assume the debts that Chile incurred during the country's liberation against Spain; this would absolve him of having to repay Hullet & Co. The second was an end to the commercial war between Valparaíso and Callao, a move that would boost his business interests. The third was that Peru and Bolivia limit the size of their militaries. The fourth was full indemnification for the costs of suppressing Freire's expeditionary force. Last of all, he demanded the Confederation's dissolution.

Santa Cruz, now known as the Protector, was anxious to avoid war, particularly with Chile, which, although relatively small, had a reputation for being tenacious. For the previous three centuries, it had been at war with the southern Mapuche tribes, and Chilean soldiers were considered fierce and seasoned. Therefore, Santa Cruz accepted all of the conditions except for the last one; he refused to dissolve the Confederation because doing so would have made his position obsolete, and it would have renewed Bolivia's port problems. Upon their return to Valparaíso, the diplomatic delegation reported to Portales, who rejected the counter offer and declared war on December 28, 1836.

With war on the way, the Machiavellian-like Portales prepared to consolidate his position at home and abroad. He introduced martial law, stripped away civil liberties, closed the congress, and introduced the death penalty for anyone accused of treason. On the external front, he launched a series of diplomatic initiatives. First, he formed an alliance with Gamarra and his Restoration Movement. Even though the Restoration Movement represented the economic elites of northern Peru, which included the rival port of Callao, Portales's main objective was to eliminate the Peru-Bolivian Confederation. To that end, he sent a Chilean squadron to blockade the Peruvian fleet and assure his navy's supremacy of the seas. Simultaneously, he appointed Admiral Manuel Blanco Encalada to prepare an expeditionary force to lead the army of the restoration. Last of all, he sent ambassadors to Ecuador and Argentina to convince them to join his campaign. The delegation to Ecuador was well received, but since the country was in the midst of a bloody conflict between Guayaquil and Quito, the government decided to remain neutral.

The diplomatic mission to Buenos Aires was more successful. For a year, Portales had courted Argentine despot Juan Manuel de Rosas, sharing intelligence that showed that Santa Cruz was aiding the guerillas launching raids into northern Argentina. Portales presented documents that showed a detailed a plan to carve the northern part of Argentina into a new sovereign state. Unitarian guerillas were also making forays from Uruguay, and Rosas was afraid that their combined activities would destabilize his country.[43] He was at the start of his mandate and under constant attack from his political enemies. Therefore, the information convinced him to declare war on the Confederation.

Portales did not yet know that his biggest threat would come not come from abroad, but from within his own ranks. Even though Portales had purged the high command of the 136 senior officers who had fought alongside Freire, there were still many midranking and junior officers who supported the liberal cause. In June 1837, Portales travelled to inspect the military barracks at Quillota. Many officers thought that the war against the Confederation was just a pretext to clear out the remaining liberal elements from the ranks. As the soldiers passed in review, Colonel José Antonio Vidaurre arrested Portales and clapped him in irons.

The news of the mutiny soon got out, but the uprising did not spread. On the contrary, Encalada stopped his invasion preparations and put down the insurrection. Realizing that his gambit had failed, Vidaurre forced Portales to write a letter ordering the General Encalada to surrender. However, the general refused to do so, realizing that the request had been written under duress. As the two sides were getting ready for battle, the rebels decided to transport Portales to a new location. Along the way, his carriage was detained and he was executed.

Portales's authoritarian style was very unpopular, as was the notion of a war with the Confederation, but his brutal murder rallied the nation. The public and media blamed Santa Cruz for the assassination, stirring up a patriotic fervor that induced men to enlist. With the preparations for the invasion under way, the focus shifted to the Peruvian coast, as well as Bolivia's border with Argentina.

The first contact between Chile and the Confederation occurred at sea. The blockade of Callao was having mixed results. Although the port was not completely sealed off, maritime traffic was limited. There were also several small naval engagements, particularly off the coast of Ecuador, but the most interesting developments occurred along the Argentine border. Santa Cruz tried to placate the Argentines, but Rosas had already declared war. Given that the Bolivian border is so far away from Buenos Aires, the Confederates were able to attack first. Confederation troops, under the command of General Otto Phillippe Braun, pushed deep into the province of Jujuy. This forced the Argentines to take defensive positions, even though they had started the conflict. Soon, Buenos Aires was rushing to send troops, arms, and ammunition to prevent the collapse of the northern provinces. To make matters worse, Santa Cruz negotiated a series of favorable trade treaties with the United States, Britain, and France. In return, they diplomatically recognized the Confederation and pressured Buenos Aires to break off, but it refused to budge.

The French became incensed at the Argentine arrogance, especially since they already had a long list of grievances, such as the imposition of military ser-

---

[43]   Rojas and Berdichesky, *Guerra, Región, y Nació.*

vice on French nationals and the refusal of Argentina to grant France "most favorable nation" trading status. When Buenos Aires declined to accede to the new demands, Paris ordered the blockade of the River Plate in 1838, which only added to Argentina's economic woes. As mentioned in the previous chapter, the embargo was not lifted until after the war.

Meanwhile, in Chile, the military was preparing its attack. On September 15, 1837, the expeditionary fleet sailed from Valparaíso. The army of the restoration, which was under the command of Admiral Encalada, consisted of 3,200 Chilean troops and 420 Peruvian soldiers. Although the blockade of Callao did not curtail all trade, it prevented the Confederation naval forces from sailing out to intercept the expeditionary force. The allied invasion was also supposed to coincide with a new Argentine offensive against Bolivia. The idea was that Santa Cruz would be forced to divide his army along two fronts, with part of it deployed on the Argentine border and the other part on the shore engaging the army of the restoration. Yet, the Argentines reconsidered on the eve of the battle. Their forces had already fared poorly against the Bolivians. Afraid of endangering their northern provinces, they backed out at the last minute.

Two weeks after Restoration Movement's fleet left Valparaíso, the ships made landfall in Cobija, and the troops marched toward Arequipa. They proceeded under a number of misguided assumptions and bad intelligence from reconnaissance units: they believed that they would find volunteers along the way, that Peruvian farmers would contribute provisions, and that mass desertions from the Confederation's ranks would swell the ranks and increase their numbers. None of this turned out to be the case. As was evident during Salaverry's offensive against Santa Cruz, southern Peru was sympathetic to the Confederation cause.

A sense of foreboding began to grow as the expeditionary force moved deeper into enemy territory, retracing Salaverry's disastrous steps from a year earlier. As it approached Arequipa, the force found Santa Cruz's troops waiting on the other side of the Paucarpata River. The two armies maneuvered, but the Confederation troops had the high ground. With each squared off against the other, the Confederation leader ordered the artillery to fire a volley over the Chileans' heads. He then sent Encalada a note proposing a parley. The Chileans agreed and presented their demands. After a few days, the Confederation signed the Treaty of Paucarpata, where they agreed to meet all of the terms, including the full recognition of Chile's foreign debt, although they still refused to accede to the demand of the Confederation's dissolution.

Encalada knew that the dissolution of the Confederation was a key objective, but he perceived his situation to be dire. With Portales dead, he assumed that the government would be more interested in finding a peaceful resolution of the conflict. He was also isolated and running low on supplies. Moreover, the Argentine diversion never materialized, and the entire Confederation Army was bearing down on him. Not wishing to end up like Salaverry, Encalada moved to secure the best possible deal and retreated with his forces intact.[44]

Unfortunately, he did not get a favorable reception upon his return to Valparaíso. The admiral was ridiculed and court-martialed for having negotiated such poor terms—for having agreed to the same terms as the earlier diplomatic mission, which had already been rejected the year before. In the end, the admiral was acquitted of all charges. Nevertheless, Chile refused to ratify the treaty, and began to work on a new offensive campaign.

As dawn broke on first days of January 1838, the Chilean government launched a second invasion force, this time with General Manuel Bulnes at the helm. The beefy general came from a distinguished military family. His father, a captain in the Royal Army, obtained a commission for his son to study in the infantry corps, but when the young man was appointed adjutant to a Spanish brigadier general during the War of Independence, he refused the appointment. The Spanish correctly suspected that the younger Bulnes was sympathetic to the rebel cause, and they exiled him to a distant island in Pacific. Bulnes eventually escaped and joined the rebels, taking part in several of the most important Chilean battles. He then linked up with his uncle, José Joaquín Prieto. In addition to his powerful connections, the corpulent leader was a skilled tactician. By the time of the War of the Confederation, he was a senior officer; he was given the command of the Second Restoration Expedition and assigned the command of the United Restoration Army, which included Peruvians who were fighting under the ever-opportunistic Gamarra.

Confident that the Protector was still in southern Peru, Bulnes decided to concentrate his efforts on capturing Lima. By leapfrogging over the south, he could lay siege to the capital and cut off the Confederation's supply lines. However, he first needed to neutralize the naval force they had deployed along the southern coast of Peru. On January 12, 1838, a squadron of frigates led by Admiral Robert Simpson, an English mercenary, surprised and attacked a smaller detachment of Confederation warships in the port of Islay, off the coast of Arequipa. The two groups exchanged broadsides, but the Confederation forces were badly outgunned. As dusk turned into night, they fled, thus allowing the invasion fleet to proceed northward. In the meantime, Lima's support for the war was waning. The ever-opportunistic President Orbegoso decided to secede from the Confederation and sue for peace as soon as the Chilean expeditionary force arrived off the port of Callao. Not surprisingly, General Bulnes distrusted Orbegoso's overture of peace, knowing his reputation for betrayal. Nevertheless, he used the negotiations to rest his troops, weary from the long voyage. On August 7, 1838, the invasion force finally debarked at Ancón, thirty miles north of Lima.

Orbegoso's troops took up defensive positions and waited for the Chileans to arrive. After two weeks, the army reached Portada de Guías, one of the entrances

[44] Fabio Galdámez Lastra, *Historia Militar de Chile: Estudio Crítico de la Campaña de 1838–1839* (Santiago de Chile: Trabajo Premiado En El Certámen Del Centenario, 1910).

to the old, walled city. A small cavalry detachment, led by a future Peruvian president, Ramón Castilla, was probing the outer defenses when it was were ambushed. Refusing to give quarter, Bulnes ordered cannons to be brought up from behind and fired into the enemies' lines. The defenders fell back and regrouped at a small stone bridge. With dusk approaching, the Chilean general did not want to lose his momentum. Therefore, he ordered a cavalry charge. The thundering horsemen bore down on the foot soldiers, instilling panic and inducing them to run.

Soldiers fled the city and Orbegoso went into hiding. These types of frontal attacks characterized Bulnes's tactics throughout the remainder of the campaign. He was bold and decisive, and he thrived on momentum, regardless of how desperate the situation seemed. The Confederation forces were in disarray, and a contingent of seven hundred troops, mostly Bolivians, escaped to the Real Felipe fortress, the citadel that guarded the entrance to the port. In the end, the Peruvians suffered a tremendous defeat. More than a thousand soldiers lay dead. Meanwhile, the army of the restoration had lost only forty.

That same evening, two major events took place. The first was Gamarra's swearing-in as president of Peru. The second was that the fortress was placed under siege. In addition to the seven hundred Confederation troops that escaped from the Battle of Portada de Guías, the fort was manned by a contingent of five hundred men under the command of Colonel Manuel de la Guarda. Therefore, the Chileans needed to be sure to keep them corralled.

Confederation troops continued converging on the fortress. The commander was more than willing to provide them with refuge, but he refused to allow their leader, Field Marshall Domingo Nieto, to enter. Like Orbegoso, Nieto had behaved in cowardly fashion at the Battle of Portada de Guías, fleeing in the middle of the fight. When he tried to enter the fort, de la Guarda exiled him, forcing him onto a ship bound for Guayaquil. Orbegoso also made his way to the fort. He was allowed to enter, but was imprisoned for his cowardly conduct. For the next two months, the twelve hundred men lived under a state of siege, blockaded by the Chilean Navy at sea and surrounded by the army of the Restoration Movement on shore.

Although Bulnes was an excellent field tactician, he was not adept at conducting static operations. The area surrounding the fort was marshy and thick with mosquitos. Many Chileans fell ill during the siege, which thinned the ranks. The general also lacked the equipment and arms needed to break the fort's formidable defenses. It had been built in the mid-1700s with thick stone walls to defend against pirate attacks. Bulnes lacked the siege engines and cannons that could breach the walls. Furthermore, his army was widely dispersed. He had a large contingent of men in the sierra to guard the western approaches to Lima, as well as a large deployment of soldiers guarding the northern and southern flanks. Chilean military organization and weapons, as well as naval support, made them a formidable force along the coastal regions, but the situation was different in the narrow mountain passes of the Andes. They had little knowledge of the territory, and they were not accustomed to the climate and altitude. Therefore, the Confederation soldiers could easily take them on.

One such engagement occurred on September 18, 1838, when 272 Chilean soldiers were ambushed in the town of Matucana, fifty miles east of Lima. The attackers, an advance column of Santa Cruz's Confederation Army, were headed north to the capital. The Chilean battalion was celebrating Independence Day by firing a twenty-one-gun salute when it was suddenly surprised. Chaos reigned as Santa Cruz's soldiers poured out of the craggy mountain passes, and it looked as though the Chileans were going to be routed. Fortunately, their superior training allowed them to regroup and counterattack. The battalion was able to retreat, but the clash made it clear to the high command that controlling the Andean highlands would be a difficult endeavor.

Likewise, the Chilean Navy was having problems enforcing its blockade. One of the difficulties was the constant pressure from the international community. A host of ships from the United States, France, and Britain lay just beyond the Chilean fleet and demanded free access to Callao. Hence, the navy was forced to loosen its grip, allowing some traffic to move through the port. The relaxation of the blockade allowed de la Guarda to slip in supplies and equipment. By early November, word arrived that Santa Cruz was on the outskirts of Lima. Bulnes knew he would be an easy target if he did not move out, since the Protector could lay siege to the capital. Not only would he have to tend to the needs of his men, he would also have to feed the population of Lima. Therefore, he decided abandon the city and find a more favorable place to engage the enemy.[45]

On November 8, Bulnes ordered his infantry and artillery to embark; meanwhile the cavalry was ordered to march north. A small squadron was left on blockade duty, while the rest of the fleet transported the army. A week later, the amphibious force arrived in Trujillo. The men disembarked and rendezvoused with the cavalry. The now-reunited Restoration forces proceeded deeper into northern Peru. Their escape allowed the Confederation to retake Lima, liberate the besieged fort, and begin plans for a new offensive campaign.

Santa Cruz knew that the Chileans' main weakness was their supply lines, and harassing the fleet was the best way to undermine the invasion force. To bolster his own naval resources, the Protector issued letters of marque offering foreign ships the opportunity to legally raid Chilean vessels and take the spoils. Several captains took up the offer. On November 24, 1838, under the command of French Captain Juan Blanchet, a small squadron of British, Mexican, and Peruvian raiders set sail from Callao.

For many months, the blockading squadron had been on duty, under the command of Jorge Bynnon, a Welsh mercenary. Bynnon's ships were in bad shape, sup-

---

[45] Gonzalo Búlnes, *Historia de la Campaña lel Perú en 1838* (Santiago de Chile: Imprenta de los Tiempos, 1878).

plies were depleted, and morale was low. The day before the engagement, Bynnon sent word to the admiralty requesting supplies and reinforcements because he knew that his squadron could not repel an attack in its current state. When Blanchet's privateer raiders approached, Bynnon had no choice but to lift the blockade, and then escape the safety of the open sea.

With the blockade broken, Santa Cruz prepared his men for the final offensive. Thinking that Bulnes was low on supplies, the Confederation troops followed in hot pursuit. However, the army of the restoration was not in bad shape. Northern Peru was sympathetic to the rebel cause, and they were willing to provide assistance. All Santa Cruz needed to do was to scout the right place to do battle.

As he moved north, Bulnes tried to slow Santa Cruz's advance by cutting bridges and laying ambushes. On December 17, a squad of ten Chilean soldiers prevented a company of fifty Bolivians from taking the bridge at Llaclla. A month later, the rear guard of the Restoration Army came in direct contact with the Confederation's vanguard at the bridge over the River Buin. The Chilean general ordered three battalions to delay the Confederation forces, while his men advanced toward Yungay, a town in the middle of a canon, the Callejón Huaylas, or Alley of Huaylas. The skirmish was a draw, but Santa Cruz lost one of his better men, General de la Guarda—the valiant colonel who had held off the siege in Callao.

Two weeks later, the two armies finally met up at Yungay. The sides were evenly matched, with about six thousand men each. They had undergone weeks of forced marches, and morale was low. Roughly a quarter of Santa Cruz's troops were Bolivian, while a fifth of the Restoration Army was Peruvian. Therefore, the commands were a mix of nationalities and officers.

Bulnes was assisted by Ramón Castilla, the cavalry officer who had engaged the enemy at the Portada de Guías. The Protector, who had been assisted previously by generals Braun and O'Connor, was alone this time. Nevertheless, his intention was not to engage the enemy. With the enemy cut off from their supply ships, Santa Cruz thought they would negotiate. However, the Chileans knew that this was not an option. Having seen the receptions that their predecessors had received when they returned empty-handed, they knew that they had no other option but to defeat the Confederation or die trying.

To goad Bulnes, Santa Cruz made the situation appear ominous. His troops took the high ground by occupying Punyan and Pan de Azúcar, two prominent hills that commanded the valley. The Callejón Huaylas, or Alley of Huaylas, is a long, narrow valley between two mountain ranges: the snowcapped Cordillera Blanca (White Mountains) on one side, and the towering Cordillera Negra (Black Mountains) on the other. The terrain offers very little chance to maneuver or escape. The Santa River runs through the narrow canyon. The much smaller Ancash River flows right across the base of the Pan de Azúcar and empties into the Santa.

In controlling Callejón Huaylas, the Confederation controlled the most strategically optimum position in the valley. The battlefield was indeed grim for the

Restoration Army. The defenders held the high ground, but Bulnes thrived in such conditions, so he held firm. His previous successes had occurred when he had attacked decisively and kept the offensive going, regardless of his losses. He planned to follow the same strategy in the Battle of Yungay.

Bulnes's army attacked at dawn, and all of the pieces began to fall into place. Bulnes ordered the Aconcagua Battalion to take Punyan, the smaller of the two hills that straddled the valley. Colonel Pedro Silva was at the head, with three battalions in reserve. The hill was slightly sloped, and Colonel Eusebio Guilarte was waiting at the top with a battalion of Confederation defenders. He also held three companies in reserve. As the Chileans made their way up the summit, Guilarte suddenly ordered his men to abandon the high ground—without firing a shot. In many ways, the War of the Confederation was a civil war between northern and southern Peru, and switching sides was not completely unusual. With this desertion, the Chileans quickly took the hill, boosting the men's spirits and morale.

At nine in the morning, Bulnes started his second attack. This time it was against the more formidable Pan de Azúcar. The task was assigned to Colonel Jerónimo Valenzuela, who was assigned a column of four hundred men. The equatorial sun was starting to blaze as the soldiers clawed up the steep cliffs. Many of them used their rifles as pick axes to ascend. Confederation soldiers fired on the attackers and hurled stones. Wounded men plunged to their deaths or rolled down helplessly crashing into those below them. Within minutes, a third of the attackers had been wiped out, including Colonel Valenzuela. Yet, the Restoration forces persevered. Fewer than half made it to the top, but those who did jumped over the parapets, fixed bayonets, and charged. The result was a bloodbath. The enraged Chileans tore into the defenders' lines, stabbing even surrendering soldiers. One of the companies was led by Candelaria Pérez, a young Chilean girl who had enlisted when the Restoration Army entered Lima. Until then, she had worked as a housemaid for a Dutch family who had relocated to Callao. In the army, she rose to the rank of sergeant. During the assault, all the officers in her company were killed, which made her in command as the ranking officer. She led her company through a hail of gunfire to help take the hill, in the process becoming a national hero.

The Chilean losses on Pan de Azúcar were high, but they continued to press the attack. Company after company charged up the hill, overcoming enormous odds to reach the Confederation troops. The onslaught worked, and as the day wore on it appeared that the Santa Cruz's forces were all but defeated, so the Protector ordered his Fourth Battalion to cross the Ancash River and attack the Chileans from behind. Santa Cruz imagined that trapped between the defenders on the hill and the Fourth Battalion, the Chilean assault would crumble, but he was wrong. Bulnes countered by ordering his Colchagua Battalion into action. The troops fell into formation and fired into the attacking Confederation forces, dropping a third of the men.

With the situation clearly turning in favor of the Chileans, Santa Cruz decided to engage the main part of his army, which was dug into a set of trenches and fortifications on one side of the Ancash River. Even though the river does not have much flow during the end of the year, the steep banks present a formidable obstacle. Nevertheless, the Protector ordered the Confederation soldiers to fix bayonets and charge. Now, the Chileans were on the defensive, and Bulnes called for reinforcements to repulse the attack.

The Confederation regrouped on the other side of the Ancash, but the Chileans counterattacked before pulling back to their side of the river to reload. So much blood was lost in the endless crossings and recrossings of the river that the water began to flow a dull shade of crimson. Suddenly, the seesaw came to an abrupt stop when the last Confederation defenders of Pan de Azúcar surrendered, and the Chilean colors were unfurled on the hilltop. As a roar of euphoria broke out among the ranks, Bulnes realized that he had regained the momentum. He prepared one last frontal attack. With a new artillery battery deployed on Punyan pummeling the Confederation forces, the army of the restoration lined up and prepared to charge.

High on the opposite bank, the Confederation troops were waiting behind a hastily arranged bulwark of defenses. Bulnes figured that his tactic had a 10 percent chance of success, but even those odds of success were high enough for him to press forward. As the Chileans and northern Peruvians advanced, the cavalry maneuvered behind them. All at once, they pounced, breaking the Confederation lines and stirring mayhem. Seeing his troops splinter and disintegrate, Santa Cruz abandoned the field of battle.

Under disguise, Santa Cruz made his way back to southern Peru and Bolivia. All was lost. He was no longer the Protector. He no longer had the support of the people, and he was forced to flee the country, never to return. Bulnes, however, returned as a hero. His military success helped launch his political career, and he was swept into the presidency two years later.

Like a dream that melts away at the first light of dawn, the Battle of Yungay marked the end of the Confederation. When the Restoration Army returned to Lima, the troops filed proudly through the city. There were no acts of animosity or unrest; that would be left for a later war. In the end, Chile's military performance transformed the nation. Not only did it stir a strong sense of patriotism that healed the rifts that had developed during the civil war, but also it gave the country a sense of vigor that would allow it to compete against competitors above its weight class for the next two centuries.

Chile was able to take on an alliance that was much larger in size, population, and wealth. The conflict would whet its appetite for the mineral riches embedded in the northern desert, and it would give the country the confidence to take on the same two adversaries again before the end of the century. The war also convinced the country's elite to maintain a large standing army and a formidable navy to project its power at home and abroad.

The War of the Confederation became the crucible of fire that allowed the warring states to forge their national identities. Fractured by years of colonization, caste segmentation, and civil strife, the war allowed disparate people to unite under a single flag. Sadly, it also sowed seeds of animosity that would lead to national rivalries that still mark the lack of communication and cooperation among members of a region despite sharing a similar origin.

The war torpedoed the Bolivian-Peruvian Confederation, and the protagonists would soon be at each other's throats. Moreover, the idea of a union between Bolivia and Peru remains an idea that is still very much alive today. Prior to taking office in 2011, Peruvian President Ollanta Humala once again raised the issue of uniting the two countries. The War of the Confederation may have been an obscure conflict that occurred two centuries ago, but its theme resonates to this day.

Last of all, the war highlighted forces that triggered South American conflicts. Territorial disputes were at the heart of the problem. This time, it was Bolivia's access to the Pacific Ocean, and whether it should it go through Arica or Cobija. Meanwhile, a panoply of external powers acted as instigators that helped stir the state of animosity. However, these external forces would play a more overt role during subsequent engagements.

4 THE WAR OF THE TRIPLE ALLIANCE: ALL AGAINST ONE

THE WAR OF THE TRIPLE ALLIANCE: ALL AGAINST ONE

On March 1, 1870, Paraguayan President Francisco Solano López paused on the banks of the Aquidabán River. He was on the run, hiding in the rainforest of his devastated country. His small detachment of two hundred soldiers was all that remained of the once-mighty Paraguayan patriotic army. During a skirmish in Cerro Corá earlier that day, he had been wounded in the stomach and head, and now he had become separated from his men. Suddenly, he was ambushed by Brazilian General José Antônio Correia da Câmara and a squad of six soldiers. Refusing to surrender, Solano López rushed at the enemy, and was mortally wounded in the process. This violent end closed the bloodiest war in Latin American history, and consigned a promising nation to the ash heap of history.

Like the American Civil War (1861–1865) and the Franco Prussian War (1870–1871), the War of the Triple Alliance was a conflict that heralded some of the deadly weapons and techniques that would be deployed during the twentieth century. Armored warships, Gatling guns, observation balloons, telegraphs, and trench warfare were staples of the conflict. It was also an early example of total war, with three hundred thousand soldiers from four belligerent countries meeting on the battlefield. In the end, Paraguay was devastated. It lost more than 60 percent of its population, 40 percent of its territory, and most of its dignity—leaving it with a memory that still smolders in the national psyche.

Paraguay had belonged to the viceroyalty of the River Plate. Bereft of mineral resources, it was best known for its large population of Guaraní Indians. For that reason, it was placed under the auspices of the Catholic Church, which set up a system of missions in order to proselytize and use the indigenous labor to produce products for the miners of Potosí.[46] Once the War of Independence started, Paraguay, like Bolivia, split off and became isolated. There were attempts by the rebels in Buenos Aires to claim them. Argentine General Manuel Belgrano was assigned the futile task of recapturing the territory, but failed. The revolutionary leaders eventually lost interest and turned to the more pressing issue of eradicating the Spanish threat from the western flank.

After the war, the United Provinces devoted their attention to resolving their internal disputes, leaving the issues of Paraguay and Bolivia aside. At the same time, Brazil preferred to maintain a buffer between itself and Argentina. The Pla-

---

46   Nelsy Echávez-Solano and Kenya C. Dworkin y Méndez (Eds.), *Spanish and Empire* (Nashville, TN: Vanderbilt University Press, 2007).

tine and Cisplatine Wars had been painful experiences. Tensions had eased with a buffer between the two neighbors. This was why Brazil was the first country to recognize Paraguay as an independent and sovereign nation.

Paraguay lacked large deposits of precious metals, but it had an abundance of fertile land and a large labor pool. Still, it had one major disadvantage: it was landlocked. Brazil lay to the north and east, Bolivia to the west, and Argentina to the south. Paraguay's only access to the rest of the world was through the rivers that drained into the River Plate. This forced its government into a dependent relationship with Argentina, which became a constant source of political stress. Surrounded by such large and powerful nations, Paraguay's military needed to be on a constant war footing. For that reason, like ancient Troy, the small nation had a long tradition of authoritarianism, militarism, and centralized power.

The Paraguayan system of administration had been hierarchical ever since its days as a Jesuit colony when small groups of clergy governed the large indigenous population. This imbued the country with a legacy of autocracy, but with a humanistic bent that facilitated the rise of strong paternalistic leaders.[47] José Gaspar Rodríguez de Francia was the first, followed by his nephew, Carlos Antonio López, and then Carlos's son, Francisco Solano López.

There are two popular versions of their historical legacies. Some historians present them as feudal lords who enslaved the indigenous population to become fabulously wealthy. Others depict them as utopian visionaries who used state ownership to advance the nation's development. In fact, they were a combination of both and, whether despotic or patriarchal, autocratic. Paraguay's macroeconomic policies could be characterized as autarkic, statist, and mercantilist; they limited imports, private enterprise, and foreign investment. As a result, the country was forced to rely on higher rates of savings and import-substitution for its growth.

The mainstays of the economic model were the state-owned plantations; soon after independence, the government had nationalized the land belonging to Royalist officers, sympathizers, and political enemies, converting them into huge, state-owned farms producing yerba mate, tobacco, grains, cotton, and timber for export, which generated the revenues needed to build the region's first railroad and telegraph. It also allowed the government to establish shipyards, ironworks, and the largest standing army in South America. The Paraguayan Army was well outfitted and trained in the latest technology and techniques by European mercenaries.

The organization of the Paraguayan economy was very different from its neighbors, and it was also more prosperous. Its state-led economic model created a more equitable distribution of income, which contrasted sharply with the great concentration of wealth that characterized Argentina and Brazil. Paraguayan society was also structured differently. Unlike many of the other Latin American colonies, which re-

[47] Edberto Oscar Acevedo, *La Intendencia del Paraguay en el Virreinato del Río de la Plata* (Buenos Aires: Ediciones Ciudad Argentina, 1996).

strained access to education in order to preserve schisms in their social hierarchies, the Paraguayan government fostered public education. It even gave scholarships to members of the lower classes to study abroad, thus facilitating social mobility.

There are also contrasting views on Paraguay's foreign policy. Many depict it as an expansionist state, with aspirations of gaining direct access to the Atlantic, while others see it as defensive, with genuine concerns about its large and hegemonic neighbors. The latter group argues that the aggressive tendencies demonstrated by Argentina and Brazil threatened the sovereignty of the smaller regional nations. For that reason, they say, the War of the Triple Alliance was not so much a land grab by Paraguay as it was a necessary move in the struggle for survival.

This dichotomy in perception is crucial to the depiction of the conflict. History is written by the victors. In this case, Brazil, Argentina, and Uruguay have typically depicted Paraguay as the aggressor rather than as the victim of a genocidal war. To perpetuate that viewpoint, the allies torched the national archives in Asunción. Most of the surviving histories of the conflict were written in Buenos Aires and Río de Janeiro. Nevertheless, many newspaper chronicles, diaries, and letters survived, and they paint a much more complex picture than the common narrative.

The first major milestone of the conflict occurred in 1862, when the presidential baton was passed to Francisco Solano López. Spoiled as a young boy, he was impetuous and autocratic. At the age of eighteen, he was promoted to the rank of brigadier general. At twenty-six, he was sent to Europe, with plenipotentiary powers, where he spent a year and a half in Britain, France, and Italy. He became enraptured with tales of Napoleon, and developed a romantic fascination for the Napoleonic Wars, ordering similar uniforms for his troops and an exact replica of Bonaparte's gold crown. In Paris, López met Eliza Lynch, an Irish courtesan, and brought her back to Asunción to be his mistress and conjugate. Upon his arrival in 1855, his father named him minister of war, and he served in that position until he assumed the presidency seven years later.

The regional balance of power was in flux when Solano López donned the presidential sash in 1862. A year earlier, the military forces of Buenos Aires, under the command of Bartolomé Mitre, came to blows with the army of the Argentine Confederation at the Battle of Pavón. The Confederation forces, led by José Justo de Urquiza, had been winning the engagement when Urquiza suddenly quit the field of battle. Realizing that his opponents were melting away, Mitre, who had been retreating, turned and gave pursuit. This marked a pivotal turning point in the country's history. Since its independence a half century earlier, Argentina had been ravaged by a contest between Unitarians and Federalists. When Urquiza decided to abandon Pavón, the Federalist movement came apart at the seams, and the country consolidated under the Unitarians' model.[48]

<hr>

[48]   Isidoro J. Ruiz Moreno, *El Misterio De Pavón: Las Operaciones Militares y sus Consecuencias Políticas* (Buenos Aires: Claridad, 2005).

One of Mitre's most trusted officers was General Venancio Flores, a Uruguayan with an extremely violent streak. A month after the victory at Pavón, his men surprised a contingent of three hundred Federalist troops at Cañada de Gomez. Instead of taking prisoners, he ordered their throats slit. Bloodthirsty and ambitious, he burned with a desire to pilfer the presidency of his country. As discussed in an earlier chapter, Uruguay had been wracked since its independence by a struggle between the two leading political factions, the Blancos and Colorados. Tired of the bloodshed, they signed a truce in 1860 and created the Fusionist coalition, appointing Bernardo Berro, a Blanco, as head of state.

The end of the Argentine civil war convinced Flores that it was time to return home. He petitioned Mitre for assistance in overthrowing the legitimately elected government. The Argentine leader agreed, and he provided him with funds, arms, and soldiers. On April 19, 1863, Flores debarked at a small Uruguayan landing aptly named Rincon de las Gallinas (Chickens' Corner), slightly south of Fray Bentos, where he began to assemble a new insurgency called the Liberating Crusade. The resumption of the hostilities led to the collapse of the Fusionist coalition, when the Colorados decided to join Flores. However, he was not able to overthrow the government.[49]

Berro's hand was strong. An aristocrat from a large, landowning family, he had been the country's first president. Now, he was serving for a second time. Flores may have landed with men, equipment, and ammunition, but it was not enough to win the nation over. Therefore, he was forced into a guerilla campaign. In March 1864, Berro ended his term, but the ongoing conflict impeded elections. Therefore, he was replaced on an interim basis by the president of the senate, Atanasio Aguirre, also from the Blancos. He managed to keep Flores at bay, but the situation was about to change.

Uruguay's relations with Brazil had been stormy ever since the end of the Cisplatine War. Contraband trading was rampant, and bandits attacked farms on both sides of the border. In May 1864, the imperial government of Brazil presented Uruguay with a list of incidents and demanded indemnification; Aguirre refused. Brazil's emperor responded by ordering an invasion of Uruguay. The objective was to occupy the river port of Paysandú, the country's second-largest city, to exact retribution.

The enterprise was put under the command of the Marquis of Tamandaré, Admiral Joaquim Marques Lisboa, who ordered a squadron of five Brazilian warships to sail up the Uruguay River. Given that the river was shared by Uruguay and Argentina, the Brazilians requested safe passage from Buenos Aires, which happily acceded to the petition. This came as little surprise to the Uruguayan government, given that Argentina was openly assisting Flores's subversive actions. Squeezed by the hegemonic forces of Argentina and Brazil, Berro appealed to his neighbors, Solano López and Urquiza.

Urquiza's forces were formidable, despite his reversal at Pavón. He was by far the richest man in Argentina. Tens of thousands of gauchos were at his command,

[49] Gordon Ross, *Argentina and Uruguay* (New York: Macmillan, 1916).

and the province of Entre Ríos was his domain. An Uruguayan delegation traveled to his home and informed him that Montevideo had no chance of standing up to Argentina and Brazil; they warned Urquiza that what was happening in Uruguay was a precursor of what would happen to him. Urquiza, however, was exhausted with the Federalist cause, and the constant bickering between the various political factions. He had resigned himself to accepting the supremacy of Buenos Aires, and he was refocusing his efforts on enlarging his enormous wealth.[50]

Solano López was not as complacent. Paraguay was a sovereign country, and he knew that was occurring in Uruguay heralded what lay ahead for him. Buenos Aires had been distracted for fifty years by its internal disputes, but with the civil war over, it was now going to lay claim to the territories of the old viceroyalty. Brazil was also on a similar mission, wanting to dominate the smaller states along its southern flank. Therefore, Solano López decided to act. On November 12, 1864, the Paraguayan Navy captured the Brazilian steamer *Marqués de Olinda* as it was sailing north on the Paraguay River. Such an aggression constituted an act of war, and there was no turning back.

Solano López had been gearing up for such a situation ever since he had became minister of war. A few years earlier, he had ordered Paraguayan spies to reconnoiter the southern regions of Brazil, laying out tactics and plans for a preemptive invasion. His troops were well prepared for the fight. Although his neighbors were larger and richer, their land forces were not as well organized. Paraguay had a standing army of forty-four thousand men. After its civil wars, Argentina's army had been reduced to fewer than five thousand soldiers, with most of them deployed along the southern frontier to defend against Indian attacks. Brazil's army was larger, with more than sixteen thousand troops, with a great concentration of them in Río Grande Do Sul, where they had been deployed since the Farroupilha uprising. Uruguay's army was the smallest of three allies, with fewer than two thousand men.

The situation was different on the naval front. Thanks to its shipbuilding program and foreign acquisitions, the Paraguayan Navy had twenty-nine warships. The Argentine Navy had a total of five vessels. Uruguay had none. Meanwhile, the Brazilian Navy consisted of forty-two warships; its fleet had shrunk significantly since independence, but it was still formidable. As was mentioned in the chapter on the Cisplatine and Platine wars, the Portuguese legacy of a strong navy provided a decisive military advantage.

Despite Paraguay's initial act of aggression, Brazil was largely focused on exacting its revenge on Uruguay.[51] On December 1, 1864, Brazil attacked the Uruguayan city of Paysandú with a combined force of twenty thousand soldiers and sailors, assisted by Uruguayan rebels led by Venancio Flores. Shelled from land and sea,

[50] William Hartley Jeffrey, *Mitre and Urquiza: A Chapter in the Unification of the Argentine Republic* (Madison, NJ: Library Publishers, 1952).

[51] Guido Rodríguez Alcalá and José Eduardo Alcázar, *Paraguay y Brasil: Documentos sobre las Relaciones Binacionales, 1844–1864* (Asunción: Editorial Tiempo de Historia, 2007).

the city was reduced to rubble. A week later, women, children, and the elderly were evacuated to a nearby island. There was still hope that Urquiza would join the fight and turn the tide. Many Argentines from Entre Ríos volunteered to defend against the siege, but Urquiza would not budge. On the contrary, he betrayed his neighbor by selling thirty thousand horses to the Brazilians at a greatly inflated price, thus buying his neutrality.

Witnessing the impunity with which Brazil, with the assistance of Argentina, was treating Uruguay, Paraguay decided to act more decisively. Proclaiming that the invasion of Uruguay was a clear act of aggression, it declared war on Brazil on December 13, 1864. Ten days later, a battalion of forty-two hundred soldiers boarded seven military transports and headed north on the Paraguay River. Their destination was the Brazilian city of Coimbra in the state of Mato Grosso do Sul.

On December 27, they launched a surprise attack against a garrison of 155 men. The Brazilians held out for two days before escaping upriver to the military city of Corumbá. This fortification was larger, and it was defended by five hundred soldiers, but the commander, realizing that he was grossly outmanned and outgunned, decided to retreat to Cuiabá, the capital of Mato Grosso, where he could count on more resources. Because the river was too shallow for their steamships to proceed, the Paraguayan troops installed themselves in Corumbá, digging trenches and emplacing artillery pieces—where they remained until the end of the war.

A separate Paraguayan column launched a simultaneous incursion into the southeastern flank of Mato Grosso do Sul. They arrived at the military outpost of Dourados, which was defended by a small company of sixteen men. After a bloody fight in which all the Brazilian soldiers perished, the invasion force continued north, halting in Miranda. As a result, the Paraguayan Army had established two separate fronts deep within Brazilian territory. Their strategy was to create a diversionary attack that would distract the imperial forces from the larger operation that was about to push south across Argentina and join forces with Uruguay.

Back in Paysandú, the situation was growing desperate. Totally outgunned and outnumbered, the city surrendered on January 2, 1865. When the garrison leader, Leandro Gómez, approached the Brazilians to ask for terms, he was apprehended and handed over to Flores. Ignoring the conventions of war, the Uruguayan general ordered Gómez shot, thus marking the end of the siege. Next, Flores led his rebels and a force of eight thousand imperial soldiers toward Montevideo.

In the interim, Aguirre's term had ended. He was replaced with an interim president, Tómas Villalba, by the senate. Fearing a bloodbath and a repeat of Paysandú, Villalba began negotiating. The two sides agreed to allow the savage general to take over until elections could be called, while pardoning all of the Blancos and Colorados to avoid reprisals. The installation of Flores as the legitimate head of Uruguay reduced the country to puppet-state status, under the complete command of Argentina and Brazil.

The unfolding of events in Uruguay worried Solano López. While Brazil's position was clear, he was unsure what to do with Argentina. Buenos Aires continued to claim neutrality, but Mitre's compliant attitude toward the transit of Brazilian warships through Argentine rivers and his open support for Flores suggested something else. In order to probe Argentina's true intentions, he requested permission for the Paraguayan Army to cross through the Argentine province of Corrientes to assist the beleaguered Uruguayans. Mitre refused, claiming that Argentina was neutral and could not allow belligerents to enter.

The Paraguayans pointed out that Mitre had allowed Brazilian warships to sail up the Uruguay River to assist in the siege of Paysandú, and asked how he could call that neutral behavior, but there was no response from Mitre. The die was cast. War with Argentina was inevitable, but first Solano López had one more diplomatic card to play. He sent an emissary to Urquiza, proposing an alliance against Buenos Aires, going so far as to promise him the presidency of Argentina if they won, but the caudillo was no longer interested in championing lost causes.[52]

Left with no other option, Solano López called on the Paraguayan congress to declare war on Argentina. They debated for more than a month and finally issued the declaration of war on March 13, 1865, vesting him with martial powers and the command of the Paraguayan Army. His strategy was to invade the province of Corrientes in the hope that the local population would join his cause. Brimming with Guaraní Indians and their descendants, the province shared a great kinship with Paraguay and the Paraguayans. The invasion consisted of two prongs. One would push down the Paraná River toward the city of Corrientes; the other would thrust down the other side of the province, along the Uruguay River.

The campaign was directed from Humaitá, a fortress that sat at the confluence of the Paraguay and Paraná Rivers, controlling the fluvial access to the capital of Asunción; in other words, Humaitá was the front door to the nation. The impregnable fortification was defended by rings of thick walls and separate artillery batteries. As soon as the conflict started, Solano López relocated his headquarters there to direct the campaign.

The city of Corrientes was an important Argentine commercial hub. The capital of the province of the same name, the large port city sat on a set of bluffs. With hostilities imminent, the governor requested arms and troops from Buenos Aires, but Mitre ignored the requests. He was still dealing with insurrections in the west, and needed to ration his resources. Moreover, he was ignorant of Paraguay's declaration of war, since the document was still on its way. As a precaution, he sent two aging gunboats to assist in the city's defense. Little did he know what awaited.

On Holy Thursday, 1865, a squadron of five Paraguayan warships carrying five thousand soldiers was sent to take the city. The flotilla, under the command of

---

[52] Miguel Angél de Marco, *La Guerra del Paraguay*, 1st ed. (Buenos Aires: Planeta, 2003).

General Wenceslao Robles, slipped past the city docks under the cover of night, only to turn around and take it by surprise.

The fall of Corrientes triggered seismic tremors in Buenos Aires, especially when it was revealed that the city had fallen without a shot in self-defense. As Solano López thought, the population had welcomed the Paraguayans. A delegation of prominent citizens had even received the invading troops, waving Paraguayan flags. Afraid that his newly consolidated nation would fragment into pieces, Mitre pledged to end the conflict, and to be inside Asunción in less than three months. In the meantime, Solano López redoubled his efforts, adding an additional twenty thousand troops to the invasion force. Robles left a contingent of fifteen hundred soldiers to guard the city and continued down the Paraná River.

Mitre was in shock. Paraguay had to be destroyed before the situation spiraled out of control. Knowing his limitations, he invited his country's nemesis, Brazil, to join the enterprise, as well its new client state, Uruguay. Brazil, as it would soon become evident, needed the war to suppress its own secessionist groups. The tripartite treaty, which had been signed on May 1, 1865, was kept secret, since it endorsed an overwhelming use of force against a much smaller nation. The treaty was the formalization of the improvised alliance that had taken shape the year before in Uruguay, and it played out true to Solano López's fears of Brazil and Argentina's proclivity for hegemonic dominance. Formally known as the Triple Alliance, it named Mitre as the head of the expedition.

Mitre now had to rally his country. To do so, he changed the national political narrative. Up to that moment, the ideological debate had focused on the Unitarian versus Federalist forms of governments. However, the Battle of Pavón had made that argument moot. After the battle, Buenos Aires agreed to a revenue-sharing scheme known as coparticipation, which would distribute the customs revenues to the provinces. As a result, a hybrid form of administration emerged, with revenues split in a Federalist manner, but with Buenos Aires unilaterally commanding the nation. Needing to shift the public's attention away from this reality, Mitre created a new discourse, arguing that the war against Paraguay was a struggle against barbarism. Argentina's quest was to liberalize it, in the economic and political sense, and to put an end to the "savage tyranny" represented by state ownership.

As a result, Mitre framed the enterprise against Paraguay as a liberal crusade. This gave the conflict an economic dimension that was particularly attractive to Brazil—and Great Britain. Paraguay's more egalitarian form of economic organization was an embarrassing contrast to the private property arrangements that were employed in Brazil and Argentina, along with great concentrations of wealth they produced. It was also an obstacle to British attempts to make commercial inroads into the country, either through the capital markets or through direct foreign investment. It was one of the first times that economic ideology had been used as a justification for war.

The opening act of the allied offensive took place in Corrientes, when a squadron of eight Brazilian warships and two Argentine steamships retook the city. Mitre planned the operation, which was led by Argentine General Wenceslao Paunero. The invasion was bloody, with vicious house-to-house fighting that resulted in about five hundred casualties on each side. Much to their surprise, there was no welcome reception.

Afraid that the inhabitants would turn against them when the Paraguayans counterattacked, the allies retreated and reboarded their vessels. When they did so, the Paraguayans reentered the city and reinforced their defensive positions. Nevertheless, the Brazilian fleet remained anchored slightly south. From the middle of April, it set up a blockade. Not only did the blockade impede trade, it prevented the transport of munitions and weapons destined for Paraguay. This became an important setback for Solano López, who had wanted to procure more equipment from Europe and the United States. He needed find a way to break the blockade.

In June 1865, Solano López launched an operation that would become the largest naval battle in Latin American history. His plan was to take the Brazilian squadron by surprise; he hoped to capture several large vessels and use them to break the blockade. The mission was given to Commodore Pedro Ignacio Meza, one of the Paraguay's most senior and experienced naval officers. Lacking the proper resources, Meza's improvised squadron consisted of eight steamships armed with thirty cannons. In addition to the steamships, the Paraguayan squadron towed seven gun barges that could be anchored to provide fire support. Only the flagship, *Tacuarí*, had armored plating. Most of the remaining vessels were wooden paddle ships, including the Brazilian merchant vessel, *Marquês de Olinda*, which had been captured a few months earlier. In addition to the 492 sailors on board the vessels, the forces included a battalion of five hundred soldiers to serve as boarding parties. They were supported by twenty-two cannons, which were under the command of Lieutenant Colonel José María Bruguez and deployed along the heights of the city. Last of all, a regiment of two thousand reinforcements was at the ready. The Brazilian squadron consisted of nine armored steamships, fourteen hundred sailors, and thirteen hundred hundred soldiers.[53]

The mighty Paraná River is the second-longest waterway in South America, and it carries more water than the Mississippi. The river drains the central part of the continent, making it a major conduit for trade and communications. It bends past the city of Corrientes, which is a thousand kilometers from the mouth of the river, with a width of more than three kilometers. The name of the city refers to the currents that swirl as the river courses past it. The presence of large islands creates a Bernoulli effect that accelerates the velocity of the water while creating a cascade of whirlpools that are difficult to navigate.

Every night, the Brazilian fleet quit its station twenty kilometers south of Corrientes to bivouac on the opposite bank. The crew dropped anchor and disem-

53 Leslie Bethell, *The Paraguayan War, 1864–1870* (London: Institute of Latin American Studies, 1996).

barked, meanwhile keeping an eye on any traffic that approached. The Paraguay-ans knew that they were outgunned, so they decided to use the element of surprise to catch the Imperial Navy unaware. The plan was to sail down the Paraná under the cover of night. The raiding parties would then capture the ships before the Brazilians could reboard and counterattack.

The operation was launched on the night of June 10, 1865. Everything started well. The squadron sailed out of Humaitá and steamed down the Paraguay River. After midnight, the vessels had just entered the Paraná River when the propeller of the *Yberá* was damaged by underwater debris. Although it was not the lead ship, it was one of Meza's larger vessels—and one of the few that used a propeller pro-pulsion system. The admiral decided to press on, but at a slower pace. As a result, the squadron arrived abreast of the Brazilian fleet at dawn, although cloaked by a dense fog. Meza assumed that the ruse was up. The river current was also faster than he had expected, and he felt that the anchors would not hold enough to give the raiding parties sufficient time to board the ships. Therefore, he decided to push past the Brazilian squadron and rake the ships with cannon fire as he passed. His decision unleashed a groan of discontent among the members of the raiding party, who were poised to disembark.

The thundering broadside heralded their arrival, and the imperial sailors quickly reboarded. Better armed, they seriously damaged one of the marauding steamships and sank one of the barges. Several of the other attacking ships also sustained hits, producing heavy casualties within the raiding party. As he made his way past the anchored enemy, Meza realized that he was in a bind. He had lost the element of surprise, his only tactical advantage, and now he was in a vise. Upriver was a superior force, and downriver was an even larger enemy squadron on block-ade duty. Therefore, he had no other option but to fight. He ordered his ships to stop and prepare for a counterattack.

The Brazilian fleet immediately weighed anchor and sped downriver. Under the command of Commodore Francisco Manuel Barroso, the crews were ordered to battle stations. The heavy cruiser *Belmont* was the first in line. As it approached the enemy squadron, the shore artillery opened fire and engulfed the ship in flames. The next cruiser, the *Jequitinhonha*, turned away to avoid being drawn into the trap, but it ran aground. The Paraguayan artillery reacted by raining down a hail of fire on the second vessel. The Brazilian fleet was in disarray.

The Paraguayan admiral ordered three of his ships to engage the *Belmont*. He also signaled the sailors on the *Marquês de Olinda* to board the *Jequitinhonha*. To keep his squadron from disintegrating, Barroso ordered them to regroup upriv-er. Knowing that Meza's wooden ships were no match for his armored cruisers, the imperial commodore signaled his flagship, the *Amazonas*, to ram Meza's sec-ond-largest ship, the *Paraguarí*. The Brazilian warship pushed deep into the side of the wooden vessel, forcing it out of action. This allowed the momentum to turn in favor of the Brazilians. Seeing how easily his ironclad vessel had sliced into the

Paraguarí, Barroso ordered the *Amazonas* to ram two additional ships, including the *Marquês de Olinda.* He also ordered his gunners to aim at the Paraguayan side-wheelers, leaving them dead in the water. Having destroyed more than half of the enemy squadron, the imperial gunners turned their sights on the remaining barges and sank all of them. The battle had lasted the entire day, but the Brazilian Imperial Navy did not press the attack as dusk descended. They allowed the surviving Paraguayan ships to slip away and return to their base in Humaitá. On the deck of the retreating *Tacuaré,* Meza laid mortally wounded. He died a week later.

The engagement, which became known as the Battle of Riachuelo, was the largest naval battle in Latin American history, with the largest number of combatants and vessels. It marked an important milestone by establishing Brazil's naval superiority and its command of the river systems. Brazil's superior equipment and technology had been decisive. It was clear that Paraguay needed better vessels if it planned to take on the enemy. However, with the Brazilian blockade, Paraguay would be unable to receive additional equipment, and it would therefore be forced to rely on its own factories, foundries, and shipyards to meet its war needs.

Despite the setback, the Paraguayan Army continued its campaign. Robles slowly advanced down the shores of the Paraná River, even shelling the Brazilian squadron when it steamed south after its victory at Riachuelo. The general continued all the way to Goya, where the bulk of the Brazilian fleet was on blockade duty. At the same time, a contingent of twelve thousand Paraguayan soldiers moved south along the Uruguay River, which marked the line of demarcation between Brazil and Argentina. The eastern bank of the waterway marked the border of Brazil, while the western shore was Argentina. The two campaigns effectively separated the provinces of Corrientes and Missiones from the rest of the country, thus marking the largest invasion of Argentine territory.

The expeditionary force that advanced along the Uruguay River was under the command of Lieutenant Colonel Antonio de la Cruz Estigarribia. His first stop was the Brazilian city of São Borja, which fell the day after the Battle of Riachuelo. The colonel was under strict orders to halt his advance at the town of Itaqui, but he decided to press on after he saw the enemy running away. In late June 1865, he split his force into two groups and resumed the invasion, with a column on each side of the waterway. On the Argentine side of the river, a column of three thousand men was placed under the command of Major Pedro Duarte. Estigarribia controlled the rest of the force on the Brazilian side. The two columns finally halted a hundred kilometers south of Itaqui, when their resupply lines became dangerously overstretched. Duarte stopped at Paso de los Libres and Estigarribia halted at Uruguaiana, which was on the opposite side of the river.

In the meantime, the allies were preparing their offensive. The new center of operation was the Argentine city of Concordia, two hundred kilometers downriver from Paso de los Libres and Uruguaiana. The city hummed as tons of weapons, uniforms, and supplies arrived from all over the country. Foreign ships filled the docks with imported munitions. Thousands of Argentine recruits arrived each week. There was a great deal of excitement, as if the campaign was going to be a grand adventure. Sons of prominent politicians and wealthy families volunteered, but not everyone was as excited about the war. A month earlier, in the Entre Ríos town of Basualdo, an army of ten thousand mounted gauchos led by Ricardo López Jordán had deserted when they learned they were going to fight Paraguayans. They had been assembled by Urquiza and volunteered thinking that they were going to take on the Brazilians who had laid siege on Paysandú. As was evident during the fall of Corrientes, the population of northeastern Argentina had more in common with the Paraguayans than with the Brazilians. They shared the same language, customs, and ancestry of the Guaraní who populated the region.[54]

The Guaraní culture also penetrates deep into southern Brazil, which is was one of the reasons why so many Brazilian towns fell to the Paraguayan invaders without putting up much of a fight. The people of Río Grande do Sul had little in common with the European-based nobility of Río de Janeiro, as became evident during the Farroupilha uprising. Moreover, the imperial high command was panicking because desertions were becoming rampant. Hence, the rapid surrenders of Corrientes, São Borja, Itaqui, and Uruguaiana confirmed the fears in Río de Janeiro and Buenos Aires that Paraguay was an existentialist threat that needed to be eradicated because the invasion could provide the pretext for other states to secede.

This was the essence of the War of the Triple Alliance. It was never an effort to contain the expansionist ambitions of Solano López or to eradicate his statist policies; it was a joint effort by two mortal enemies, Argentina and Brazil, to wipe out a successful independent entity within their common domain. This was a conclusion that became apparent to Urquiza, and it explained why he abandoned the Federalist cause. He realized that he could never counter the immense power of Buenos Aires. Therefore, he acquiesced and dedicated himself to his commercial interests. However, Solano López never had that option. With the invasion of Uruguay and the massacre at Paysandú, he knew that it was only a matter of time until his country would suffer the same fate.[55]

Given that Paraguay was the center of Guaraní culture, its existence was the threat. Therefore, it needed to be wiped out—its economy destroyed, its leadership eradicated, and its population decimated through nothing less than a genocidal campaign. That was why the economic and political elite in Río de Janeiro decided that it needed to pay more attention to the conflict. Therefore, against the wishes of the congress, Emperor Dom Pedro II decided to decamp for the field of battle.[56]

[54] Barbara Anne Ganson, *The Guaraní Under Spanish Rule in the Río de la Plata* (Palo Alto, CA: Stanford University Press, 2003).

[55] Moniz Bandeira, *La Formación de los Estados en la Cuenca del Plata: Argentina, Brasil, Uruguay, Paraguay*, 1st ed. (Buenos Aires: Grupo Editorial Norma, 2006).

[56] Lília Moritz Schwarcz, *The Emperor's Beard: Dom Pedro II and the Tropical Monarchy of Brazil*, 1st American ed. (New York: Hill and Wang, 2004).

In August 1865, the allies launched their campaign, with Flores and Mitre at the lead. They set out from Concordia with an army of twelve thousand soldiers and thirty-two cannons. Their first objective was Duarte's force of three thousand men in Paso de los Libres. As the allies approached, he sent an urgent message to Colonel Estigarribia, requesting reinforcements. The colonel did not just dismiss Duarte's request; he belittled him for his cowardly impertinence. Thus, not only was Duarte outmanned, but all his artillery was on the other side of the river; he knew that his odds of survival were slim to none.

The Paraguayan Army had been on the offensive up to now, launching a series of surprise attacks that had allowed them to make deep inroads into Brazil and Argentina. Now, they were on the defensive and facing superior forces. Scouting for the best ground, Duarte positioned his troops on the banks of the Yatay Creek, so their only option was to fight or swim. On the eve of the battle, tensions were running high when a detachment of Argentines from Corrientes called out in Guaraní for the Paraguayans to flee because they would be massacred the next day. The Paraguayan soldiers responded that they needed to do their duty.

At ten the next morning, on August 17, 1865, the attack began with a thunderous cavalry charge. The Paraguayans held out for three hours against far superior forces. Half of the men were killed in battle, except for a few hundred who escaped by swimming across the river. Duarte tried to launch a final counterattack, but his horse was shot out from under him, and he was captured. The colonel was brought to the bloodthirsty Flores, who ordered him executed. Fortunately for Duarte, his life was spared by Paunero, the Argentine general who had attempted to retake the city of Corrientes a few months earlier.

Not every one else was as lucky. Upon interrogating the prisoners, Flores found that many of the soldiers were Uruguayans who had joined the Paraguayan Army, as well as Argentines, thus confirming the notion that the Paraguayan cause enjoyed a broad appeal. Therefore, he ordered them to be shot or garroted. Many Argentine soldiers and officers were aghast at the atrocities, with Mitre bitterly complaining to the Uruguayan general. Those prisoners of war who were not slaughtered were impressed into the Uruguayan Army, which was low on soldiers, and forced to take up arms against their brethren.

The focus of attention shifted to the town of Uruguaiana after the defeat at Yatay. A Brazilian division launched a siege on July 16, 1865. With the battle ended on the Argentine side of the river, several regiments were sent to increase the siege force to seventeen thousand men. The Brazilian Navy had also taken position a month earlier, preventing the Paraguayan Army from escaping or being resupplied. The lack of food weakened the men. Many took sick and desertion was on the rise. On September 11, 1865, Dom Pedro II arrived on the battlefield. He met with Mitre and Flores to discuss the progress of the campaign. The British ambassador, Sir Edward Thornton, also participated in the discussions. Britain had a great deal of interest in the war; not only was it keen on opening the Paraguayan economy to foreign lending and investment, but the US Civil War was still raging, and the British desperately needed alternate sources of cotton. Paraguay had begun to export cotton a few decades earlier, but Solano López refused to allow foreigners to buy land. Last of all, the British wanted to monitor the war since some of its banks were financing the Brazilian campaign.

On September 18, Estigarribia was given a final ultimatum: surrender, else the allied assault would commence in two hours. Outnumbered two to one, with almost no possibility of making it back to Paraguay, he asked for terms. He requested that the senior officers be allowed to escape to wherever they wanted, even Paraguay if they chose. He also requested that the soldiers of Uruguayan birth not be handed over to Flores. The allies agreed. Hence, the Paraguayan general who had belittled his subordinate for seeking aid before facing an allied force that was four times larger capitulated without firing a shot.

Solano López wept upon receiving the news. With a third of his professional army gone, his hopes and ambitions for limiting the hegemonic might of Brazil and Argentina evaporated. His was similar to Hitler's position after the fall of Stalingrad; nothing stood between him and the enemy, and it was only a matter of time until the four horsemen of the apocalypse would be at his doorstep. Many people secretly reproached him for failing to take direct command of his army. The sovereign leaders of Brazil, Argentina, and Uruguay were at the front, witnessing firsthand what was going on with their forces. Had Solano López done the same, he might have prevented the blunders that were made, such as overstretching the supply lines, and Estigarribia's capitulation at Uruguaiana.

Despite assurances by the allies, many of the atrocities that were witnessed in Yatay were repeated. Scores of prisoners were killed as they surrendered. An estimated eight hundred to a thousand captives were taken away by Brazilian officers as slaves, and the rest were impressed into the newly created Paraguayan Division of the Uruguayan Army to fight against their own countrymen. Even Duarte, the valiant colonel who had led the defense of Yatay, was carted away as chattel.

The allies rested for two months before departing for the city of Corrientes. The Paraguayans were now in full retreat, with Robles retracing his steps. On several occasions, Argentine officers tried to bribe the Paraguayan general to abandon his command. Although Estigarribia refused, the rumors made their way back to Solano López. He immediately relieved the general of his duties, had him arrested, and brought him back to Paraguay for execution. With the campaign deteriorating, Solano López was becoming a tragic figure. Paranoia began to set in, and he isolated himself as his strategy shifted from conducting an offensive campaign to saving his nation. On October 3, the Paraguayan leader ordered all of the remaining troops to abandon Argentina. An allied invasion was inevitable, and he needed to prepare for the onslaught.

Entire Argentine cities, towns, and villages were sacked as the soldiers moved out. Fully laden Paraguayan steamships hauled away furniture, machines, and even church bells. Many Argentine women and children, particularly the families of senior officers and politicians, were carried away as hostages. On October 22, the last Paraguayan soldiers departed Corrientes.

The allied war effort was now at a fever pitch. The immense financial and manufacturing resources of the two largest countries in South America were being brought to bear against one of the continent's smallest nations. The Paraná brimmed with transports carrying war supplies for the front, and recruiters fanned across Argentina and Brazil. However, things took an unexpected turn on November 8, when a mutiny by six thousand recruits in the northern part of Entre Ríos exploded. The initial enthusiasm for the war effort had faded, and young men were taking to the hills or going under cover when recruiters approached. The sandy islands of the Paraná and Uruguay Rivers became outposts for deserters and draft dodgers. Many had been forced into the army at gunpoint, and there were stories of men being brought to the front lines covered in chains. The governments in Buenos Aires and Río de Janeiro were afraid that this new mutiny could spread to other parts of the army. Therefore, they decided to give a lesson in discipline. Brazilian and Argentine troops were used to put down the insurrection, and half a dozen of the ringleaders were summarily executed.

In the meantime, Solano López was preparing for the allied assault. He ordered the mobilization of the peasant population. He also moved his headquarters to Paso de Patria, the traditional ferry landing used for crossing the Paraná from Argentina, next to the impregnable citadel of Humaitá. By moving to Paso de Patria, Solano López could personally oversee and direct all military operations.

A mass of fifty thousand allied troops took up positions on the Argentine side of the river as 1866 dawned. On the other side, the remnants of the Paraguayan Army waited for the assault to begin. They were deployed in the heavy fortifications of Itapirú, Curupayty, and Humaitá, three forts that had been designed and organized for mutual support and to deny riverine access to the Asunción. The fort of Curuzu was used as a redoubt to protect the rear.

The invasion of Paraguay was going to be extremely difficult, and the allies needed to prepare. For the past year, the war had been a blur. The invasion of Mato Grosso do Sul, the Corrientes Campaign, the defeats at Riachuelo and Yatay, along with the capitulation at Uruguaiana had occurred in rapid succession. However, the conflict was now in a prolonged lull. For more than three months, the allies sweltered under the tropical sun. The encampments, which were divided by nationality, were thick with merchants, camp whores, and black cabichui (wasps). The soldiers idled their time gambling and drinking, or making excursions to the city of Corrientes. Although Mitre was at the head of the war effort, the Brazilian Navy refused to move from its anchorage off the city until Admiral Lisboa, Marquis of Tamandaré, returned from his prolonged sojourn in Buenos Aires.

The Paraguayans used the lull to sap the enemies' morale. At night, scores of fully laden canoes would depart the fortified shores of Paso de Patria to raid allied camps. The attacks were little more than a harassment of the troops, but they infuriated Mitre. He asked the Brazilian Navy to intercept them, but they refused. Finally, he decided to teach the enemy a lesson. On January 30, 1866, he ordered General Emilio Conesa, who was at the head of the Buenos Aires division, to ambush the marauders.

That night, 250 Paraguayans crossed the river. A few kilometers inland, behind the stream of Pehuajó, Conesa lay in wait with sixteen hundred men. Although he had the element of surprise and the advantage of numbers, he wasted both by rallying his men with a thunderous yell, to which they all replied as they broke into a charge. Alerted of the ambush, the Paraguayan marauders fled. Most of them were barefoot and familiar with the swampy terrain, and were thus able to flee nimbly through the streams and dense undergrowth. The Argentines were mainly gauchos who had recently arrived from Buenos Aires, unfamiliar with the topography and wearing heavy boots that became stuck in the thick bog. Hearing the tumult, the Paraguayans sent two hundred reinforcements, and then an additional seven hundred soldiers. The result was a bloodbath.

Paraguayan sharpshooters and snipers hid in the trees, taking aim at the Argentines. Dozens fell in the space of a few seconds. Mitre heard the mayhem from his bivouac, but he refused to send additional troops. Many people speculated that there was bad blood between him and Conesa because the latter had fought on Urquiza's side during the battle of Caseros. The result was nine hundred Argentine casualties against 170 Paraguayans.

The Battle of Pehuajó was not a major engagement. It did not mark a reversal in the war or alter its outcome. It did, however, show the tenacity of the Paraguayans. Despite their defeats at Riachuelo, Yatay, and Uruguaiana, they remained devoted to the cause, and were even more fervent because they were defending their homeland. The battle was a precursor of the carnage that lay ahead.

On March 20, the Marquis of Tamandaré finally moved his fleet to the mouth of the Paraguay River. For three weeks, four armored cruisers pummeled Fort Itapirú, reducing it to rubble and allowing the landings to begin on April 17. The first men off the boat were one hundred Paraguayan prisoners, followed by ten thousand soldiers, twenty-five wooden transports, and eighty-seven artillery pieces. The invasion force unloaded troops and supplies within view of Solano López's headquarters at Paso de Patria. Once the beachhead was secured, an additional fifty-seven thousand men crossed the river and moved into position.

The invasion coincided with the start of the rainy season. Torrential downpours drenched the fighters, many of whom were forced to sleep without shelter. Although the Argentine and Brazilian governments were dedicating countless resources for the war effort, not all of the funds were being spent wisely or fairly; many of the suppliers cut corners to maximize profits, sending defective guns and munitions, rotten food, and diseased cattle. Land barons like Urquiza, José Gregorio de Lezama, and Anacarsis Lanús profited handsomely from the war effort, while allied soldiers died from the lack of equipment, armaments, and food.

Solano López moved his headquarters to Paso Pucu, four kilometers inland. The new command post was on a hill, and it was connected to the larger forts of Curuzu and Curupayty, as well as Humaitá. The allies established their main camp at Tuyutí. Much blood would be shed there as the Paraguayans tried to eject the enemy from their homeland.

From his perch at Paso Pucu, Solano López followed the allied preparations. He witnessed the endless arrival of troops and supplies, but he also saw their hesitation. At first, Mitre had been anxious to get the campaign over as quickly as possible, but he acted far more circumspectly after he arrived on Paraguayan soil. He lacked intelligence on the enemy. He was short on maps and knowledge about the terrain. During the Argentine portion of the campaign, he had had plenty of information about the topography, but now he was lost. This led to tensions with the Brazilian high command, which wanted to get the war over as quickly as possible.

Solano López used the lull as an opportunity to launch a counteroffensive. On May 2, 1866, he ordered a surprise attack on a column of Uruguayans that was making its way up the Estero Bellaco—Bellaco Creek—under the command of Flores. As the Uruguayan general probed his way through the unfamiliar landscape, the Paraguayans attacked. Along the banks of the creek, thousands of soldiers armed with swords, lances, and bayonets jumped from the bushes. The two sides slammed into each other in an orgy of blood and gore. Some of the worst acts of savagery ever recorded took place at the Battle of Estero Bellaco, as the soldiers engaged in hand-to-hand combat. Limbs and mutilated corpses littered the ground. More than four thousand dead and dying men covered the field before the day was out, marking it one of the bloodiest engagement of the war.

Both sides claimed victory at Bellaco, but Solano López lost more men—resources he could ill afford to lose. Nevertheless, three weeks later he decided to double down and launch another surprise attack. Solano López needed a decisive victory to negotiate an end to the war. He also needed to raise morale to obscure the fact that he was running out of troops and supplies. Against the advice of his senior officers, who stressed that the allied forces were superior and the swampy ground impeded the use of cavalry, López Solano decided to attack Tuyutí on the morning of May 24.

The plan was to assault the allies along three sides, with a column of troops harassing the left, another probing the right, and a third charging head on. After the infantry attack, the cavalry would bulldoze through the middle of the allied formation and divide it in two, thus limiting the troops' ability to support each other.

At eleven that morning, twenty-three thousand Paraguayans took the field. They represented the last of Solano López's professional infantry and cavalry. The attack began well, but the allies dug in to prepare the onslaught, and the Brazilian artillery wheeled into action. Although the Paraguayan cavalry charge almost succeeded in cutting the allied camp in half, a Brazilian barrage sliced into the riders.

The Argentine infantry also moved into phalanxes, thus frustrating the mounted attack. As the smoke cleared, five thousand Paraguayans lay dead; another seven thousand had been mortally wounded. The allied casualties totaled five thousand. So many cadavers littered the field that the soldiers threw thousands into river. This contaminated the waters of the Paraguay and Paraná Rivers, igniting a cholera epidemic downriver that spread into the littoral communities of lower Argentina.

The Battle of Tuyutí stands as the largest land battle in Latin American history, with almost sixty thousand combatants and twenty thousand casualties. It also marked an important milestone. Although the turning point of the war occurred in Uruguaiana, the defeat at Tuyutí erased Solano López's ability to negotiate a favorable peace. His decision to override his most senior officers' recommendations caused his ultimate defeat, and it sealed the destruction of Paraguay.[57] Yet, it is important to stress that the allies did not make any meaningful territorial gains. While the battle had been a humiliating defeat for the Paraguayans, the allies lost thousands of men but gained only a few kilometers. The tenacity of the defending soldiers confirmed that there was still more bloodshed ahead. Sadly, the end of the war was three years away.

Hubris makes for great bedfellows. The victory at Tuyutí imbued the allies with a sense of invincibility, but three months later, they would face their biggest defeat. On September 3, they launched an attack against Curuzu, the next fortification along the Paraguay River. The fort was defended by twenty-five hundred soldiers, most of them dug into a network of trenches. The fort, considered one of the strongest emplacements, fell without much resistance, thus convincing the allies that the enemies' resolve was broken. They were preparing to move on Curupayty when a lone soldier approached the front lines carrying a white flag. Solano López was requesting a parley.

The Paraguayan leader appeared early the next day. He was regally clothed, even wearing a small gold crown. Mitre approached, dressed in his combat gear, muddy boots, and his presidential sash. Brazilian Field Marshal Polidoro Quintanilha Jordão refused to attend the conclave because he had no orders or powers to enter into negotiations. Flores joined the group for a short time, but retreated after Solano López berated him for having started the war by allowing Brazil to invade his country. This left only Solano López and Mitre, who spoke for five hours.

The Paraguayan leader proposed that Argentina withdraw, thus allowing Paraguay to continue fighting against Brazil—which he saw as the main aggressor. With Argentina out, the Brazilians could no longer use the Paraná to transport their troops or cross through Argentine soil, which meant that they could only support the war effort through Mato Grosso do Sul, which was virtually cut off from the rest of the country. When this offer was rejected, Solano López followed up with a

---

[57] Christopher Leuchars, *To the Bitter End: Paraguay and the War of the Triple Alliance* (Westport, CT: Greenwood Press, 2002).

series of very generous indemnifications. Although Mitre may have been disposed toward the idea of ending the war, he was bound by the terms of the Triple Alliance, and could not act unilaterally. Brazil's emperor, Dom Pedro II, flatly refused. He convinced the Argentine leader that Paraguay remained an existential threat to the hegemony of Brazil and Argentina. Therefore, it had to be destroyed.

In contrast to his nickname, "The Magnanimous," Dom Pedro II's burning determination to continue the campaign against a much smaller and already defeated nation, despite its entreaties for peace, underscored the genocidal nature of the campaign. Brazil, and eventually Argentina, understood that a prosperous Paraguay was a serious threat because it proved that independent ethnic group could be successful.[58] That sort of successful self-determination could incite other renegade regions to break away. Brazil and Argentina were extremely large landmasses, incorporating a broad spectrum of social clusters that were brimming to break free of the hegemony of Río de Janeiro and Buenos Aires. Therefore, they had to be shown that any state outside the dominion would suffer the worst consequences.

It was clear that the war would need to be prosecuted to its bitter conclusion. Moreover, Solano López's peace overture was seen as a sign that the country was on the verge of collapse. Hence, Mitre decided to make haste and take Curupayty. He ordered an artillery barrage to break down the enemy defenses. For days, the allies hammered away at the fortification. When the allies finally ceased shelling, the Paraguayans understood that an attack was imminent, and they began digging a series of new set of trenches. The excavations, which were performed under the direction of an English engineer named George Thompson, went on day and night, while marching bands played martial music to conceal the sound.

On the dawn of September 22, the allied assault began. At eight in the morning, the Marquis of Tamandaré maneuvered his fleet close to the fort and unleashed his cannons. The plan was to bombard the fortification and follow up with an infantry attack from the main camp at Tuyutí. The bombardment was done from a distance, and most of the shells fell wide of the mark. As the Brazilian Navy continued shelling, the allied troops, mainly Argentines, began to form up. Mounted officers donned their dress uniforms and moved into the front, followed by endless lines of infantry. The Uruguayan lines were thin, with many of the soldiers having deserted or been massacred at Bellaco. The rest of the attacking force consisted of Brazilians. Many soldiers carried siege gear, including ladders, ropes, and sapper bags. They were a formidable foe.

The preparations made by Thompson, however, turned out to be fortuitous. As the allies marched into the field in front of the fort, the Paraguayan defenders popped out of their trenches and opened fire with cannons and Gatling guns, mowing down thousands of men. Shrapnel sliced through members of the most promi-

---

[58] Mário Maestri, *Guerra no Papel: História e Historiografia da Guerra no Paraguai, 1864–1870* (Porto Alegre, Brazil: PPGH FGM Editora, 2013).

nent families of Buenos Aires, including the son of Vice President Marcos Paz and the son of a future president, Domingo Sarmiento. Dozens of senior officers were killed, virtually decapitating the high command. In total, more than ten thousand allied soldiers were killed—eight thousand Argentine and two thousand Brazilian casualties. The Paraguayans lost almost none. The catastrophe at Curupayty revealed one of the inherent problems with the alliance. There was no unity of command, with the Brazilian fleet operating independently and Mitre being forced to coordinate through the hierarchy of three national armies. The only successful joint operation was the allied defense of Tuyutí, where the disparate forces had been able to coalesce together under a withering attack. The humbling defeat at Curupayty brought the war effort to a standstill for the next year and a half.

The calamity at Curupayty coincided with a new uprising in western Argentina. As Dom Pedro II had feared, Argentina and Brazil were very loose federations, which could easily disunite. In November 1866, a strike by police officers claiming back wages exploded into an outright rebellion. Faced with the financial demands made by the war, the government went into arrears with many of its obligations, such as paying civil servants. The Argentine population was also tired of throwing so many of its young men into the meat grinder, with tens of thousands of casualties produced by the conflict.

The mutiny spread, with 280 recruits destined for the Paraguayan front joining the rebellion. They opened the jails in Mendoza and set free scores of subversives who had been captured. Carlos Juan Rodríguez, a young lawyer who had been arrested in 1863, was among them. He quickly became the leader of the revolt, which moved into other provinces—particularly San Luis, which was under the leadership of the Saá brothers, and La Ríoja, which was under the command of Felipe Varela. Hence, Buenos Aires was forced to act. Vice President Marcos Paz ordered General Wenceslao Paunero to return from the front to put down the rebellion, but Paunero was not very successful. On January 5, 1867, a Federalist detachment in Rinconada del Pocito was overrun. The setback forced Mitre to abandon the war and return with a detachment of four thousand seasoned soldiers to subdue the uprising.

As was the case in the past, when the forces of Buenos Aires confronted a provincial rebellion, they made alliances with the provinces that were not part of the dissident group. In this case, Mitre joined forces with Santiago del Estero. Together they began to beat back the rebels. By July, the last of the rebel forces had been defeated, thus allowing Mitre to return to the front.

For the months that Mitre had been away, the allies had sat in their trenches, bored to distraction. Soldiers slumped in stupor, taking to drink. They played pranks on each other and whiled away the time reading the scores of trench newspapers that proliferated. Things changed when Mitre's return allowed the offensive to resume.

In August, the Brazilians began to bombard Humaitá, Paraguay's strongest fort and the home port of the navy. In addition to its strategic position at the mouth of the Paraguay River, a series of sharp bends in the riverbanks formed a fishhook shape right in front of the fort. This forced transiting ships to reduce speed or else run aground, which would leave them exposed to the numerous shore batteries. Furthermore, the Paraguayans strung a series of large chains on barges that stretched across the width of the river to prevent anyone from sneaking past it under the cover of night or fog.

For the next months, the Brazilian warships shelled the enormous naval base. The steeple of San Carlos, which proudly flew the Paraguayan flag, was a favorite target. Every few days, a shell would hit the church, knocking down the national standard; the Paraguayans raised it again on the following day in open defiance. The newly raised banner would snap in the hot breeze, underscoring the defenders' resolve. The gunners also aimed at the barges that held the chains that barred access to the river. Life for the defenders was grim, with the soldiers suffering from the constant shelling. In order to keep the redoubt supplied, convoys of barges brought in fresh munitions and supplies from Asunción. In the meantime, the allies pressed their attack on Humaitá, slowly tightening the noose.

Eventually, Solano López grew convinced that the fort was in danger of falling, and he ordered another attack on Tuyutí on November 2. A force of nine thousand Paraguayans took the allies by surprise and they overran the fort at Tuyutí, but when the men reached the supply depots and discovered the abundance of food, supplies, and drink, they abandoned all discipline and began to loot. After months of privation, the abundance of basic nourishment was too much to ignore. Many carried away crates full of coats and boots. Others hauled away sacks of money and mail. The breakdown of the offense and the collapse of discipline allowed the allies to regroup and counterattack, thus slaughtering the soldiers while they ate, drank, and looted. As a result, seventeen hundred soldiers died, and the attempt to break the encirclement of Humaitá failed.

Solano López decided to escape across the Paraguay River and move the bulk of his army into the arid scrubland of the Chaco. He proceeded to Timbo, a small fort inside the Chaco, leaving behind a detachment of troops to hold Humaitá. The survivors marched through the arid wilderness until they reached the town of San Fernando. Upon their arrival in January 1868, they heard the news that Argentina's Vice President Marcos Paz had succumbed to the cholera epidemic that was devastating Buenos Aires. They also learned that Mitre was being forced to return home; his term in office was ending, and it was time to pass the presidential sash to someone else. In the meantime, the Duke of Caxias, Luís Alves de Lima e Silva, was left in charge. Solano López believed that this could buy him some time to organize a defense of Asunción. However, the Brazilians jumped into action as soon as the Argentine president left. They had grown tired of his dilatory approach, and a rift had developed. With him out of the picture, the campaign entered a new phase. Brazilian officers were put in charge of the operation and imperial troops led the way until the end of the war.

The allied force in Tuyutí was given orders to prepare for a final assault on Humaitá. The Brazilian Navy redoubled its artillery barrage. Up until then, the navy had acted somewhat cautiously. The fleet was one of the country's most important assets, and there was no way that it would ever be placed at risk. Nevertheless, on February 3, the allies made their move. At three in the morning, they opened fire. The intent was to distract the enemy while the Brazilian fleet dashed past the guns. The Brazilian cruiser *Barroso* was the first to make it through. Next, came the *Bahia* and third was the *Alagoas*, which broke down fifty meters from the shore. The gunners at Humaitá opened fire, and the ship was hit 180 times, but somehow the crew managed to get her boilers restarted, and *Alagoas* escaped upriver. Simultaneously, the Duke of Caxias ordered a frontal attack on Humaitá, which produced twelve hundred allied casualties, with only one hundred victims among the defenders.

The fort did not fall, but the cruisers had managed to get past the base, so it was now only a matter of time before they would arrive at the capital. Therefore, Solano López ordered the evacuation of Asunción. Hordes of refugees and government officials moved east to the town of Luque. When the fleet finally arrived on March 22, the Brazilian cruisers took up stations abreast of the capital and opened fire. The gunners took aim at the presidential palace and the main train station, raining a hailstorm of shrapnel on the passenger wagons evacuating innocent civilians. Dozens of shells exploded over the city, sowing panic and carnage. When the ships moved closer to shore, a Paraguayan artillery battery opened fire, forcing the squadron to temporarily escape downriver.

Solano López's messianic personality had by now been transformed into paranoia and desperation. The allies' decision not to occupy Asunción made him think that a conspiracy was afoot. His fears turned into nightmares in August, when the garrison that had been left to defend Humaitá surrendered. On July 23, Solano López ordered the final evacuation of the fort. With martial bands playing as loudly as they could to mask the noise, a small fleet of canoes began to shuttle the survivors to the other side of the river, where they were supposed to assemble and escape to San Fernando. However, the allies gave chase and hunted down the fleeing soldiers. It was a massacre. Most of them were starving and unarmed. To avert further bloodshed, Argentine General Ignacio Rivas offered Colonel Pedro Martínez a chance to surrender. The Paraguayan officer accepted on the condition that his soldiers would not be forced to fight against their own country. Upon hearing the news, Solano López flew into a rage. He declared the colonel a traitor and arrested his wife, Juliana Insfran de Martínez, who was then tortured and shot by firing squad.

The fall of Humaitá meant that there was nothing left to hold back the invaders. The war was lost, and many Paraguayan elites proposed surrendering. Some officers deserted, stealing weapons, plans, and maps. Determined to hang on until the bitter end, Solano López began a witch-hunt. He chased down every rumor, imprisoning, torturing, and executing members of the high command, clergy, and even members of his own family. He held tribunals at his headquarters in San Fernando, with almost five hundred executions.

Soon afterward, Solano López moved his command post to Lomas Valentinas. This marked the last phase of the bitter war, and it has been called the "Diagonal of Death." It was the last retreat, as the entourage marched toward the upper corner of the country. All along the way, soldiers deserted, only to be replaced by women, children, and old men who sought refuge from the unstoppable onslaught of the allies.

On December 6, the Duke of Caxias launched a series of attacks, which became known as the "Decembrada." In an effort to outflank the forces in Lomas Valentinas, the duke ordered his forces to cross the river and move up the Chaco to a position halfway between Solano López's headquarters and Asunción. He then crossed the river and engaged the Paraguayans in a series of three skirmishes that produced four thousand casualties. This cleared the way to Lomas Valentinas. With a defense force of seven thousand troops, mainly consisting of wounded soldiers, old men, and young boys, the battle was lost before it started. The Paraguayan leader managed to escape with a detachment of ninety men toward Cerro León. There was no way that Solano López was going to submit. Even though he had written his last testament, he was not surrendering. He perceived himself as consubstantial with Paraguay. He was the embodiment of the state.[59]

Solano López's getaway was no coincidence. The duke allowed it as a sign that the war was over, and that a manhunt was all that was left. The allied forces turned north and marched into Asunción on January 5, 1869. Brazilian soldiers sacked the town, looting and wreaking destruction without regard for whether the properties belonged to foreigners or locals. The duke soon received orders to hunt down Solano López, as well as to destroy Paraguay's industrial capacity. However, he refused. Declaring that he had completed his assigned mission, he relinquished his command, embarking on a transport bound for Río de Janeiro.

Dom Pedro II, however, was not going to allow the Paraguayan leader to remain on the lam. He agreed with Solano López's concept of consubstantiality, and he was determined to kill him in order to destroy the country. Therefore, he turned to his son-in-law, Prince Gaston d'Orleans, the Count of Eu. The count was the grandson of French King Louis Philippe I. The family had been forced into exile in 1848 when his grandfather abdicated. The count trained as a military officer and distinguished himself during the Spanish-Moroccan War of 1859. In September 1864, he arrived in Río de Janeiro after his uncle, King Ferdinand II of Portugal, suggested that he marry Dom Pedro II's eldest daughter, Isabel. After some hesitation—Gaston thought her unattractive—he agreed, and the couple wed just as the War of the Triple Alliance was getting under way.[60] The count soon petitioned to

59 James Schofield Saeger, *Francisco Solano López and the Ruination of Paraguay: Honor and Egocentrism* (Lanham, MD: Rowman & Littlefield, 2007).

60 Heitor Lyra, *História de Dom Pedro II, 1825–1891* (São Paulo: Companhia Editora Nacional, 1940).

be deployed to the front, but the Royal Council refused. The sudden departure of the Duke of Caxias created the perfect opening for him. It also created an excellent opportunity for Dom Pedro II to raise the public profile of his son-in-law, the consort to the heir of the throne.

On March 22, 1869, the Count of Eu took command in Asunción, where he unleashed the four horsemen of the apocalypse: conquest, war, famine, and disease. He launched a combined expedition of searching for Solano López and laying waste to Paraguay's industrial capacity. He razed the city of Luque, turning it into a giant funeral pyre. He then burned the ironworks in Ybicui and destroyed the munitions factory at Valenzuela. His scorched-earth policy led to the collapse of Paraguay's farming system, triggering famine; the dead began to accumulate, and a new epidemic of cholera swept the country, infecting Paraguayans and allies alike.

Meanwhile, Solano López continued his march into the northwest, accompanied by his common-law wife, Eliza Lynch, and their children. The group took refuge in the town of Piribebuy, where the remnants of the Paraguayan government and army had congregated.[61] On August 10, the Count of Eu appeared with a force of twenty thousand men to take on the ragtag defense force of sixteen hundred women, children, and mutilated veterans. For three days, the allied forces assaulted the town, while the residents fought house to house in a desperate act of survival. The attack turned into a massacre after the count's good friend, General João Manuel Mena Barreto, was killed by a young boy. In his rage, the Prince Gaston ordered all captured officers to be drawn and quartered, and the women and children to have their throats slit. The Brazilians torched the hospital without evacuating the wounded. Piribebuy also held the national archives. The count ordered all the documents to be incinerated, officially robbing the nation of its memory and identity.[62]

Somehow, Solano López managed to escape yet again. The Paraguayan leader attempted to delay the Brazilian advance at Acosta Ñu on August 16 with an elaborate ruse, amassing a defensive force of three thousand children, aged nine to fifteen, dressed as soldiers and wearing false beards. The conflict was no longer an example of total war; it was a holocaust.

The fugitives rested for a few days in Curuguaty, before skirting along the Brazilian border and moving north to Punto Porã. They turned inland to Cerro Corá, which would soon be Solano López's final resting place. With his entourage reduced to a small detachment of personal guards and camp followers, the Count of Eu dispatched Brazilian General José Antônio Correia da Câmara with a regiment of twenty-six hundred imperial soldiers for the final assault. The Brazilians pounced on the Paraguayan camp on March 1, 1870, turning it into a charnel house.

[61] William E. Barrett, *Woman on Horseback: The Biography of Francisco López and Eliza Lynch* (New York: Fredrick A. Stokes Company, 1938).

[62] Robert Bontine Cunninghame Graham, *Retrato de un Dictador: Francisco Solano López, 1865–1870* (Buenos Aires: Inter-Americana, 1943).

The attacking soldiers slaughtered everyone they came upon, whether they fought or surrendered. Solano López tried to flee again, accompanied by his personal guards—a group of soldiers wives and children known as "Las Residentas" and led by Eliza Lynch—but he had been wounded in the head and stomach. Coming to rest on the banks of the Aquidabanqui River, he was ambushed by General Correia da Câmara and a squad of six men. The general offered him the opportunity to surrender, but the Paraguayan leader drew his sword and charged, screaming, "I will die for my country." The general ordered him killed.

Such was the end of both Solano López and the War of the Triple Alliance. Once framed by Bartolomé Mitre as a campaign against barbarism, the war was the most brutal war in South American history, with the largest land and sea battles, as well as and the largest number of casualties. Paraguay lost 40 percent of its territory and more than 60 percent of its population. The war devastated one of the most developed countries of the continent, and transformed a relatively prosperous corner of the continent into a cesspool of poverty, ignorance, and inequality.[63] It has taken more than 140 years for the country to recover.

It also left most of the country's assets in foreign hands. Many of the state-owned farms were sold to Brazilians, Argentines, and British nationals at knock-down prices. For example, one such winner was the Anglo-Paraguayan Land Company, which became one of the largest landowners in the country, with more than twenty-one thousand square kilometers. In total, more than twenty-five million hectares of the country's incredibly fertile land were sold to foreigners. The government was placed in the hands of individuals who took their orders from Buenos Aires and Río de Janeiro until 1936, when the military took over for the next fifty-five years. The victors suppressed Paraguayan culture, outlawing the use of the Guaraní language. Yet, the devastation of the Guerra Guazú, or the "Great War," as it is known to the Paraguayans, transcended the borders of the small nation.

The devastating effects of the war were not limited to Paraguay. Five years of fighting burned through almost all of Brazil's gold reserves and left it highly indebted. The economic weakness produced by the campaign eventually led to the downfall of Dom Pedro II and the empire. Argentina's costs were even higher. In addition to the economic burdens of the war itself, epidemics of cholera and yellow fever ravaged most of Buenos Aires, forcing residents to abandon the neighborhoods of Boca and San Telmo for new dwellings in Recoleta and Barrio Norte. The war also cemented Uruguay's role as a small buffer state.

Venancio Flores never lived to see the end of the conflict. He was murdered in broad daylight in Montevideo, a victim of all of the atrocities he had committed. Even Urquiza, the great caudillo from Entre Ríos, found himself in an ignominious end. A month after the war ended, assassins broke into his palatial estate and mur-

---

[63]   Harris Gaylord Warren and Katherine F. Warren, *Paraguay and the Triple Alliance: The Postwar Decade, 1869–1878* (Austin, TX: University of Texas at Austin, 1978).

dered him in front of his family. The operation was organized by Ricardo López Jordán, the gaucho who had led the mass desertion in 1865, as payback for Urquiza allowing Brazil to maraud freely inside Argentina and Uruguay.

In the end, the War of the Triple Alliance was partially an extension of the Cisplatine and Platine conflicts, since Uruguay was the catalyst that triggered the conflict. Hence, there was a territorial dimension to the conflict. The war also had to do with the determination of Britain to access the Paraguayan economy and its natural resources, particularly cotton. Last of all, the war showcased the martial capabilities of South America, and it was a precursor to the death and destruction that would soon lay waste to the Pacific side of the continent.

5 THE WAR OF THE PACIFIC: SAND LOT RULES

THE WAR OF THE PACIFIC: SAND LOT RULES

In 1909, German chemists Fritz Haber and Carl Bosch artificially synthesized ammonium nitrate. The procedure required the application of high temperature and pressure to combine atmospheric nitrogen and hydrogen into active substances. Although the first reactor only produced a few ounces per hour, by 1913 German companies were churning out twenty tons per day.[64] Nitrates are essential components in the production of fertilizers, gunpowder, and explosives.

Until the Haber-Bosch process, the main sources of the nitrogen-based agents were naturally occurring depots found in sodium and potassium nitrates, which were naturally abundant along the coastlines of northern Chile. European and South American miners harvested these deposits during the latter half of the nineteenth century, generating vast fortunes. The competition for these salts, also known as saltpeter or *salitre*, culminated in the War of the Pacific (1879–1884). However, the development of synthetic nitrate inundated the market a quarter of a century later. As a result, prices fell by more than 85 percent, making the enormous loss of life an exercise in abject futility.

South American conflicts have always been territorial in nature. Governments have long sought to resolve border disputes brought about by the collapse of the Spanish colonial system. The clashes have also had an international dimension that gradually became more pronounced as external powers competed for the continent's industrial commodities. Britain was one of the principal instigators in South America. Given that it was one of the most industrialized countries, it was very concerned about securing access to the raw materials that were essential in feeding its manufacturing base.

Nitrates were the main reason behind the War of the Pacific, but there remained a great deal of resentment in the region. The War of the Confederation (1836–1839) had left an indelible mark on the belligerents. There were some instances of cooperation after the war. For example, in 1865, Spain dispatched a battle group to regain some of the territories and influence it had lost in the Americas. The force was under the command of Admiral Luis Hernández Pinzón, who tried to intervene in Peru's domestic affairs. Chile quickly allied itself with Peru and defeated the Spanish fleet, but the wounds of the old conflict were still fresh, and territorial ambitions burned brightly. Bolivia's access to the sea also remained un-

---

[64] Daniel Charles, *Master Mind: The Rise and Fall of Fritz Haber, a Nobel Laureate Who Launched the Age of Chemical Warfare* (New York: Ecco, 2005).

resolved. Although the war ended the Confederation, Chile remained wary about the close relationship between its two neighbors.

The latter part of the nineteenth century was a period of economic transition. The collapse of the viceroyalty system allowed the governments to open their ports. South American entrepreneurs scoured the hinterlands for products to export. Guano was one of the success stories since there were large deposits of the bird excrement scattered along the Pacific coast. Its chemical composition, which was rich in nitrates, phosphates, and potassium, allowed the replacement of nutrients, particularly nitrogen oxide, that were depleted through intensive farming. Its agricultural application had first been discovered by the Incas, who considered guano so valuable that they used it as a unit of payment. The biggest guano deposits were found on several small islands in southern Peru. Other deposits were found along the Bolivian and Chilean coastline. The fertilizer boosted the Peruvian economy and produced a large increase in exports.[65]

The new arrivals began to prospect after they arrived in the desert, and soon discovered other mineral deposits. During the 1830s, a silver lode was discovered in the Norte Chico Mountains. Another one was found in Caracol in southern Peru. The attention then shifted to the immense salt flats that covered the floor of the Atacama Desert. Chemists realized that the minerals had similar properties to guano, but with a wider range of commercial applications. The deposits were mainly sodium and potassium nitrates, and they could also be used in the production of gunpowder and explosives. Their applications addressed two of the largest growth areas of the nineteenth century, the industrialization of farming, and the mechanization of war.

The most abundant nitrate deposits were in Tarapacá, Peru's southernmost province. A host of local and foreign investors established large processing facilities, known as *oficinas*, or offices. As the sector flourished, Lima became eager to take the entire benefit for itself. Therefore, it nationalized the industry in 1875, but it had to indemnify the owners, which limited the windfall. Still, the earnings were enough to allow the government to invest heavily in infrastructure. The government used the funds to complete the country's first railroad, erect streetlights, and build bridges. The military also modernized its equipment, artillery, and ships. Nevertheless, the episode showed how governments were willing and capable of expropriating privately owned business operations.

The nitrate deposits in Tarapacá were immense, but there were also large salt beds scattered between the twenty-third and twenty-fourth parallels, deep in the Atacama Desert. As we saw earlier, Simón Bolívar had allocated most of the area to Bolivia, but the country's leadership neglected the region because it was inhospitable and difficult to access. The discovery of the salt deposits fueled a great deal of

---

[65] David Hollett, *More Precious than Gold: The Story of the Peruvian Guano Trade* (Madison, NJ: Fairleigh Dickinson University Press, 2008).

commercial interest, but the country lacked the capital and labor to develop it. The collapse of the silver mines of Potosí had impoverished Bolivia. Furthermore, most of its indigenous population lacked the basic educational and language skills needed to become economically active. Therefore, any capital and labor would have to come from abroad.

Chile, however, was in a better position. It was small, but scrappy. The country's territory was a fifth of what it is today, covering a thousand kilometers from Coquimbo to Concepción. Fortunately, it had a thriving entrepreneurial base in Valparaíso. The port had evolved into an important business hub after the California Gold Rush of 1849, when transiting prospectors and adventurers decided to homestead. Foreigners set up shop, earning fortunes in trade, warehousing, and finance. John North was a good example. The young Englishman arrived in the mid-1860s with a few shillings in his pocket. He began working as a riveter in Tarapacá, and used his savings to invest in waterworks, transportation companies, and processing mills. In the span of two decades, North controlled much of the nitrate industry.[66] Still, he needed more capital to expand his empire.

Great sums of money were needed for the construction of the calcination furnaces, crushing presses, and rail lines. Gladly, Chilean financial institutions, such as Banco de Valparaíso and Casa Gibbs, were willing to help.[67] Large London financiers, such as Rothschild & Sons, as well as rich Chilean landowners, also participated in the funding. Meanwhile, Chilean laborers travelled to Peru and Bolivia to operate the new mines. La Paz welcomed the investment and immigration. In 1868, it established the port of Antofagasta to attend to the administrative needs of the new arrivals.[68]

The Atacama mining operations thrived, and by the mid-1870s more than half of Chile's public revenues came from taxes on nitrate-related activities. One of the largest companies was Compañía de Salitres y Ferrocarriles de Antofagasta. British citizens and Chileans were the main shareholders, with a large participation from Casa Gibbs. The success of the mining operations induced the government to update the bilateral trade agreement with Bolivia. The new treaty stipulated that La Paz would not levy any taxes on Chilean mining companies for the next twenty-five years. In return, Chile surrendered its territorial claim to the Atacama Desert. According to Chilean colonial maps, the border was at the 23rd parallel, along the Bay of Mejillones. However, maps presented by Bolivia showed that the border was the Paposo River, which flowed along the twenty-sixth parallel. In ex-

---

[66] William M. Mathew, *La Firma Inglesa Gibbs y el Monopolio del Guano en el Perú* (Lima: Banco Central de Reserva del Perú, 2009).

[67] The owners of Banco de Valparaíso would later change the name of the bank to Banco Edwards—an institution that would be one of the guiding forces in the country's economic and political development.

[68] Manuel Ravest Mora, "La Casa Gibbs y el Monopolio Salitrero Peruano: 1876–1878," *Historia* 41, no. 1 (2008): 63–77.

change for a promise not to raise tariffs, Chile surrendered its claim to more than three hundred kilometers of coastline, but it decided not to blindly trust Bolivia's word. Peru had already nationalized its nitrate sector and it was using some of the proceeds to rearm. Hence, Chile decided to follow a similar course. The navy was given funds to purchase two new cruisers, the *Almirante Cochrane* and *Blanco Encalada*. Army officers were sent to Europe and the United States to acquire the latest guns and artillery pieces. Meanwhile, Chilean mining companies were encouraged to turn over survey data to the army so it could assemble detailed maps of the region.

Relations between the two countries remained friendly, but tensions rose when General Hilarión Daza toppled Tomás Frías from the Bolivian presidency in 1876.[69] Daza had been backed by Bolivian businesses, principally the owners of the Huanchaca Company, who wanted to evict the Chilean miners from the coast. A year after taking office, President Daza levied a tax of ten cents per quintal on all exported nitrates.[70] He stopped short of expropriating the industry, but in many ways, it was a furtive nationalization. The mining companies were ordered to pay back taxes on the products they had already exported. Otherwise, their properties would be confiscated. The new rules had serious implications for Compañía de Salitres y Ferrocarriles de Antofagasta. Among the assets it could lose was the railroad it had recently completed. The Bolivians could seize these assets without having to pay indemnifications, as the Peruvians had been forced to do. Not surprisingly, the Chileans began an intense lobbying campaign against the new tax. They argued that La Paz was going back on the border treaty, and they refused to comply with the measures. The Bolivian government responded by threatening to place an immediate embargo on all nitrate exports.

The showdown electrified the political atmosphere in Chile. Not only were lobbyists exerting a great deal of pressure on the president and congress, the economy was weakening. Europe and the United States were in the midst of an economic depression. The United States was trying to stabilize in the aftermath of the Civil War, sending deflationary pressures abroad. The Franco-Prussian War had devastated the French economy, exploding into the Paris Commune. As a result, the global financial malaise was spreading. Moreover, Chile was suffering from its own problems. The phenomenon of El Niño in 1876 had led to a series of floods that destroyed many of the country's bridges and roads. The following year, a powerful earthquake and tsunami in northern Chile wrecked much of the mining sector. Therefore, the population was under a great deal of stress. Yet, there was still no legal justification for a declaration of war against Bolivia.

---

[69] Javier Romero, "The War of the Pacific," *Strategy and Tactics* 262, no. 5 (2013): 6.

[70] The word "quintal" refers to **a unit of weight equal to from 100 to about 130 pounds.** The prevailing price at the time was about 1.70 soles per quintal. Therefore, the increase was not so significant.

The Chilean government, led by Liberal President Aníbal Pinto, pushed for the invasion of the Bolivian coast to protect the country's economic interests. At the same time, the initiative was challenged by the conservatives, led by Senator Benjamín Vicuña Mackenna, who opposed a policy of aggression as being expensive and morally wrong. Nevertheless, the measure was overwhelmingly approved by the congress. On February 14, 1879, the day that the mining concessions were supposed to be seized, the *Blanco Encalada* appeared off the coast of Antofagasta. It was soon joined by the *Almirante Cochrane* and the *O'Higgins*. At the same time, a diplomatic mission arrived in La Paz. The Chilean ambassador argued that Bolivia's decision to abrogate the trade treaty allowed Chile to reinstate its territorial claims without a proper declaration of war. As a further justification, he pointed out that most of the region's population was Chilean. Out of seventy-two hundred inhabitants in the Atacama, only twelve hundred were Bolivians. Therefore, Chile claimed sovereignty over the territory. The Bolivians rejected the arguments as specious.

With diplomatic options exhausted, the troops began to disembark. An invasion force of eight hundred sailors and marines immediately took control of the city. Two days later, a small amphibious force landed at Mejillones. The soldiers followed the railroad tracks inland and captured the undefended silver mines of Caracol, where they erected a set of defensive fortifications. The news of the Chilean occupation arrived in La Paz on February 25, as the city dwellers were celebrating Carnival. The festivities suddenly turned grim. Thousands of Bolivians took to the streets in protest. Women wept openly, knowing that the war would soon bring death and destruction, while the newspapers poured bile on the aggressors and called for retribution. Within this frenzy of nationalism, the Bolivian congress declared war on February 28. Daza ordered the imposition of martial law and the confiscation of all Chilean private property, thus unleashing the dogs of war.

Antofagasta was used as a launch pad to put the entire province under Chilean control. The first operation was led by Colonel Emilio Sotomayor. He was sent with two companies of infantry and a cavalry detachment to take Calama, a large market town at the foot of the Andes. Like Antofagasta and Caracol, it was undefended. Upon hearing that a Chilean force was on its way, landowners and merchants assembled their workers into an armed militia. On March 14, the Chileans sent a peace delegation entreating the garrison to surrender. Mayor Ladislao Cabrera informed the militia that they would fight until the end. The defense force had prepared for the attack by demolishing two of the three bridges that crossed the Loa River, thus forcing the Chileans to focus their attack on the Topáter Bridge. Its defense was left to Eduardo Abaroa, a forty-one-year-old mining engineer. On March 23, the Chileans attacked, marking the official start of the armed conflict. The resistance force did not have enough guns for all of the men, and many had to wait until one of their compatriots fell in order to pick up a weapon.[71] Still, the militia fought valiantly, repulsing several charges. Abaroa died heroically at his post. Surrounded and out of ammunition, he was told to give up. His famous reply was, "Surrender? Tell your grandmother to surrender, dammit!" Yet, despite countless acts of bravery and selflessness, the improvised militia was no matched for the well-armed aggressors. The last survivors escaped into the desert and made their way north. The same day that the Chileans were overrunning Calama, a naval squadron invaded the ports of Tocopilla and Cobija, in effect, completing the invasion of the province.

The Chilean troops were well organized and led, but they often lost their discipline when dealing with civilians. The War of the Pacific was riddled with atrocities, most of them perpetrated by Chilean soldiers. Homes were looted, women raped, and prisoners executed. One of the reasons for this behavior was that many of the soldiers were former miners, and they held a deep grudge against the Bolivians for the expropriation of their property. It was with good reason that the Bolivian authorities in Antofagasta were in such a hurry to leave after the arrival of the Chilean troops that they made no attempt to destroy official documents and correspondence.

Upon inspection of the government offices, a platoon found a cache of documents alluding to a secret pact between Bolivia and Peru. The agreement, better known as the Riva Agüero–Benavente Treaty, had been signed in February 1873 after the two countries became acutely concerned about Chile's territorial ambitions. The agreement was also the product of intense diplomatic maneuvering. As Chile's interests in the Atacama grew, Santiago made repeated overtures to form an alliance with Bolivia against Peru. Chile promised to help Bolivia oust Peru from Tarapacá in order to gain control over Arica. In return, Bolivia would cede Antofagasta to Chile. This would allow the two governments to get what they most coveted: Bolivia would obtain a deepwater Pacific port, and Chile would gain full control over the mineral deposits in the Atacama. Upon hearing what the Chileans were offering, Lima pushed Bolivia to sign the mutual defense pact. The idea was proposed to Adolfo Ballivián, the newly appointed president of Bolivia, when he passed through Lima on his way to his inauguration. The Chilean proposal was interesting and pragmatic, but Bolivia had a better disposition toward Peru.[72] Nevertheless, the treaty was kept secret because the two parties knew that Chile would react violently to such a pact. The memories of the War of the Confederation were still fresh, and Santiago made it clear that it would never tolerate a union between them.

---

[71] The valor of the Bolivians came to be known because of Chilean newspaper correspondents who wrote about the militia's valor at the Bridge of Topáter and the Battle of Calama.

[72] The diplomatic intrigue was not limited to the three countries. As was mentioned earlier, in the run up to the War of the Confederation, Argentina and Ecuador were also part of the equation. Buenos Aires was invited to sign the secret defense pact. An alliance between Chile and Bolivia would alter the region's balance of power and create a menace.

It has never been clear whether the letter was authentic, but its publication triggered a political uproar. Up to this point, the Chilean government had no pretext for its aggression against Bolivia other than avarice. Whether the invasion of Antofagasta was sufficient grounds was debatable. However, the apparent discovery of the secret pact between Bolivia and Peru spurred the public's imagination, and it gave Santiago the legitimacy it needed to go on a full offensive against its neighbors. On the same day that the Chilean forces were overrunning Calama, Ambassador Joaquín Godoy was demanding to know whether the secret pact between Bolivia and Peru really existed. When the government affirmed its existence, Chile recalled its ambassador and prepared for war.

Two weeks later, on April 5, 1879, Chile presented Peru with a declaration of war. Finally, it could extend its sights beyond the patchy fields of the Atacama and focus its efforts on the endless bounty of Tarapacá. The ensuing war would consist of two phases, a naval campaign followed by a land operation. The military high command understood that it needed maritime supremacy before committing to a ground war. Given that there were few roads through the desert, marine transportation was the only way to sustain a land operation. Therefore, the Chilean Navy needed to establish control of the seas to bring in supplies and reinforcements. Likewise, Peru understood that its navy was its most important defense against an invasion of the homeland.

In April 1879, the Chilean Navy dispatched a squadron of cruisers to blockade the port of Iquique. Command was given to Rear Admiral Juan Williams, who had orders to draw out, engage, and eliminate enemy forces. The idea was that Lima would send its fleet to protect the economically important port. The decision to focus on Iquique was partly because there were more than eighty thousand Chileans working in the region, and they could be counted on to serve as part of a militia. Some Chileans began to riot when the blockade commenced, forcing the local authorities to intern fifteen hundred of them in warehouses.

The port's defense was led by Coronel Juan Dávila, who was given a division of fifteen hundred soldiers and militiamen, along with a mobile artillery battery. In order to force the defenders to capitulate, the *Esmeralda* delivered an artillery barrage that destroyed the city's desalinization plant, thus eliminating the town's main source of potable water. A railroad line connected Iquique with the hinterlands, but the authorities were afraid that trains ferrying water supplies would make an easy target for the ships' cannons. Therefore, mule trains were brought in under the cover of night. Water rationing was also put in place, allowing individuals a liter of water per day. Fortunately, the engineers at the nitrate plant assembled a pipeline to bring in fresh water, which averted the city's collapse. Nevertheless, the Chilean ships continued to weaken its defenses. They dragged the ocean floor near the port until they found and cut the submarine telegraph line that was used to communicate with Lima.

Rear Admiral Williams grew frustrated with the lack of results, so he dispatched some of his ships to harass other Peruvian towns that lined the coast. On

April 15, 1879, the guano facility at Pabellón de Pica was bombarded. Three days later, a raiding party destroyed all of the small boats that were anchored in Pisagua. Finally, on April 30, the navy blasted the harbor in Mejillones, sinking all of the vessels that were at anchor. Yet, the Peruvian fleet was nowhere to be found. What started as a short campaign was becoming an extended engagement.

The Bolivian and Peruvian allies were also preparing for a protracted ordeal. Bolivian President Daza and Peruvian President Mariano Ignacio Prado established a joint headquarters at Arica to personally direct the war effort. At the same time, Chile stepped up its recruitment efforts, but the public's initial enthusiasm for the war faded. Many people saw the conflict for what it was—a proxy fight instigated by British merchants to steal Peru's and Bolivia's nitrate fields—and they were not eager to die for someone else's economic gain. The recruitment process was reduced to the impressment of vagrants and delinquents. Without public support, the military needed to bring a rapid end to the conflict. Therefore, a great deal of pressure was heaped on Rear Admiral Williams.

He dispatched his four cruisers toward Callao. Unbeknownst to the Chilean admiral, the reason why the Peruvian fleet had been absent was that its main ships had been in dry dock, undergoing boiler repairs. Peru had only two armored cruisers, the *Huáscar* and the *Independencia*, while Chile had four, *Almirante Cochrane*, *O'Higgins*, *Magallanes*, and *Abtao*. Even though the Peruvian economy had benefitted enormously from the guano and nitrate boom, it had not dedicated as much of its windfall to the acquisition of warships. Chile had taken the lessons of the War of the Triple Alliance to heart. Naval supremacy was essential for keeping the sea-lanes of communication open. The government understood how decisive a powerful navy could be in determining the outcome of a conflict.

Williams left his two oldest ships, the corvette *Esmeralda* and the schooner *Virgen de Covadonga*, on station. While the Chilean squadron was steaming north, Peru's two armored cruisers finally made their way south. They were escorting a group of transport ships headed for Arica. The convoy was under the command of Admiral Miguel Grau, Peru's best naval tactician. The two groups crossed each other, but never came in contact. The Peruvian admiral delivered his transports, and then made way for Iquique. He learned that the Chileans had left two older ships on picket duty, and believed that they would be easy targets for his gunners. On the dawn of May 21, as the morning mist parted, the Peruvian fleet appeared on the horizon.

Commander Agustín Arturo Prat was in charge of the small Chilean detachment. A graduate of the Chilean Naval Academy, he came from humble origins. He had served with distinction during the war against Spain in 1865, on board the *Esmeralda*. In 1870, he undertook law studies and sat for his final exams. However, the war soon broke out, and he was back in service as a line officer.

The Peruvian squadron was led by the *Huáscar*. The state-of-the-art warship had been built in Birkenhead, England, four years earlier. A small, ironclad turret ship built similar to the monitor design, it was protected by a 4½-inch-thick iron belt and armed with two ten-inch cannons housed inside a rotating turret. It had been named for the hapless Incan king who was murdered by his brother, Atahualpa, during Pizarro's invasion. Now, the fate of the nation was resting on the ignominious name. The second ship of the squadron, the *Independencia*, was an ironclad corvette built in 1864. Commanded by Juan Guillermo More, it bristled with rifled muzzle-loading cannons. Unfortunately, the two Chilean vessels were much older and inferior.

Prat rallied his men and maneuvered his vessels to the middle of the bay. Commander Condell, who was in charge of the *Virgen de Covadonga*, took up position astern of the *Esmeralda*. At 8:15 a.m., the two sides exchanged the first broadside. Ten minutes later, they reengaged. A shot from the Huáscar ripped through the stern of the *Esmeralda*, killing several crewmembers in the ship's infirmary. Realizing that they were outgunned, the *Virgen de Covadonga* moved closer to shore. Prat did the same. This created a dilemma for Grau. Although his armament was superior, the rounds that were aimed at the *Esmeralda* could end up damaging Iquique—the very port he was supposed to defend. Therefore, he needed to use a parabolic attack to bombard the enemy, a skill that was beyond the reach of his gunners. For an hour and a half, the *Huáscar* tried to hit the *Esmeralda*; finally, the gunners scored a direct hit on the bow, killing the crew of a machine gun nest. In the meantime, Dávila had moved his artillery battery into position and begun shelling the *Esmeralda*. Attacked from sea and shore, Prat ordered his ship's engines to full speed. Unfortunately, the sudden increase in steam was too much for its old boilers, and one of them exploded. With the Chilean warship almost dead in the water, Grau ordered the *Huáscar* to ram it.

Prat used the little bit of headway he had left to maneuver out of the way. Nevertheless, the *Huáscar* fired its two ten-inch cannons at point-blank range, killing more than forty sailors. It is not clear whether Prat died in the broadside. Chilean folklore says that he led a boarding party, consisting of himself and another sailor, onto the Peruvian flagship, only to be killed moments later. Seeing the desperation of the situation, Grau offered the *Esmeralda* to strike its colors. The new acting captain, Lieutenant Luis Uribe Orrego, refused. Therefore, Grau rammed the Chilean ship a second time. Simultaneously, the *Huáscar* fired another volley at point-blank range, massacring more of the crew. The collision damaged the ramming ship's armor, but the *Esmeralda* was mortally wounded. Seawater poured in, flooding the ammunition hold and drowning scores of sailors. Another Chilean party made another attempt to board the *Huáscar*, only to be gunned down. Grau ordered his ship to ram the *Esmeralda* one last time. This time, the old wooden vessel slumped forward and slipped below the waves.

A few miles away, things were going differently for the *Independencia*. The *Virgen de Covadonga* was a smaller ship and could move closer to shore without much trouble, but still the larger Peruvian ship remained in close pursuit. Suddenly, it ran aground. With no ability to maneuver, the Peruvian corvette became an easy target for the Chilean gunners. They pummeled the ship with an endless barrage of shells, forcing the crew to abandon ship and escape on lifeboats. The Chileans gave no quarter and continued to shell the survivors as they rowed away. Eventually, Grau showed up and the *Virgen de Covadonga* sailed away. The admiral realized that nothing could be done for the stricken ship, so the *Independencia* was torched. Flames licked the darkening sky, as the proud warship burned. In the end, the Battle of Iquique turned out to be a major victory for the Chilean Navy. Although they lost the *Esmeralda*, it was an old wooden ship. Meanwhile, Peru lost half of its armored fleet. Before the engagement, Chile's naval superiority was two to one. Now, its edge was four to one.[73]

The news of the *Esmeralda*'s loss stunned the nation. An air of defeat swept Santiago and Valparaíso. However, Vicuña Mackenna used the setback as a rallying cry. He transformed Prat into a martyr, extolling his humble beginnings and selfless devotion, and urged the population to take up arms to defend their nation's honor. The naval officer's background and bravery touched a nerve in the Chilean psyche, and a wave of patriotism swept the country. Men turned up in droves to join the war effort. So many people showed up, in fact, that the recruitment centers were forced to turn hundreds away. The national leadership converted a bitter defeat into a fervor that carried it to victory. Many consider the death of Prat to be the catalyst that allowed Chile to form its national identity.

While Santiago was focused on enlarging its territory to the north, it was about to face a major setback in the south. Ever since the collapse of the viceroyalty system, Chile and Argentina had claimed Patagonia. For the most part, the region was Argentine, but Chile's competing claim made it difficult to define borders and limits. With Chile was preoccupied with its Pacific campaign, Buenos Aires maneuvered deftly.

The Chilean invasion of Antofagasta had triggered a massive outcry in Buenos Aires and several other large cities. There were calls, particularly in the northern provinces of Jujuy and Tucumán, for retaliation against the Chilean aggressors. Several prominent Argentines, including future president Roque Sáenz Peña, offered their services for the war effort. As in the War of the Triple Alliance, cultural loyalties transcended sovereign lines of demarcation. Bolivian blood ties penetrated deep into Argentina. Many Argentines volunteered to join the cause or contributed funds. There was also a booming business, as arms merchants in Buenos Aires sourced weapons for the Bolivian Army, thus circumventing Chile's blockade of the Pacific coast. However, the Argentine government was hesitant to join the fray. It had more pressing interests. Buenos Aires promised that it would remain neutral in the affair if Chile agreed to drop its claim to Patagonia. Outfoxed, the government agreed, surrendering a claim to a million square kilometers. Santiago knew

[73] Brian Vale, *Cochrane in the Pacific: Fortune and Freedom in Spanish America* (London: I. B. Tauris, 2008).

that its claim was weak, and it was also cognizant that the mineral-rich Atacama was a more lucrative prize.

For the next five months, the Chilean Navy pursued the *Huáscar*. However, the wily Grau eluded the enemy. In July, he made a midnight raid on Iquique, sinking the troop transport *Matías Cousiño* and the gunship *Magallanes*. Soon after, he captured the *Rímac*, along with a detachment of three hundred Chilean cavalry and their horses. He also bombarded Chilean coastal emplacements, while avoiding contact with the large cruisers. The admiral's luck finally ran out on October 8, 1879, when he was sailing past the town of Antofagasta with the corvette *Union*.

The Chilean high command had devised a trap. Guessing that Grau would eventually attack Antofagasta, they divided the fleet in two divisions. The first division, which consisted of heavier and slower ships, was led by Commodore Galvarino Riveros from aboard the ironclad *Blanco Encalada*; those ships were positioned close to shore. The second division, which consisted of the faster ships, was led by Commander Juan José Latorre from aboard the ironclad *Almirante Cochrane*; those ships orbited farther out to sea, but in a perpendicular pattern south of the city. The idea was to allow the *Huáscar* to move in between the two divisions and bring them both to bear. They anticipated that Grau would turn south after he spotted Riveros's division in front of Antofagasta and that would allow Latorre's second division to close the trap.

Grau's squadron passed Antofagasta in the middle of the night, searching for easy targets. When he saw that there were none, he continued on his northward track. As dawn broke, a lookout on the *Huáscar* saw the black smoke produced by the Riveros's division. The Peruvian admiral immediately ordered his ships to turn south. His vessels were passing Point Angamos, very close to the port of Mejillones, when he saw the smoke of the second Chilean division on the horizon. The Peruvian commander immediately realized that he was in a trap. He signaled the *Union*, which was one of the fastest ships in the Pacific, to escape.[74] Simultaneously, he ordered his men to battle stations.

The Peruvian gunners had not improved their marksmanship since the Battle of Iquique. Therefore, they missed as the *Almirante Cochrane* bore down and maneuvered into firing range. At two thousand meters, the Chilean cruiser opened fire. One of its armor-piercing shells sliced through the turret, disabling the two main cannons. Another armor-piercing round penetrated the steel belt and disabled the ship's rudder. Not only did this leave the ship adrift, the *Huáscar* began to list to starboard. In the meantime, the *Blanco Encalada* was moving into position. All the while, the *Almirante Cochrane* continued to pummel away, landing a shell on the bridge and incinerating Admiral Grau.

The crew of *Huáscar* continued to fight, despite the hopelessness of the situation. Likewise, the two Chilean cruisers poured round after round into the ship,

74   Romero, "The War of the Pacific."

killing scores of officers and sailors. With most of its guns disabled, the Peruvian crew decided to scuttle the vessel. The officers of the *Almirante Cochrane* and *Blanco Encalada* realized that the ironclad was adrift and an easy target. Therefore, boarding parties were ordered to take it by force. As the Peruvian crew was moving to the lifeboats, a boarding party made its way onto the vessel. They proceeded to the engine room and closed the seacocks in time to prevent the scuttling, thus capturing the flagship.

The Battle of Angamos was the decisive turning point of the war. With full maritime supremacy, the Chilean Army had free range to move up and down the coast unopposed. At the same time, the Peruvians were cut off from Lima. Still, the war would still take another four years to finish. The sea campaign took less than a year, with limited loss of life. However, the land war would be a bloody and protracted affair. Not only would the defenders put up a strong fight to protect their homeland, but the war would rage in the middle of the Atacama, one of the most hostile environments in the world, with temperatures that reached the extremes from blazing heat to freezing nights, and a scorching sun that blinded soldiers. The featureless desert made navigation almost impossible. There was a complete lack of water, except for the occasional oasis, and there was no grass for the horses to forage.[75]

Antofagasta was the center of Chile's land operations. It had already been under Chilean control for more than a year. A force of twenty thousand men was at the ready, armed with the latest equipment and technology. In addition to British and American carbines, the artillery companies counted on modern French and German cannons, as well as American Gatling guns. More than seven hundred kilometers to north, the allied headquarters at Arica was also bustling with activity, but they were not as well prepared. Bolivia's standing army consisted of four divisions with twenty-three hundred soldiers total; half of them were officers, which created a cumbersome fighting organization. Bolivia's armament was outdated and in poor shape, and included such an enormous variety of guns that keeping the right quantities and caliber of ammunition on hand was a logistical nightmare. There was also virtually no cavalry or artillery. In order to bolster the ranks, more than four thousand volunteer and conscripts were added, but many of them could only speak Quechua or Aymara, the ancient Inca dialects. Peru's army was in better shape, with a standing force of thirteen thousand soldiers and forty-five hundred militia. However, the units were not well organized. Much of its armament was outdated, with large numbers of muzzle-loading rifles from the US Civil War. Therefore, Chile's army enjoyed a huge advantage in technology, hardware, and training.

The allies decided to base their strategy on the defense of Arica and Iquique. Each port would be protected by a brigade of a thousand soldiers. The rest of the

[75] Claude Michel Cluny, *Atacama: Ensayo Sobre la Guerra del Pacifico, 1879–1883* (México, DF: Fondo de Cultura Economica, 2008).

army would be organized into a mobile unit that would quickly support any of the coastal cities that came under attack. The less-important ports would be defended by smaller garrisons of a few hundred men each.

The Chileans knew that the large ports were well almost impregnable. Therefore, they decided to begin the invasion of Tarapacá with an assault on the small port of Pisagua, for four reasons. First, it was defended by a detachment of nine hundred Bolivians. Second, it was economically important, as it was the main embarkation port for Peru's nitrate exports. Third, it was halfway between the main allied military bases of Arica and Iquique, so a landing at Pisagua would effectively cut off Iquique from the rest of the country. Fourth, Pisagua had a rail line that the invaders could use to move their troops inland.

The Chilean invasion force consisted of fifteen ships, which included four armored cruisers and eleven transports with ninety-five hundred soldiers and 850 horses.[76] General Erasmo Escala, the army's chief of staff and a veteran of the War of the Confederation, was put in charge of the operation. The defenders had a pair of heavy artillery pieces that were placed high in the cliffs, but these were no match for the Chilean armaments. At seven in the morning, on November 2, 1879, the Chilean Navy took up position and opened fire. A bracket of accurately placed rounds immediately silenced the defenders' guns and allowed the transports to enter the harbor.

The amphibious operation consisted of two prongs. The first was a landing at Junin, which was offset from the main beach. This allowed a small group of soldiers to move inland and attack the Bolivians from behind. The second was the main landing force, which would take the city. The landing at Junin began as the ships started to bombard the shore installations. They established a beachhead and took position behind the allied forces. However, the main landings were slower than expected. The Bolivians had moved to the shoreline to engage the invaders. After several hours of vicious hand-to-hand fighting, which turned the surf into a crimson froth, the Chileans fought their way inland. Finding themselves outgunned and outmanned, the surviving Bolivians retreated into the mountains, burning the nitrate warehouses as they departed, which filled the air with thick, black smoke.

General Escala located the nearest allied force. Upon interrogating the prisoners, he learned that Peruvian General Juan Buendía commanded the Army of the South, but they were unsure of his location. Therefore, he sent out a small reconnaissance mission, led by Lieutenant Colonel José Francisco Vergara, to find its position. The detachment advanced to an oasis called San Roberto and found the pump station intact. They secured it as a source of potable water and returned to Pisagua, where Vergara recommended that the Chilean general send out a much

---

[76] Several foreign warships, including French and British vessels, accompanied the amphibious operation. Their official role was to act as observers, but large European banks such as Rothschild & Sons had loaned money to Chile, and they wanted to keep close tabs on the evolution of the war.

larger reconnaissance force. A few days later, Escala dispatched a company of 180 cavalry to probe the desert and secure any wells they could find. On the afternoon of November 6, 1879, they chanced upon the Army of the South's cavalry resting on the plains of Germania. The Chileans feinted as if they were retreating, inducing the allies to attack. Most of the riders were Bolivians. The Chileans quickly reversed and sprung a trap, killing half of the allies. With much of the allied cavalry destroyed, the Army of the South was severely handicapped.

The landing at Pisagua had caused a great deal of consternation at allied headquarters. President Daza decided to lead a Bolivian expeditionary force to join Buendía's Army of the South, which was positioned a few days from the Chilean beachhead. Together, they would outnumber the invaders and push them back into the sea. Therefore, Buendía moved his army north toward the oasis of Dolores to await Daza's arrival. As he waited, disparate groups wandered in, including the survivors from Pisagua and several straggling units of the Bolivian cavalry. All of the forces would congregate before attacking the Chileans.

Daza's march through the desert turned into a nightmare. Although flamboyant and arrogant, he had no military experience. In his haste to leave, he left his artillery behind. Afraid that his soldiers would desert if they moved at night, he ordered his troops to march during the day, but the searing heat of the Atacama was brutal during the daylight hours. The indigenous Bolivians were more accustomed to the cold climate of the altiplano, and they wilted under the unforgiving sun. Daza had turned down the offer of Peruvian scouts to guide him through the desert, which left him at a loss as to how to find water. With dehydration setting in, the Bolivian president decided to break out the liquor stores, allowing the soldiers to fill their canteens with wine and rum. The result was mayhem. Soldiers stumbled drunk through the scorching sand. More than two hundred died of alcohol poisoning, and all discipline broke down. Five days into the expedition, near Camarones Creek, the men began to desert. Many fled into the mountains, and others returned to Arica. Upon hearing of the calamity, President Prado suggested that Daza return to headquarters and allow Buendía to proceed with the attack. At first, the Bolivian president refused to comply, but his officers voted in favor of retreating. Therefore, they returned home.

Bolivia's woes were made worse by the country's political instability. General Narciso Campero was leaving La Paz with the elite Fifth Division when he heard of Daza's debacle. Thus, he decided to return home. Not only were his men ill equipped for desert conditions, he had presidential aspirations. There was, therefore, no point in helping out his beleaguered opponent. Moreover, there were powerful economic interests, particularly those from the mining operations of Huanchaca, who were lobbying to keep the Fifth Division close at hand to protect them from a possible Chilean invasion. This left Buendía at a loss. No longer able to count on Daza's expeditionary force, he had to make do with what he had. His combined army consisted of almost ten thousand men, which was considerably larger than Escala's force of sixty-five hundred Chilean soldiers. But, the latter had twice as many artillery pieces, much better training, and unity of command. These factors proved to be pivotal when they met on the field of battle.

On November 19, the two sides came head to head at Dolores. Sotomayor, the Chilean colonel who had taken Calama, sent out a reconnaissance group that sighted the allies advancing toward the oasis. He ordered his cavalry regiment to make haste to beat them there. Upon their arrival, they took position along the surrounding hills in order to secure the vantage point. He moved a fifth of his forces to the northern side of the position in anticipation of Daza's arrival—and arrival that would never occur, given that the Bolivian general had abandoned the fight and returned to Arica.

Buendía was an old veteran, but senility was setting in. He relied heavily on his chief of staff, Belisario Suárez, and several other senior officers. The allied battle plan was to divide into three groups. A Peruvian column, led by Buendía, would take the high ground of San Francisco. The second column would attack the heights around Dolores. A third force, consisting of Bolivian soldiers, would wrap around the back and attack the Chilean from the rear.

The allies halted their march as soon as they arrived in Dolores. The soldiers had started moving at three in the morning, and they were exhausted. They used the time to make bivouac, taking water from the well, eating rations, and preparing their weapons. The delay allowed the Chileans to receive reinforcements, but the artillery unit was unsure what was going on. A cavalry reconnaissance was misinterpreted as the start of the attack, and the Chilean gunners opened fire. The infantry jumped to their feet and charged in a disorderly manner. In the mayhem, the allies advanced on the enemies' artillery pieces.

Fortunately, the Chileans were able to regroup. Armed with Winchester repeating rifles, and supported by their Krupp artillery pieces, they were able to hold back a much larger attacking force. The discipline of the allies began to break down when many of the munitions turned out to be defective. At five in the evening, a new Chilean battalion arrived, destroying the allies' will to fight. They also received news that the Bolivians had retreated to Arica. Distraught with the news that Daza's army would never arrive, the allies retreated—with many of the Bolivians chanting "back to Oruro," their border town. In the process, the allies abandoned precious cannons, guns, and munitions that they could ill afford to lose. Once again, the unity of command would be a major problem. The coordination between soldiers of different nations was difficult to manage, leading to breakdowns in communication, organization, and discipline.

The Chileans dug in as night fell. They braced for a counterattack the next morning, but it never came. The Army of the South regrouped in Tarapacá, and Buendía ordered the garrison that was defending Iquique to join him. This left the port completely undefended, and it was snatched by a small, amphibious force. In a short period, the Chileans had gained command over half of the wealthy province.

The men were in high spirits, and an air of invincibility stirred in the ranks. Meanwhile, Buendía's men were in bad shape. They had lost much of their equipment and armament, but they still were a fighting force of forty-five hundred soldiers. Sometimes, high levels of confidence can degrade into hubris and disaster.

Overconfident, General Luis Arteaga hurriedly prepared a battalion of twenty-three hundred Chileans to finish off the allied survivors. Lieutenant Colonel José Francisco Vergara was given a battalion to attack their position at Tarapacá. When he arrived at the oasis, he realized that his men were exhausted, dehydrated, and hungry after the grueling march through the unending sand; in their haste, they had departed with very little food or water. The only way to remedy their situation was by capturing the allies' supply wagons. Early on the morning of November 27, the Chileans attacked. The strategy was to divide the force in three columns, similar to the failed plan that the allies used at the Battle of Dolores. The first column would make a frontal attack on the town, with the second one making a flanking maneuver, and the third advancing to the rear, preventing any escape.

Unexpectedly, a thick fog descended as dawn broke, making it difficult to establish their position. Meanwhile, Buendía was waiting for the attack, occupying the surrounding high ground. As the enemy approached, the Peruvians held on. Two Peruvian officers, Colonel Andrés Avelino Cáceres and Colonel Francisco Bolognesi, led the defense and became national heroes. The former became renowned for the actions of his Zepita Battalion, the Second Peruvian Division (Batallones Zepita and 2 de Mayo, or Second of May Regiment) in defending the heights. Meanwhile, Bolognesi became famous for his tenacity in holding onto the town.

The two sides fought savagely until late in the afternoon, when the allies began to fade. When the allies began to retreat, the Chileans ran to the well to fill their canteens, which is when the allies suddenly reappeared and charged into the unsuspecting men. Panic spread throughout the ranks. A group of fifty Chilean marines managed to detain the advancing force, but the battle was lost and the survivors retreated in disorderly fashion. Unfortunately, without a cavalry to give pursuit, Buendía could do nothing more than watch the enemy recede into the night. He realized that he had no other choice but to retreat to Arica. He was out of munitions and supplies. Although the Chilean casualties at Tarapacá were higher than his, he would lose more than half of his men as they made their way home.

Upon his arrival in Arica, he was arrested by Rear Admiral Lizardo Montero for having lost the Army of the South. Peru's vast mining wealth was now in Chile's hands, and there was little that the country could do. The loss of income added to the nation's woes and sapped its ability to continue fighting. The capture of Atacama and Tarapacá also added to Chile's coffers and bolstered its ability to buy armament and recruit soldiers.

The sequence of events in Tarapacá triggered seismic waves in Peru and Bolivia. Realizing that they were completely outgunned by Chile's superior firepower and modern technology, President Prado obtained congressional permission to travel to Europe. His mission was to secure loans for new guns and cruisers to break Chile's edge. He was fifty-three, impetuous, and arrogant. He thought that as the nation's head of state he could secure better terms for the loans. Prado left his vice president, Luis La Puerta, in charge. The aging politician had been managing the country's affairs while Prado was at the front, yet he was not prepared to deal with the political unrest that soon swept the nation. The political opposition had grown stronger with the loss of Tarapacá. An opposition faction, led by Nicolás de Piérola, accused the president of abandoning the country and absconding with national funds. He whipped the public into frenzy and toppled the government on December 21, 1879, three days after Prado's departure. Two days later, he proclaimed himself president. With an order of capture if he returned to Peru, the ousted president decided to remain in Paris until the political situation stabilized. It had been a poor decision for the commander in chief to leave his country with the enemy at his nation's doorstep.

Similar political pressures were convulsing Bolivia. Daza was immediately ousted for his disgraceful performance in desert. The government then cycled through a series of leaders, including as Eliodoro Camacho and Uladislao Silva, before passing the mantle to Narciso Campero on January 1, 1880. He had been the general who decided to abandon the campaign after hearing of Daza's plight in the desert. Seeing the instability that Peru and Bolivia were undergoing, the Chilean high command decided to press the attack. Their new objective was the complete destruction of the Army of the South.

The change in Bolivia and Peru's governments led to important changes in their military command structures. President Piérola's main military leaders were Rear Admiral Lizardo Montero and Pedro del Solar, a high-ranking civilian official. The allies had a fighting force of eleven thousand men, with ten thousand soldiers based in Tacna. Preparations were helped when the *Union*, the warship that once accompanied the *Huáscar*, ran the blockade and resupplied the garrison with much-needed arms and reinforcements. As noted earlier, the *Union* was considered the fastest ship in the Pacific, and it could easily outrun anything the enemy had.

The Chilean high command also underwent important changes. General Escala was replaced by Brigadier General Manuel Baquedano. His mission was to destroy the allied presence in Tacna and Arica. He began the campaign by dispatching an expeditionary force on December 31 to take the small port of Ilo, which was north of Arica. The invasion force captured the port and severed the telegraph line to Moquegua, a nearby town that served as a waypoint to the Peruvian hinterlands. They proceeded to commandeer the train and rode it into the village, which immediately surrendered. With the northern flank neutralized, Baquedano began to disembark the bulk of his army. A total of 14,500 men were landed between February 18 and 25, 1881. At the same time, Arica was put under siege. However, the port was well prepared. Ever since the start of the war, new fortifications had been constructed, along with the preparation of new gun batteries. The siege was led by the *Huáscar*, once the pride of the Peruvian fleet and now flying the Chilean standard.

Although the town of Moquegua had been neutralized, Baquedano felt that his northern flank remained vulnerable. The port of Mollendo was 134 kilometers to the north, and it was connected by rail line to Arequipe, one of Peru's largest cities, where a division of twenty-five hundred Peruvian soldiers was preparing to mobilize. They could pose a serious threat to his invasion force. The trek to Tacna was more than 150 kilometers across the scorching desert. Baquedano's men and the supply lines would be vulnerable. Therefore, he ordered Colonel Orozimbo Barbosa to take Mollendo and clear out any Peruvian forces.

On March 9, the colonel disembarked with a regiment of eight hundred men. A company of Peruvians had retreated, offering no resistance to the landing force. They regrouped at a nearby train depot and called for reinforcements. Barbosa made way for the station, but came under fire as he moved closer. Chilean sappers planted charges and damaged the rail lines, but they decided to regroup in the port before renewing the attack. Upon their return to Mollendo, they found that all discipline had broken down. The troops had broken into the warehouses and ransacked the liquor stores. Drunken soldiers were on a rampage, looting and discharging their weapons. Endless atrocities were committed, with civilians murdered and women raped. Barbosa ordered his men to board the ships, but many deserted. Concerned that he could face a mutiny, he ordered his ships back to Ilo on March 12. As had happened so many times before, the Chileans were well trained, but they could easily turn into an unruly rabble.

In the meantime, the Peruvian threat to the invasion force became real. Colonel Andrés Gamarra advanced with a force of fifteen hundred Peruvian soldiers to Los Angeles, a prominent fort halfway to Arequipe. Hearing the news, Baquedano set out with a division of forty-five hundred men to clear his northern flank once and for all. Although the Peruvians had no cavalry or artillery, they still posed a meaningful threat. The installation at Los Angeles was formidable, and it would be difficult to take. It was ensconced at the end of a narrow valley, and the Chileans would need to launch a frontal attack. However, the wily Baquedano advanced under the cover of night and positioned his soldiers at the foot of the hill undetected. As dawn broke, he unleashed an artillery barrage, which he followed with an infantry and cavalry charge. His men fixed bayonets and ran up the hill, catching the defenders completely unaware. With the redoubt about to be overrun, Gamarra ordered his men to retreat. This removed the last threat to the Chilean invasion force, and they could now safely advance on Tacna.

The attack against Tacna would be massive. Baquedano set out with a contingent of 13,500 soldiers, leaving a thousand men to guard the rear and the baggage train. The invasion force would march across some of the most inhospitable parts of the Atacama. Every drop of water and blade of grass for the horses had to be carried. Carriages, heavily loaded with water, food, and ammunition, sank deep into the scorching sand. The same happened to the caissons and artillery pieces. With the army trudging along, the allies had plenty of time to prepare. However, there was a great deal of infighting within the high command. The main dispute was over who was going to be in charge. A few weeks earlier, Bolivian President Narciso Campero had finally arrived with the elite Fifth Division. Under the terms of the mutual defense pact, the army would be led by the heads of state. Since Campero was the only head of state present at Tacna, he argued that he should be in charge, but there was resistance from the Peruvian senior officers, particularly from Rear Admiral Montero. He argued that they had more experience since they had done most of the fighting since the start of the war. Montero finally acquiesced under pressure from Lima, but his resentment smoldered like a burning ember.

With the chain of command settled, Campero mapped out his defensive plan. His strategy would begin with an ambush of the invasion force on the outskirts of Tacna. Regrettably, things went wrong. On the night of May 25, he led an allied regiment to Quebrada Honda to lay in wait, but there was a dense fog and he lost his way. The soldiers marched around the desert until they realized that they had made a large circle. He decided to retrace his footsteps to Tacna, thus leaving the engagement until the following morning. When the men arrived at the fortification, he deployed them along the top of the Alto de la Alianza, or Alliance Heights, at the edge of the city. The hill was formerly called Intiorko, but it had been renamed as a way to motivate the men. The breaking dawn revealed the two armies facing each other. Both sides were exhausted from marching all night. They were evenly matched, but, as in the past, the Chileans were better armed and led. The only tactical advantage the allies had was their command of the high ground.

The Battle of Tacna turned out to be the largest engagement of the land campaign. It began with an artillery exchange, which turned out to be ineffective. The soft desert sand prevented the fuse caps from detonating. As a result, the ground was strewn with unexploded ordnance. The Chileans then launched a simultaneous frontal assault on the center and left flanks, which was repulsed by allies. Campero ordered his men to pursue the retreating soldiers, but they were ambushed and caught in a hail of crossfire. Scores of men were massacred. With the allied line wavering, Baquedano ordered his reserves to launch a frontal attack. The move worked. The fresh reinforcements slammed into the exhausted soldiers, and the allied line collapsed. By six that evening, Chilean troops were moving into the town of Tacna. Both sides suffered huge losses, with about twenty-five hundred casualties each. Realizing that his country was now vulnerable to an invasion, Campero ordered his surviving men to return to Bolivia. Lima was now left alone to face its old nemesis in a war that it did not even start.[77]

[77] Valentín Abecia Baldivieso, La *Dramática Historia del Mar Boliviano* (La Paz, Bolivia: Librería Editorial "Juventud," 1986).

The Battle of Tacna marked the end of Bolivia's participation in the War of the Pacific. As the surviving Peruvian soldiers melted away, the ebullient Chilean troops surged into the town, looting and raping indiscriminately. The wounded were murdered and many prisoners were shot. Chile's deplorable behavior during the War of the Pacific goes a long way to explain the long-standing animosity from its Andean neighbors.

With the Army of the South destroyed, the port of Arica had little hope of withstanding a Chilean attack. Baquedano was also in no mood to waste time. A week later, he ordered a force of fifty-two hundred men to lay siege on the citadel. The port was defended by nineteen hundred men, with Bolognesi, the indefatigable hero of Tarapacá, in charge. He had requested assistance from Lima and Arequipe, but it never came. The city was cut off and isolated. Furthermore, President Piérola was afraid that a victory by Bolognesi, who was already a prominent national figure, would constitute a political threat, and he therefore held back reinforcements and supplies.

This left the Bolognesi in dire straits. The Peruvians were grossly outmanned and outgunned. Therefore, the general convened a war council to discuss how to proceed. He asked his most senior officers if they wanted to surrender or keep on fighting, even though their chances of success were nil. All of the officers vowed that they would "fight until the last bullet," and they set about to prepare the port's defenses. The first line of defense was established at the bridges over the River Lluta on the outskirts of town. The defenders held on tenaciously, but they were eventually overwhelmed. As they retreated into the city, a Chilean delegation approached and offered them a last opportunity to surrender. They were given an hour to lay down their arms. Otherwise, the assault would commence. The defenders refused, repeating that they would "fight until the last bullet." The Chileans began their attack. The onslaught began on June 6, with an artillery barrage from land and sea. The Chilean fleet had moved into position and was pummeling the fort. For four hours, the two sides underwent an artillery duel, with the Chilean guns enjoying the advantage of larger caliber and longer range. Nevertheless, the Peruvian gunners fought bravely, and delivered direct hits on the *Almirante Cochrane* and the *Virgen de Covadonga* that forced the fleet to maneuver back to sea.

As dusk turned into night, the Chilean infantry began to move silently into position. Baquedano turned to his old tactic of dawn attacks. When daylight broke, the soldiers pounced. The Peruvians fought valiantly, but they were outnumbered three to one. The attackers fixed their bayonets and jumped over the hastily constructed berms to engage in hand-to-hand fighting. Overcoming the defenses, the bloodthirsty soldiers lustily chanted, "There will be no prisoners today." Their prediction was true. They slaughtered civilians, prisoners, and the wounded. The surviving defenders moved up into the prominent bluff that sits at the entrance of the port. The Chileans followed in pursuit, moving up the hill in just fifty-five minutes. Sensing that all was lost, Bolognesi ordered the surviving cannons to be spiked.

The remaining force of nine hundred men fought valiantly. The Peruvian colonel was bludgeoned to death on the edge of the precipice. As in previous engagements, the victors perpetrated countless atrocities on the hapless survivors.

The fall of Arica marked the last segment of the Tarapacá Campaign. Bolivia was out of the war. Peru had lost its southernmost and richest province, but it refused to sue for peace. Peru was much larger than Chile, with an extensive territory that pushed deep into the Amazon and a large population embedded across the Andes. On one hand, Peru did not feel that it had to surrender just because it had lost one of its provinces. On the other hand, Chile was anxious to consolidate its plunders of war. For four months, the two sides were at a standstill. Finally, in early October 1880, the US government convinced the warring sides to meet for a peace conference aboard the USS *Lackawanna*, which was anchored off the coast of Arica. The industrialized economies of Europe and North America were under a great deal of pressure to end the protracted conflict because it was affecting the global supply of phosphates and nitrates, which were essential raw materials.

The Chilean delegation quickly presented five major demands. They refused to return the provinces of Tarapacá and Atacama. They insisted on the restoration of all Chilean property that had been confiscated, a war indemnity for the cost of the conflict, the abrogation of the alliance between Peru and Bolivia, and a promise by Peru never to rebuild the fortification of Arica. The Bolivians and Peruvians acceded to the demands, but they had their own conditions. The Chileans had to abandon all Peruvian and Bolivian territories, the *Huáscar* needed to be returned, and Bolivia insisted on indemnification for the province of Atacama. Unfortunately, the Chilean delegation refused to concede on this last point. They saw the region as rightfully theirs, and they were not going to pay for it. Therefore, the talks collapsed and the war resumed.

Faced with the resumption of hostilities, Santiago decided to increase the economic pressure on Peru. In addition to blockading the port of Callao, an expedition force was sent to ravage the northwestern coast. An amphibious force of twenty-three hundred soldiers was placed under the command of Captain Patricio Lynch, a classmate of President Pinto and General Baquedano. He had orders to disembark at Chimbote and raid the large sugar plantations scattered along the coast to demand war reparations. Many of the largest mills were owned by British and French companies, and they were Peru's only remaining source of foreign revenues. When President Piérola learned of the extortion, he ordered the owners to suspend all payments. Lynch responded by torching the fields and dynamiting the presses. He then proceeded north along the coastline, sacking and destroying the small ports along the way. Many Chinese coolies who were working at the plantations joined the ranks of the Chilean Army as porters. The raiders marched 130 kilometers north to Trujillo before reembarking on November 1.

Lynch's success led to his promotion to rear admiral and a new mission, the invasion of Lima. The question was, how was that going to be done? An invasion through Callao was out of the question. The port was heavily protected, and Peruvian engineers had mined the approaches. The Chilean Navy had already lost several major ships. The *Virgen de Covadonga* and the *Loa* had been sunk by mines. Given Lynch's operations along the northwestern coast, President Piérola thought that the invasion force would disembark north of the capital, in the same way that the Chileans had during the War of the Confederation. Therefore, he ordered defenses to be prepared along the northern front. That was why Lynch decided to outmaneuver them by launching his invasion south of the city.

The landings commenced at the port of Pisco, two hundred thirty kilometers south of Lima. An armada of fifteen ships, escorted by two corvettes, disembarked nine thousand soldiers on November 20. Colonel Anselmo Zamudio was waiting with a force of three thousand defenders. However, seeing that he was grossly outnumbered, he retreated without engaging the enemy. The Chileans proceeded to move up the coast, but the way was treacherous. They lacked the detailed maps that they had of Tarapacá and Atacama, and, they were not able to find the oases and springs that would allow them to survive in the desert. Therefore, they were forced to return to Pisco.

It was evident that the Peruvian military presence was sparse. Therefore, Baquedano decided to leapfrog up the coast and make a new landing at Curayaco, a small port sixty kilometers south of Lima. He dispatched a fleet of twenty-nine transports, with fifteen thousand soldiers. He also ordered a landing at Chincha, giving the army full access to the coastline. The Peruvian high command responded by dispatching Colonel Cáceres, the other hero of Tarapacá, to receive the enemy. However, the Chileans advanced to Lurín, a town on the outskirts of Lima, by the end of December 1880. There well several small skirmishes and the invaders sacked the surrounding ranches. Hundreds of additional coolies were pressed into service, carrying off satchels of food, money, and cattle. Seeing their property at stake, the residents decided to form militias to engage the aggressors.

They joined the military preparations that were being made along the southern approaches to the capital. After Piérola realized that the attack was not coming from the north, he ordered a set of trenches to be constructed between the towns of Chorrillos and Miraflores. An artillery battalion was moved to the top of San Cristóbal Ridge, and fresh troops were moved into position. While the members of the militia were well armed and motivated to fight, the bulk of the army was composed of indigenous recruits who had recently arrived from the highlands. They were illiterate and could not speak Spanish, so their contribution was limited. At the same time, Baquedano's four divisions were well equipped, battle hardened, and itching to get their hands on the spoils of Lima, one of the most affluent cities of South America.

The Battle of Lima began on January 13, 1881, as the Chileans advanced on the neighborhood of San Juan. As was Baquedano's style, his soldiers advanced under the cover of night, but this time Cáceres was waiting. Lynch personally led the frontal attack, engaging the enemy at 4:30 a.m. Backed by artillery and cavalry, the Chileans drove the defenders back, forcing the Peruvians to take refuge behind the line of defenses that connected Chorrillos and Miraflores.

The next morning, the Chileans resumed the onslaught. The fighting was now on the outskirts of the capital. Faced with the dangers of house-to-house fighting, the Chileans decided to burn the town. Naval gunboats also moved into position and opened fire upon the rear of the Peruvian defenders. The fighting was savage, with more than eight thousand casualties. The Chileans fought desperately to capture the town of Chorrillos, which served as a seaside resort for many of the wealthier residents of Lima. As happened in the past, all discipline broke down when the Chilean soldiers broke into the homes and found large stores of food and liquor. Fearing another breakdown of discipline, the Chilean high command offered a truce to restore order in the ranks. The Chilean government was under a great deal of international pressure because of the destruction that was being inflicted on foreign-owned property. French, British, Spanish, and American businesses had been sacked. Many warehouses in Lima and Callao were in danger of being destroyed. Therefore, the two sides met on December 15, 1881, to begin negotiations.

Foreign delegations joined with the peace talks to ensure the protection of their property. Baquedano repeated the demands that had been presented aboard the USS *Lackawanna* and added the unconditional surrender of Callao and the fleet as a precondition for the cessation of hostilities. Suddenly, fighting broke out. This time the center of action was the affluent neighborhood of Miraflores. Observing the Chilean forces taking advantage of the truce to maneuver into a better tactical position, the defenders spontaneously opened fire. The invaders responded in kind, and the gunboats began another artillery barrage. For the next six hours, the two sides fought savagely, with cavalry charges and hand-to-hand combat. When night fell, the defenders erected barricades and mined the streets of Miraflores.

The Chileans reacted by setting the neighborhood ablaze. The ecstatic soldiers' depredation shone through as they looted and raped. Immigrant families joined the fray, with hundreds of Italians taking up arms against the invaders. However, the battle was lost. Seeing the last redoubt fall, the Peruvian Navy decided to scuttle the fleet rather than see it fall into enemy hands. Two days later, the mayor of Lima requested that the Chileans take command of the city in order to avoid a collapse of all order, but it did not help much.

The occupation of Lima marked one of the saddest chapters in Latin American history. In addition to looting and committing atrocities, the occupying force carried off much of the national library and priceless works of art. The richest families of Lima were forced to pay indemnities. As in the War of the Confederation, the Peruvian government fled into the high sierra, and Cáceres directed the resistance campaign from there. Chile's naval superiority allowed the army to control the coastline, but it could not do anything in the hinterlands. The war would last for another two years, before the two sides signed the Treaty of Ancón on October 20, 1883.

In the end, Chile expropriated six hundred thousand square kilometers, including some of the richest mineral deposits on the planet. Yet, the biggest winners were not Chilean, but British. Before the start of the war, 58 percent of the nitrate mines in Tarapacá had been controlled by Peruvians. The British had 13 percent and Chileans 19 percent. After the war, the Chilean government nationalized all of the mines and then leased them out under concession contracts. Of the total, 55 percent were obtained by British companies, 15 percent by Chileans, and the rest by investors from other countries. The result was a massive redistribution of wealth that served as the foundation for one of today's largest mining companies in the world (Antofagasta); the war converted Chile into one of the richest countries in South America, and consigned Peru and Bolivia into the ash heap of poverty.[78] Therefore, the war had all of the essential ingredients for a South American conflict: uncertainty about boundaries and territorial rights; a region that nobody cared about until it was discovered to be rich with valuable minerals; and a clash aided, abetted, and financed by an external power.

There were other winners and losers in the War of the Pacific. Argentina was one of them, when Chile surrendered its claim to 1.25 million square kilometers of Patagonia. This was more than twice as much land as it gained along the Pacific coast. With the Chilean claim out of the way, General Julio Argentino Roca launched a genocidal campaign to sweep the Indians out of the pampas and divide the land among the most politically powerful families in Buenos Aires. The operation, which became known as the Conquest of the Desert, produced a cadre of immensely rich landowners who shaped the course of country for the next seven decades.

The War of the Pacific underscored the role of leadership in determining military outcomes. Issues of command were highlighted during the War of the Triple Alliance. One problem was the absence of leadership. One of Solano López's flaws was that he did not personally direct his forces at the start of the conflict. Had he been there, Estigarribia probably would never have divided his forces or surrendered at Uruguaiana without putting up a fight. The other problem was unity of command. Although Mitre was at the head of the allied force, he had to deal with three separate chains of commands. The problems with communication and coordination became painfully clear during the disaster at Curupayty.

Many of the same mistakes were repeated by the allies during the War of the Pacific. Constant bickering between the Bolivians and Peruvians prevented the two groups from coalescing into a unified command. Most of their successes, such

---

[78] Ricardo Salas-Edwards, *The Liquidation of the War on the Pacific: Nitrate and the War. A Fantastic Indemnity. The Government of Chili and the Creditors of Peru. The Question of Arica and Tacna. The Relations between Chili and Bolivia. What Chili Spends On Armament* (London: Dunlop & Co., Ltd., 1900).

as the Battle of Tarapacá, occurred only when one of the allies was in command. The War of Pacific also showed the important role that the domestic political environment could have on the military leadership. Chilean leaders rallied around the campaign, with the opposition converting the Battle of Iquique into a moment of glory. At the same time, Bolivia's and Peru's domestic instability created serious problems. Political leaders were willing to risk defeat at the hand of the enemy rather than to allow their rivals to win political victories.

Another important lesson of the war was the pivotal role played by the navies. As we saw in the War of the Triple Alliance, control of the waterways was essential for the transportation of troops and equipment, communications and naval gunfire support. During the War of the Triple Alliance, the rivers were the main centers of battle and control. During the War of the Pacific, the fighting was done in the open seas. Last of all, logistics played a critical role in deciding the outcome. Chile's ability to transport large amounts of troops, animals, and material across great distances allowed it to overcome an enemy that was much larger.

The War of the Pacific sowed the seeds of regional animosity across the southwestern coast of South America. A deep-seated hatred against Chile still burns brightly in Peru and Bolivia. The latter's loss of its littoral province helped confine it to a destiny of poverty. It is true that Bolivia had always neglected the Atacama, but the loss of its seaboard made it more difficult and expensive to interact with the global economy. Last of all, the war defined Chile's national identity. Not only did it give them a national hero, it gave the nation the mineral riches that would make it prosperous. The conflict would also transform Chile into one of the most militaristic societies of the region. Thereafter, the country dedicated vast resources toward gaining and maintaining cutting-edge technology and training. The military would begin to take on an increasingly important role in the nation's political development, playing a central part in a civil war that would shake the nation before the end of the century—and in the dictatorships of the 1970s and 1980s. Yet, in the end, tens of thousands of lives were obliterated for a precious mineral that would soon enough be cheaply synthesized. This senseless sacrifice would soon be repeated in next set of South American wars.

6 THE RUBBER WARS: RUMBLES IN THE JUNGLE

THE RUBBER WARS: RUMBLES IN THE JUNGLE

In 1876, an English adventurer by the name of Henry Wickham smuggled seventy thousand rubber tree seeds out of Brazil. Rubber was indigenous to the Americas, and latex had been harvested by Indian tribes since well before the arrival of the Spanish. The tree was prolific throughout most of the rainforests of South and Central America. Latex is a defensive product made by the trees to gum up the mandibles of prowling insects. In the ancient language of the Nahuatl, "olmec" means rubber. "Olmec" was also the appellation given to the great civilization that preceded the Mayan Empire. They harvested the latex to make boots, capes, and the rubber balls used in ancient hoop sports.[79]

Spanish colonists brought rubber products to Europe, but it was not until the onset of the Industrial Revolution that scientists found ways to make the elastic properties of the material more applicable. The addition of turpentine allowed it to dissolve and be molded. In 1838, Charles Goodyear, a surgeon and merchant from Philadelphia, invented the process of vulcanization. By mixing rubber and sulfur under high heat, the substance became durable. Nevertheless, the industrial uses for rubber were limited. It began to play an important role in providing seals for joints and fixtures after steam engines began to proliferate. Yet, it was the growing popularity automobiles and electricity that led to the rubber boom: automobiles needed inflatable tires to cushion their rides, particularly as velocities increased, while electrical wires needed to be insulated for safety purposes.[80]

Wickham's heist of the rubber seeds was part of a larger plan orchestrated by Clements Markham, the secretary of the Royal Geographical Society, to transplant economically important tropical plants to British colonies. He had been responsible for collecting the seeds of the cinchona tree in Peru, which produced quinine in its bark. Quinine proved to be an effective antidote against the spread of malaria.[81] The export of rubber seeds was not technically illegal, but the Brazilians were very secretive about the industry. There was a wide variety of rubber trees, but the latex from the *Hevea brasiliensis* plant was the one with the highest quality. Wickham needed to penetrate deep into the jungle in order to obtain the right seeds to send

[79] Gary Van Valen, *Indigenous Agency in the Amazon: The Mojos in Liberal and Rubber-Boom Bolivia, 1842–1932* (Tucson: University of Arizona Press, 2013).

[80] John Tully, *The Devil's Milk: A Social History of Rubber* (New York: Monthly Review Press, 2011).

[81] Fiammetta Rocco, *Quinine: Malaria and the Quest for a Cure that Changed the World* (New York: Harper Collins, 2003).

back to Britain. In the end, he falsely told the Brazilian customs agents that he was exporting crates full of decomposing botanical substances.[82]

Interestingly, the seeds were stored at the Kew Botanical Gardens for almost two decades before being dispatched to British colonies in Asia. In contrast to South American latex, which was harvested from trees scattered throughout the jungle, the British had established highly efficient rubber plantations. The trees were well connected and organized in rows, making the raw material easy to harvest and bring to market. The largest plantations were in Sri Lanka and Malaysia. Although the new rubber facilities broke the Amazon's monopoly, no one really cared. The demand for rubber was outstripping supply due to the proliferation of vehicles and products that employed tires and electrical components.

The vast fortunes created by the rubber boom sparked an enormous interest in the Amazon basin, and it was the principal cause of several regional conflicts. By 1925, with Henry Ford's transformation of the automobile into a mass-consumption product, as well as the proliferation of copper wiring, rubber prices were soaring out of control. This prompted German, Russian, and American chemists to research how to synthesize oil polymers into synthetic alternates. The Japanese defeat of the British and French in Southeast Asia had left the vast majority of the industry in enemy hands. Scientists were put under more pressure to perfect the process—so much so that by the end of the Second World War, they had successfully created a massive petrochemical industry and a complete substitute, thus pushing down the demand for natural rubber and leading to a price collapse of 96 percent. Yet, the rubber boom had already left an indelible mark on South America, sparking three wars, thousands of casualties, and the redrawing of national boundaries.

The equatorial forest in the middle of South America is a giant no-man's-land. At five and a half million square kilometers, the Amazon is roughly the size of the continental United States. It commands 40 percent of South America's landmass, but it has less than 5 percent of its population. Nine countries share the jungle, but Brazil controls 60 percent. It is a region that abounds with mineral riches and biodiversity and it commands a central role in the world's ecosystem. Yet, it has always been an impediment to regional integration. The Andes mark the Amazon's western border. The Amazon acts as a land bridge that links the Spanish-American cultures, but the fringe, where the longest mountain chain in the world meets the largest rainforest on the planet, is a buffer that separates the continent from Brazil's Portuguese-based culture. In the middle, the dense overgrowth of the jungle acts as a barrier to the communication, trade, and interaction that is essential for social and economic integration.

Given the immense mineral riches of the region and the lack of population, it was open for incursions and land grabs. The Rubber Wars lacked the breadth and

---

[82]   Joe Jackson, *The Thief at the End of the World: Rubber, Power, and the Seeds of Empire* (New York: Viking, 2008).

scope of the previous South American conflicts. The belligerents did not employ the same number of troops or arms as the War of the Triple Alliance or the War of the Pacific. However, more than 490,000 square kilometers changed hands, representing territorial gains almost as big as what Chile appropriated from Bolivia and Peru after the War of the Pacific.

The first major conflict of the Rubber Wars occurred at the end of the nineteenth century in the Bolivian province of Acre, named after the large river that flows through it. By now, Bolivia had become the continent's punching bag. It had lost two wars to Chile, and lost its access to the Pacific. Now, it was about to be abused once more by a band of Brazilian adventurers.

Like many parts of South America, the boundaries of the Amazon were not well defined. Exploration was limited and there were few maps. Initially, Portugal's area of exclusivity was limited by the Treaty of Tordesillas, but slave hunters penetrated deep into the jungle. They established settlements, forts, and missions that allowed them to expand their territory. In 1750, Portugal gained control of these lands through the Treaty of Madrid, which used the precedent of *uti possidetis* to establish squatter rights over their possessions.

The Portuguese settlements were few and thin. They were relegated to the main rivers and tributaries. However, the War of the Triple Alliance reminded the government in Río de Janeiro that it needed to obtain a better definition of its extensive territory, given that the Paraguayan military had penetrated deep into the tropical grasslands of Mato Grosso. The government was particularly concerned about its western border where it had conflicting claims with Bolivia.

In 1867, the representatives from the two sides met at the Peruvian city of Ayacucho to hammer out their differences. Bolivia claimed a large segment of jungle that jutted like a thumb along the Peruvian border. Brazil's claim to the region was based on the settlements of Humaitá and Calama that sat on the eastern side of the Madeira River. In order to settle the dispute, the two sides came to terms with the Treaty of Ayacucho. They drew a diagonal line through the map of the region, allowing Brazil to retain control over its two towns. The Brazilian state of Acre, with its capital at Río Branco, was on one side of the demarcation, while the Bolivian state of Acre was on the other.

In addition to the territorial dispute, one of the important topics of the negotiations was the right-of-way to construct a railroad line to get around the rapids on the Madeira. Bolivia was also allowed to establish customhouses within Brazilian territory to facilitate exports. The rubber boom was starting to take off, and Bolivian entrepreneurs needed avenues to get their products to market. Unfortunately, the country would soon be distracted by the War of the Pacific, and it would not have the financial or labor resources to effectively exploit it. Most of its able-bodied men were off fighting at the front. Therefore, tens of thousands of unemployed workers from Brazil's poor northeastern region, particularly the drought-stricken province of Ceará, began to arrive.

They arrived by paddleboat through the endless network of branches and tributaries that connect the region to the Amazon River. As a result, the cities of Manaus and Belém became their main centers of administration and commerce. Access to the traditional centers of economic and political power along the coast, such as Río de Janeiro and Salvador, was virtually impossible. This helped explain why these two cities would play such a decisive role during the conflict.

From a diplomatic perspective, the Treaty of Ayacucho was an effective solution to the border dispute, but from a practical standpoint, it was not. Borders are typically defined by recognizable topological features such as rivers, mountain ranges, or shorelines. The use of an arbitrary diagonal line drawn on a map made this border very difficult to recognize, particularly by the Brazilian rabble that was arriving.

The workers initially came to harvest quinine from cinchona trees, but they switched to latex when they saw that it was more lucrative. The quality of the area's rubber is excellent. The moisture content is low since that part of the jungle sits at a higher elevation where there is less moisture. Therefore, prices for the area's latex tended to be higher. As international demand for rubber rose, the region became a replica of the Wild West, with rampant lawlessness, avarice, and violence. Eventually, Brazilian tappers spilled into the Bolivian side, taking little heed of the international border. However, no one was there to prevent the infiltration. La Paz neglected the province of Acre just as it had done with the province of Atacama. Lack of resources, along with political intrigue at home, kept it distracted from what was happening along the northern border.

The situation changed in 1890, when the rubber boom moved into full swing. The government eventually realized that it could generate a windfall from the collection of export tariffs. A look at Brazil's thriving Amazon cities said it all. In 1874, Belém inaugurated the Theatro da Paz, the largest opera house of the western hemisphere. In 1896, Manaus opened the Theatro Amazonas, an opera house designed to rival La Scala in Milan.[83] The gooey liquid had become white gold, enriching the rubber merchants of the equatorial forest, and Bolivia wanted to tap into the vein of money. Therefore, in 1899, the Bolivian government established Puerto Acre as the provincial capital and customs collection facility. More than eighty thousand Brazilian workers were already toiling on the Bolivian side of the border. Like the Chileans in Antofagasta during the War of the Pacific, the Brazilian tappers were in no mood to pay taxes to Bolivia.

The move particularly infuriated the Brazilian governor of Amazonas. The custom fees levied by the Bolivians were sapping his fiscal revenues. He hired Luis Gálvez Rodríguez de Arias, a Spanish diplomat and mercenary, to launch a rebellion in Acre and declare a breakaway republic that could be incorporated into

---

[83] Otoni M. de Mesquita, *La Belle Vitrine: Manaus Entre Dois Tempos 1890–1900* (Manaus: EDUA, 2009).

Brazil. The crafty Gálvez proceeded to Puerto Acre and mapped out the city's defensives. As had happened before in Antofagasta, the Bolivians had failed to bring any troops to defend their possession, other than a handful of police. Therefore, bringing down the governmental apparatus would be easy.

A bit of a romantic, Gálvez waited until Bastille Day, July 14, to make his move. His "rebels" quickly overcame the local authorities and proclaimed the Republic of Acre. However, the Spaniard was a bit too eccentric, and he was barely able to establish control. Finally, the Bolivian government requested that the Brazilian government arrest him and restore order. In March 1900, a contingent of Brazilian soldiers arrived by gunboat and brought Gálvez back to Manaus.

Up to that moment, the government in Río de Janeiro had harbored little interest in annexing Acre. After the debacle of the War of the Triple Alliance, in which it had been accused of carrying out a war of annihilation against Paraguay, it was not interested in taking on another small country. Yet it soon realized that its neighbor could not keep control over the province. Galvez's removal had led to a wave of lawlessness that was threatening to spill over into other parts of the jungle. Brazil began to realize that Bolivia was too poor to maintain law and order.

Nevertheless, Bolivian President José Manuel Pando made one more attempt to reassert his grip over the territory. He bought a new transport ship in Europe to sail a contingent of troops up the Amazon to establish a military presence. Unfortunately, Brazil decided to deny riverine access to the Bolivian military, forcing Pando to resort to a land expedition. He divided his force into three columns that hacked their way through the thick undergrowth, arriving at Puerto Acre four months later.

The arrival of Pando's troops sparked a new Brazilian rebellion, and Gentil Tristan Norberto declared himself president of the Second Republic of Acre. The republic lasted only four days before the rebels decided to surrender. Nevertheless, the governor of Amazonas continued to bristle at the Bolivian presence and the notion that they would deprive him of his customs taxes. Therefore, he sent a new cache of arms and instigators to whip up the tappers. They sowed rumors that the Bolivians were going to evict the Brazilians from their claims. With anger starting to boil, Pando began to fear for the safety of his men.

The Bolivian soldiers were mainly from the highlands, and they were unfamiliar with the rainforest. Tropical diseases decimated the ranks. The rebels were also growing in numbers. By early December, there were more than two thousand armed insurgents massing near Puerto Acre. On December 12, they launched a surprise attack. Fortunately, a sentinel sounded the alarm and the attack was repulsed. The disastrous experience of the War of the Pacific had forced the Bolivian Army to improve its armament, importing heavy-caliber Mausers from Germany and improving the training of its officer corps. On Christmas Eve, the rebels launched a second attack. This time they brought more troops, a small cannon, and a machine gun. They were armed with rapid-fire Winchester rifles, but the guns produced a thick, blue smoke that was easy to spot. The Bolivian officers ordered their men to aim below the dense cloud, and were thus able to inflict heavy casualties. Tight discipline and good marksmanship allowed the defenders to stave off an attack by a larger force. Although the rebels were superior in number, they were nothing more than a rabble. They eventually melted away into the jungle, but the Bolivian garrison was exhausted. More than half of the men had been killed in action or by disease.

President Pando needed to decide whether to use the bulk of his nation's military resources to defend the jungle outpost or to cut his losses and bring the troops home. It was true that the customs revenue produced by the rubber exports justified the costs, but given the constant political instability in La Paz, sending the military so far away was a bigger threat. Therefore, Pando began to devise a plan to allow a private company to administer the region and share their profits with the government. In reality, it was an early form of privatization. A group known as the Brazilian Syndicate, led by neighboring rubber merchants, was the first to come forward. Pando, reasoning that it would be safer to place the region in outsiders' hands—and dangerous to grant that power to Brazilians, who could easily convince their government to annex the province—opted for the Bolivian Syndicate of New York, composed of Anglo-American investors.[84] Unfortunately, he guessed wrong.

The Brazilian merchants in Belém, who had never backed the rebellion, interpreted the arrival of the Anglo-American group as an attempt to cut them out of the business. Therefore, they joined the governor's lobbying campaign to convince Río de Janeiro to permanently dislodge the Bolivian presence from Acre. José Plácido de Castro, a former army officer, was hired to lead the operation. On August 6, 1902, he launched a surprise attack, capturing the posse of police patrolling the port and declaring the Third Republic of Acre. A month later, a column of a hundred Bolivian reinforcements returned. The insurgents were routed, but they regrouped and counterattacked a few days later. They surrounded the column at the town of Volta da Empresa. The soldiers dug in and repelled the counterattack, but as the siege wore on, they ran low on rations, water, and ammunition. Many of them fell sick with malaria and other tropical diseases. Finally, they surrendered on October 15, and Plácido de Castro proceeded to mop up the remaining Bolivian garrisons.

This time, the Brazilian government was firmly in the rebel's court. Río was also under a great deal of international pressure to bring an end to the conflict, given the disruption that the conflict was having on global manufacturing.[85]

The shares of the Bolivian Syndicate were bought out, and Brazil's Foreign Minister José Paranhos, the Baron of Rio Branco, launched a new round of bilat-

---

[84] Francisco Bento da Silva and Gérson Rodrigues Albuquerque, "O Bolivian Syndicate e a questão do Acre," *História Viva*, January 3, 2004.

[85] Luiz Alberto Moniz Bandeira, "O Barão de Rothschild e a questão do Acre," *Revista Brasileira de Política Internacional* 43, no. 2 (2000).

eral negotiations. The Treaty of Petrópolis settled the matter once and for all. The Brazilian government offered Bolivia £2 million in indemnification, small land grants in Mato Grosso, and the promise to complete a railroad to bypass the rapids on the Madeira River. At first, Pando refused to sign the treaty, even preparing a new expedition to take back the province. But when the Baron of Rio Branco threatened war, Bolivia had no other choice but to acquiesce. The disastrous conflict with Chile had been enough, and a new confrontation with Brazil would become an existentialist threat.

The first of the Rubber Wars marked the last South American conflict of the nineteenth century. For almost a hundred years, the region had been at war, first gaining independence from Spain, and then defining its boundaries. Now, the attention would shift to more commercial matters, with a focus on struggles for natural resources. The Acre War was started by economic interests in Brazil, but foreigners played an important role in the territorial dispute as the war developed. The next conflict would be instigated by local businesses, but external forces would also play a more visible hand.

The events in Acre and the ongoing insatiable demand for rubber sparked more interest in the equatorial rainforest. Entrepreneurs and adventurers began to probe the jungles of Peru, Colombia, and Ecuador in search of the white gold. This forced the governments to reinforce their frontiers. Starting in 1902, several border incidents took place along the stretches of the Napo River, not far from the Peruvian Amazon port of Iquitos. Ecuadorian troops tried to push down the Napo to extend their territory, while Brazilian tappers made several attempts to overrun Peruvian garrisons. Given the immense success in Acre, Brazil tried to do a similar land grab in the Peruvian jungle. However, the international community was in no mood for another disruption of the rubber trade, and they put diplomatic pressure on the Baron of Rio Branco to desist.

The soaring demand for rubber multiplied as the Victorian Age waned, leading to more interest from American and European investors. The Bolivian Syndicate of New York failed, but a new venture appeared that would become the dominant player of the rubber industry. At the turn of the century, Julio César Arana had a small rubber business in Iquitos. His journeys throughout the region took him to the Putumayo River Basin, where he encountered an abundant supply of rubber trees and a large indigenous community. Lack of affordable labor was one of the problems plaguing the industry. Few workers were willing to leave their comfortable lives to labor for low pay while having to endure the harsh jungle conditions. Arana chose to address his labor woes by enslaving the indigenous community.[86] Moreover, access to the Putumayo and Caquetá Rivers allowed him to cheaply ship the rubber to Manaus and onto the international markets.

---

[86] Ovidio Lagos, *Arana, Rey del Caucho: Terror y Atrocidades en el Alto Amazonas* (Buenos Aires: Emecé, 2005).

Arana moved his operations to the Putumayo Basin and his business thrived. In 1907, he renamed it the Peruvian Amazon Company. He moved its headquarters to London, and had a capitalization of £1 million along with a board of English directors. Informally, the operation was known as Casa Arana. In addition to keeping its workers enslaved, the company drove out competitors. All Colombians were evicted from the river basin, even if they had clear title to land and property. The evictions were carried out by members of the Peruvian military, who were under company pay. Soon, the Peruvian Amazon Company held a monopoly over the region's rubber output, allowing it to set much higher prices for its products.

Rumors, however, began to spread about the company's use of slavery, leading to newspaper stories and books. In 1909, a British magazine called *Truth* published "The Putumayo, The Devil's Paradise: Travels in the Peruvian Amazon Region and an Account of the Atrocities Committed Upon the Indians Therein." The article (released in book form in 1912 by publisher T. Fisher Unwin) sparked an international outcry, as details of the work conditions in the rubber plantations became known. The Colombian government came under pressure to do something. It responded by dispatching a force of a hundred police officers, under the command of General Isaías Gamboa, to establish order and protect the indigenous community.[87]

Transportation is one of the major problems in the Amazon. Before air travel, the only way to travel from Lima to Iquitos was by sailing around the tip of South America to Brazil and up the Amazon River. This was one of the reasons why Bolivia lost Acre. Direct access was virtually impossible. Colombians also needed to travel via the Atlantic or through the jungle to reach the river basin. To this day, there are no land connections between Iquitos and Lima or the Colombian port city of Leticia and Bogotá. Both cities are resupplied by ships that sail in from the Atlantic. It is, therefore, virtually impossible to move troops in and out of the region covertly, which is why Peru had ample warning of the Colombian expedition.[88]

Lima considered the deployment of the police expedition a militarization of the border, and it decided to respond equally. The Putumayo region had been in dispute since the collapse of the Spanish empire. In 1828, the two countries had a brief war. The detonating cause was Simón Bolívar's anger at Peru's assistance in subverting his occupation of Bolivia. Lingering below the surface were competing claims for the Putumayo River Basin and the captaincy of Quito. Peru's defeat at the Battle of Tarqui brought the war to a close. The two sides signed the Treaty of Guayaquil, also known as the Larrea-Gual Treaty, to end the hostilities. The solution was the creation of another buffer state, Ecuador. However, the issue of the river basin was not resolved.

[87] Roberto Pineda Camacho, *Holocausto en el Amazonas: Una Historia Social de la Casa Arana* (Bogotá: Planeta Colombiana Editorial, 2000).

[88] Richard Collier, *The River that God Forgot: The Story of the Amazon Rubber Boom* (New York: Dutton, 1968).

The Putumayo and Caquetá Rivers run parallel for several hundred kilometers. The Putumayo is about forty kilometers south of the Caquetá. Colombia considered the Putumayo its southern boundary, while Peru recognized the Caquetá
as the border. In addition to this dispute, a great deal of hostility lingered between
the two countries. Simón Bolívar had ruled Peru for several years after defeating
the Spanish. During that time, he had implemented several measures that enraged the citizens, including the reinstitution of slavery, the reimposition of the
much-hated indigenous tax, and his opposition to the convocation of the Peruvian
congress. Therefore, Lima was not going to sit idle as the Colombian expeditionary
force sailed for the Putumayo region.

In February 1911, it sent a well-armed battalion, under the command of Major
Óscar Benavides, to dislodge the intruders, but the expedition did not go well. Unbeknownst to the Peruvians, many of the Colombian police officers had become ill
with the tropical diseases that run rampant in the region. They had encamped at
La Pedrera, on the shore of the Caquetá, and had dug a defensive ring of interconnected trenches in case they were attacked. Many of the men could barely walk,
but they were ready when the Peruvian riverboats approached. Major Benavides
had some of his men debark downstream from the encampment. He also ordered
two of his paddle boats to ford the rapids that were in front of the fortification so
that they could land the soldiers upstream, and the two groups could execute a
pincer movement against the entrenched Colombians. Both sides soon determined
that a war in the Amazon would be very difficult to manage, and ended the engagement quickly. The Colombians withdrew to the Putumayo River.

The two sides settled the matter diplomatically through the Salomón-Lozano
Treaty of 1922. The agreement established the border along the Putumayo, and
ceded a large trapezoidal region south of the river to Colombia. The objective of
this concession was to give Colombia a port on the Amazon, and an embarkation
point to export its rubber products. In return, Bogotá ceded territory at the head
of the Putumayo. Not only did this put the land between the two contested rivers
firmly in Colombian territory, but Peru also ceded the port of Leticia. This infuriated the population of Iquitos. The land between Putumayo and Caquetá, which
was used by Casa Arana for its rubber operations, was now in foreign territory.
Furthermore, many merchants from Iquitos had business interests and warehouses in Leticia. Julio César Arana, the ultrarich owner of Casa Arana, had recently
been elected senator, representing the region of Iquitos. Therefore, he could wield
enormous political influence to back up his economic interests. He did, too: he had
already delayed the ratification of the Salomón-Lozano Treaty for five years.

Senator Arana then started a public campaign against Peruvian President Augusto B. Leguía for having signed the treaty. With public opinion shifting against
him, Leguía was ousted in 1930. For the next two years, the business leaders of
Iquitos schemed to regain Leticia. More than four hundred Peruvians, all of whom
had been forced to change their nationality, still lived in the city. Many of them

bristled at their new overlords, who levied additional taxes and tariffs. Furthermore, the owners of Peruvian vessels complained that the Colombian authorities were impeding their navigation rights through the Amazon and Putumayo Rivers. Last of all, the effects of the Great Depression and the torrid competition from the Malaysian rubber plantations were pushing down prices and laying waste to the region's economy.

The Great Depression was squeezing Colombia's fiscal accounts. The low level of financial resources allowed the government to maintain only a small garrison of police in Leticia. This created an opportunity for the Iquitos business community and Casa Arana to make a move. They hired former army officer Oscar Ordóñez to prepare a militia of 212 men, along with guns and a small cannon, to take the city. On August 1, 1932, they struck at dawn, overwhelming the sleeping garrison. The attack took the governments in Lima and Bogotá by surprise. It would take several weeks to sail soldiers from Colombia to retake the city. Therefore, Bogotá hoped that Lima would send a force from Iquitos, which was only a day's sail away, to restore order. Lima ordered its garrison in Iquitos to await further orders before doing anything, but a group of army officers revolted and decided to move ahead with the annexation of the town.

This put the Peruvian government in a bind. President Luis Miguel Sánchez Cerro, who had led the coup against President Leguía, despised the Salomón-Lozano Treaty, but he did not want to fight Colombia. Bogotá had given him until September 6 to restore order in Leticia. However, he no longer controlled the military in Iquitos, and it would take his forces several months to sail around South America, or through the Panama Canal. Moreover, a wave of nationalism was spreading throughout the country, as the population celebrated the reannexation of the city. The president stalled, but in the end he opted for war. The problem was that neither country was ready. The global crisis had devastated both economies. Their weapons were obsolete, and their militaries were far removed from the field of battle.

Colombian President Enrique Olaya Herrera moved quickly when he became certain that Peru was not going to rein in the rebellion. He mobilized an expeditionary force and embarked on an extensive rearmament program. He sent government agents abroad to buy the best cargo ships, gunboats, and airplanes. He recruited mercenaries, mainly Germans, to operate the new equipment and fly the warplanes. The public also rallied in support. People donated money and jewelry, and thousands of volunteers reported to recruiting stations.

Although Peru had struck first, the momentum was moving to the Colombian camp. The army devised a strategy to simultaneously sail an invasion force down the Putumayo and a similar force up the Amazon. The former would then cross over land to the Napo River and continue to Leticia. They would then cut the city off from Iquitos.

In the meantime, Peru was making its own preparations. Lima beefed up the garrison in Leticia to a thousand soldiers, transferred the best cannons from the fortress at Iquitos, mined the approaches to the port, and deployed most of its air force to jungle airstrips. The high command also moved troops into the Putumayo, establishing a set of armed outposts to launch an invasion of the river basin and retake the Caquetá.

President Olaya Herrera appointed General Alfredo Vásquez Cobo to lead the Colombian expedition. Cobo rendezvoused all of his forces at the port of Manaus in January 1933 and proceeded with a contingent of seven hundred troops. His destination was Leticia, but he decided to sail up the Putumayo to the fort of Tarapacá to dislodge the enemies' presence from the northeastern corner of the trapezoid. The fort had been established in 1900 by Casa Arana as a way to control access to the river: all goods and individuals entering or exiting the region were subject to revision and control, which enhanced the company's monopoly powers. Although the base had been expanded after the start of the war, it was still a jungle outpost.

Cobo's force arrived at Tarapacá on February 13 and quickly convinced the ninety-four soldiers there to retreat or face annihilation. The men decided to leave, but they sent a radio message to Iquitos warning about the attack. Within a few hours, a detachment of bombers arrived and attacked the Colombian armada. The planes failed to damage any of the ships, but the attack was enough to shake many of the sailors and officers on board.

With the fort under Colombian control, engineers proceeded to beef up its defenses to prevent the Peruvians from using the river. Cut off from Leticia and Iquitos, the only way to provision the deployed Peruvian troops would be through jungle trails—an almost impossible task. At the same time, the second Colombian force coming down the Putumayo engaged the Peruvian outpost at the confluence with the Güepí River.

News of the victory at Tarapacá and the encounter with the garrison at Güepí emboldened Bogotá to seek a diplomatic solution to the conflict. On February 16, a cease-fire was declared, and the two sides entered negotiations in Geneva. For a month, they argued and debated. During that month, the army built up a great stock of equipment and supplies at Güepí. Therefore, it was ready to go if the order came to resume the attack. On March 26, Colombian troops crossed the river and took on the defenders. The combined use of naval artillery and aviation support routed the Peruvian defenders. Many fled into the rainforest. Half of the garrison was killed, while the attackers suffered only five losses.

The assault on Güepí revealed the extreme disadvantage of the Peruvians. Already far removed from their supply lines, the troops were struggling to fight with extremely outdated weapons. Meanwhile, the Colombians had bought state-of-the-art equipment. The defeats at Tarapacá and Güepí represented a loss of supplies and men that Peru could ill afford to lose. Morale fell and a sense of desperation began to permeate Lima.

President Sánchez Cerro ordered the two largest cruisers of the Peruvian Navy, as well as two submarines, to sail up the Amazon, ignoring the fact that these vessels would have limited use in such shallow water. The pessimism was made worse by the political unrest that was shaking the country. President Sánchez Cerro was aggressively suppressing the rise of APRA, a leftist political party. A year earlier, he had ordered the execution of hundreds of party members in the northern city of Trujillo, instilling a deep hatred among the radical youth. The anger boiled to the surface when nineteen-year-old Abelardo Mendoza Leiva shot the president through the heart as he was reviewing troops headed for the front.

The assassination took the country by surprise and deepened the national crisis. Given the country's conditions, the mantle passed to General Benavides, the hero of La Pedrera, to finish out Sánchez Cerro's term. Benavides had already served in the position once before, between February 1914 and August 1915. The general had recently conducted a thorough review of the country's forces, and was familiar with its immense shortcomings. Therefore, he quickly stepped up the peace negotiations before the situation became worse. He agreed to adhere to the terms of the Salomón-Lozano Treaty. Colombia would keep Leticia, but its forces needed to vacate Peruvian territory. The US government put diplomatic pressure on Lima to accept the terms, as a way to help compensate Colombia for the loss of Panama. Bogotá tried to be as graceful as possible, but anger simmered deep in the ranks of the Peruvian high command. The loss of Leticia would smolder for years.

The Colombian-Peruvian War highlighted the vast role played by logistics and technology. Both economic centers of countries were far from the battlefront, but Colombia was able to find a faster way to deploy troops and equipment. Likewise, it did not hesitate in buying the latest technology in ships, airplanes, and guns. Last of all, nature proved to be a formidable obstacle to both sides. Most of the South American wars were fought in extreme climates, from the sweltering swamps of Paraguay to the blinding heat of the Atacama to the disease-ridden dank of the Amazon. In addition to taking their toll on the troops' physical and mental health, such conditions led to equipment failure, with rusting guns and faulty munitions, thus adding to what Prussian military strategist Carl von Clausewitz called "the fog of war" in 1832.

Last of all, this was involved a territorial dispute, but was started for purely commercial reasons. The desire by Casa Arana to regain the rubber fields between the Putumayo and Caquetá Rivers, as well as the need for the merchants of Iquitos to reclaim Leticia, were the reasons why the two countries went to war. Close behind their actions was the need by foreign investors and industrial leaders to preserve their access to rubber. Ironically, the booming British plantations in Asia and the global depression had already reduced the importance of the equatorial rainforest. Nevertheless, the vast wealth produced in the Putumayo Basin was enough to ignite a passion that would be the cause of another war.

The third and last phase of the Rubber Wars shifted to Ecuador. Like Uruguay, Paraguay, and Bolivia, Ecuador was another small South American country that had evolved into a buffer state between the remnants of the largest viceroyalty system. Ecuador had been an important captaincy of the Spanish empire, with a great deal of autonomy. It had also been an integral part of the Inca world. Before his death in 1527, the Inca Lord Huayna Cápac had divided his kingdom in two parts. The northern region, with its capital in Quito, he passed to his younger son, Atahualpa, while the southern half, with its capital in Cuzco, he bequeathed to his older son, Huáscar. The two factions of the royal family were in the midst of a civil war when Pizarro and his murderous band of *conquistadores* arrived in 1532. Just before the Spanish captured Atahualpa, the Inca king had killed his older brother. Therefore, the Spanish effectively decapitated the kingdom's leadership by abducting him. In addition to the gold and silver that was sacked, the large indigenous population was the other great prize. They were essential in operating the immense plantations and mines that were now under Spanish control. Furthermore, they were taxed, thus providing an important source of revenue.

Most of the large indigenous civilizations of South America were located in the high plateaus that are scattered throughout the Andes. These highlands were very advantageous. They were easy to defend. There was a dearth of mosquitoes and other insects due to the high altitude and the cold temperatures, so there was no danger of tropical diseases. Moreover, the highlands had abundant water due to the constant rainfall. To this day, most of the Latin American capitals are located in high plateaus: México City, Bogotá, Caracas, Santiago, La Paz, and Quito.

In addition to a large indigenous population, the captaincy of Quito was an important center of power and education. Scholars at the large universities made original studies into issues of theology and medicine. Much of modern-day Ecuador is outside the original domain. Up to 1763, Guayaquil reported to the viceroy in Lima, and to this day, there is very little love between the highlanders and the coastal population. The lack of a common culture led to a great deal of social and political instability during the nineteenth and twentieth centuries. Indeed, the country is still one of the most politically unstable in Latin America. After the Colombian-Peruvian War of 1828, the southern district of Gran Colombia declared independence and became Ecuador. Although most of the population was scattered across the sierra and coast, it considered itself to be an Amazonian country. The rubber boom at the end of the nineteenth century turbocharged its jungle ambitions, inducing the military to push down the Napo toward Iquitos. However, the 1941 border war between Ecuador and Peru started far from the tropical jungle. It began along the Pacific coast.

Since the end of the colonial system, Ecuador had been in a long-running dispute with Peru over the provinces of Tumbes, Jaén, and Maynas. Tumbes was a rich coastal province. Most of its territory was inside Ecuador, but Peru had occupied the city of Tumbes since 1820, and Quito wanted it back. The province of Jaén was farther inland and straddled the Andes. The southern edge of the province sat on the Marañón River, one of the main sources of the Amazon and a key component of Ecuador's jungle ambitions. Last of all, the country claimed the province of Maynas. The territory formed a triangle with the Andes on one side and the Marañón and Napo Rivers on the other two. Since the immense region included Iquitos, Peru's jungle bastion, it was bound to be a contentious issue.

Peru's devastating defeat at the hands of the Colombians in 1933 sparked a wave of optimism in Ecuador. By now, the rainforest was less strategically important. Its share of the global rubber market had dropped to 15 percent. Nevertheless, there was still hope that Peru's defeat meant that Quito's Amazon ambitions were within reach. The media began to hype martial themes, and politicians played along. The results of the conflict also motivated the Peruvian military to modernize its weapons and improve the training of its officer corps. Peru acquired new tanks, warships, and airplanes. Therefore, when Ecuador decided to begin its aggression in July 1941, the Peruvians were ready to fight.

The Ecuadorian strategy was to bait the Peruvian forces until they retaliated and committed an act of war. The government would then claim that it was being abused by a much larger aggressor, in the hope that the international community would intervene and convene a mediation conference. During negotiations, Quito would make demands over the three contested provinces, hoping to win some concessions. Yet, instead of starting its provocations in the jungle, where Ecuador had its greatest territorial ambitions, the military decided to focus its efforts on the Zarumilla River Basin in the province of Tumbes, which was easier to reinforce and resupply.

The Zarumilla is a small river that marks the traditional boundary between the two countries. Numerous border incidents took place during the late 1930s, ranging from the firing of machine guns to the harassment of Peruvian positions by Ecuadorian aircraft. Yet, Lima knew Ecuador's true intent. Its spies had infiltrated the government, and the intelligence corps had deciphered the military's code. They would not allow themselves to be provoked. Peru ordered its soldiers to diffuse hostile incidents, and told its commanders not to mass troops along the border.

In addition to the harassment along the Zarumilla, the Ecuadorian military had also erected a new set of border outposts well inside the Peruvian part of the Amazon jungle. Sensing that the two countries were headed for war, the United States offered to broker negotiations between the two sides, but these failed to produce any results.

Thus, Lima prepared for combat. In 1940, the high command formed the North Group to push back the incursions and outposts that had been erected. While the military was mobilizing its resources, its officers continued to fend off the provocations. The Ecuadorians interpreted the response as a lack of commitment and became more aggressive in their goading. Meanwhile, the Peruvians continued massing troops along the front. They finally launched an attack on July 24, taking the coastal town of Huaquillas. Ecuador was caught completely unawares. The Peruvian Army quickly punched into enemy territory. Unlike during the War of the Pacific, Peru now dominated the seas. This allowed the navy full range of the coastline. The North Group decided to center its offensive along the littoral in order to rely on naval gunfire support. The troops moved inland toward Chacras as Peruvian bombers delivered a deluge of bombs on the fleeing soldiers. To make matters worse, the North Group sent a battalion of Czech-made tanks into action, creating a fully mechanized offensive. The defensive line disintegrated as the motorized units roared across the border. The Ecuadorians tried to regroup at Arenillas, on the outskirts of Chacras, but there was not much they could do to stem the onslaught.

The next day, the Peruvians continued to move inland, taking the entire province of El Oro. By now, the Ecuadorian Army had degraded into a rabble and the men began looting their own towns. They broke into homes, pillaging food and drink. Mobs of drunken soldiers stumbled through the streets, prompting the citizens to pine for the arrival of the Peruvian Army to restore law and order. So fast was the Ecuadorian Army's retreat that the Peruvian mechanized infantry could not keep up. Therefore, the North Group decided to leapfrog by dropping paratroopers over Puerto Bolívar.

By the end of July, Peruvian troops were in control of a thousand square kilometers of Ecuadorian territory, and Guayaquil was in danger. Desperate Ecuadorian diplomats in the United States began leaking reports that the stunning Peruvian victory was due to the participation of Japanese units, and this baseless rumor triggered a panic attack in Washington, DC.

Europe was in flames in 1941, and in less than six months, the United States would be at war with Japan. Japanese aggression was on the rise throughout the Pacific Basin, so to US government officials, it seemed possible that the Ecuadorian rumor was correct. The United States had made large advances in the development of synthetic rubber, but it was still far from entering mass production. Most of the world's rubber output was in Southeast Asia and under threat of falling into Japanese hands. The remaining friendly capacity was in the Amazon. Hence, it was logical for Washington to fear that the Japanese could be on the move in South America. There was a significant Asian community in Peru that could easily be mistaken for Japanese.

Already anxious about the war in Europe and Southeast Asia, the Americans ordered an immediate cease-fire in the hostilities between Ecuador and Peru on July 31. Instead of clarifying the misinformation and continuing the offensive, Peru agreed. Several flare-ups threatened to break the truce. Ecuadorian forces attempted to make advances in the rainforest, but they were repelled. Finally, the two sides met in Brazil to hammer out a compromise. Under the Río de Janeiro Protocol of 1942, Ecuador agreed to surrender its claim to the Marañón and Amazon River Basins, provided that Peru abandoned its occupied territory. The treaty was bolstered by the presence of the United States, Brazil, and Argentina as guarantors to the peace. The three countries had acted as observers and arbitrators in order to make it a more equitable and lasting process.

Peru's performance during the war was impeccable. Its losses against Chile and Colombia had left an indelible mark on the military, convincing the high command of the need to improve the quality of its weapons and training. However, the border conflicts with Ecuador would continue for another sixty years. The next time, the focus would shift deep into the jungle.

The Santiago and Zamora Rivers were supposed mark the border in the Cordillera del Cóndor (Cóndor Mountains) region, but the discovery of the Cenepa River at the end of 1940s added a new level of abstruseness, since jungle boundaries were typically defined by waterways. Quito said that the presence of an unbeknownst river made the treaty unenforceable and called for new negotiations. The real reason why the river became such an important diplomatic issue was that it was tributary of the Marañón, which flows into the Amazon. Therefore, by recognizing the Cenepa as the boundary, the government could claim that Ecuador was a member of the Amazon community and gain legal rights to the waterway. That was also why Lima wanted to keep the border along the ridge of the Cóndors, and prevent Ecuador from occupying the eastern slopes of the mountain range.

There were several confrontations between the two sides, but the first engagement occurred in 1981, when Ecuadorian forces started building a set of outposts in the Cenepa basin. By now, the rubber boom was a distant memory. The geometric expansion of inexpensive petrochemical products had made rubber obsolete. However, the issue of the equatorial rainforest remained an important symbol of nationalism and pride. The large rainforest was also taking on a new dimension for its diverse flora and fauna, and as the largest source of fresh water on the planet.

Peru accused Ecuador of making persistent encroachments on the eastern side of the Cóndor Mountains. Tired of outposts being erected inside its territory, Lima ordered a helicopter attack against Paquisha outpost on January 28, 1981. Two other outposts, at Mayaicu and Machinaza, also came under attack. The Paquisha War, as the incident became known, was the first major engagement there dominated by aviation, necessitated by the remote location of the jungle outposts. Helicopters played a central role in transporting troops and material, while Peruvian Cesna A-37s, supersonic Mirage 5s, and Sukhoi Su-22s provided close air support and ground attack. Ecuador deployed A-37s, Mirage 1s, and Israel-made Kfirs to support their troops. For the next two weeks, the Peruvians carried out operations to dismantle the outposts and push back the Ecuadorians. Fearing that Peru would repeat its invasion of 1941, the Ecuadorian high command mobilized, sending twenty-five thousand troops to defend the southern front. South America was in the cusp of a major economic crisis, and Lima was not about to embark on another costly war. Therefore, the leaders from the two countries met and made a "gentlemen's agreement" to remove their outposts and troops from the contested region. However, a much bigger encounter exploded on January 25, 1995.

The two sides had begun building up their forces at the end of 1994. Ecuador had an important advantage. It had established a set of roads to connect its jungle region with the rest of the country. Meanwhile, Peru needed to airlift all of its troops and supplies. Its economy was also in bad shape. Peru was exiting one of its worst economic and political crises. The country had suffered a devastating period of hyperinflation in 1990, when consumer prices rose almost 400 percent in a single month. It had defaulted on its foreign obligations and was in the midst of debt negotiations. The government was also engaged in an existential struggle with the Shining Path movement; kidnappings were widespread and bombs were a common occurrence in Lima. Alberto Fujimori, an untested college professor, was president, and many considered him politically weak. It should surprise no one that Ecuador chose that time to make another stab for the Amazon.

As in the past, the military began building a series of outposts in the Cenepa valley. Two large outposts, Tiwinza and Base Sur, were a few kilometers within the contested territory, but it was enough to whip the Peruvians into frenzy. In late December 1994, the army began airlifting soldiers and equipment to PV-1, a forward base. At the same time, Ecuador used its logistical advantage by trucking in heavy equipment and busloads of troops. They set up artillery bases along the top of the Cóndor ridge and in the valley behind it. Antiaircraft installations lined the tops of the mountains, converting the valley into a virtual killing field for low-flying aircraft.

The Peruvian high command was preparing for a repeat of the 1981 Paquisha War, where its troops would dismantle the Ecuadorian outposts. However, they were attacked before they could complete their preparations. On January 26, 1995, a work detail clearing a new helicopter landing strip found itself under attack by a company of Ecuadorian Special Forces. The men regrouped and returned fire, but they were no match for the elite corps. Most of the survivors were forced to flee into the jungle. Two days later, the Peruvians counterattacked, using air support from helicopters. Unfortunately for the pilots, they had flown into a trap. Missiles streaked out of the ground, taking out helicopter, and the air force called off a bombing run. For the next three days, the Peruvians continued to lose helicopters and airplanes to antiaircraft fire. Finally, they decided to change tactics by refocusing their efforts on the major artillery bases that lined the top of the mountains. Yet, they were not able to make much progress. To make matters worse, the outposts were surrounded by thick minefields, causing large casualties.

Even though Ecuador started with the upper hand, Peru's larger size allowed it to move more resources to regain the momentum. Peru sent groups of Special Forces to PV-1, and they were able to take the outposts of Tiwinza and Base Sur. With its objective completed, Peru agreed to a cease-fire on February 28. They signed the Montevideo Declaration and settled the border dispute. Ecuador agreed to use the Cóndor Mountains as the line of demarcation, ending its Amazon aspirations. In return, Peru ceded the military base of Tiwinza in perpetuity.

The Rubber Wars marked almost a century of warfare in parts of the South American rainforest. The territorial conflicts were highlighted by the presence of rubber trees and the use of the latex in modern industry. The conflicts were also witness to the immense advances in military technology, from riverboats and German rifles to tanks and paratroopers to supersonic fighters and antiaircraft missiles.

The wars evolved along with the development of the rubber industry. During the Acre Conflict, commercial applications for rubber were still modest. The conflict was mainly fought by a rabble of Brazilian peasants against a small Bolivian militia. The border war between Colombia and Peru was more sophisticated in both weaponry and tactics. At stake were the large rubber operations of Casa Arana. By the time of the Ecuadorian-Peruvian war, latex was no longer the principal source for rubber or plastic products. Nevertheless, the rainforest remained an important symbol for both countries, as well as signifying a potential source of wealth and power.

7 THE CHACO WAR: FIGHTING FOR SCRUBLAND

THE CHACO WAR: FIGHTING FOR SCRUBLAND

The next war was fought by two of the most dysfunctional sovereign entities in South America: Paraguay and Bolivia. They were landlocked states that emerged from the disintegration of the viceroyalty system. They suffered devastating defeats at the hands of powerful neighbors, with enormous losses of territories, population, and wealth. Not only did Bolivia lose its seaboard, but it was also plundered of its enormous riches in nitrates and rubber. Meanwhile, Paraguay lost all of its industrial capacity, most of its people, and almost half of its territory.

One of the inherent problems with both countries was their inability to consolidate their societies by fully incorporating their indigenous populations. While previous South American conflicts had been fought by a mix of European descendants and natives, this was mainly going to be a war between the largest surviving indigenous groups of South America.[89] Bolivia's Quechua and Aymara people were direct descendants of the Incas, while Paraguay's Guaraní were the nomadic tribes that inhabited the southeastern plains. Both had been reduced to semifeudalistic arrangements and allowed few civil or economic liberties. Electoral laws ensured that only select groups of people—mainly those of European descent—were allowed to vote. Voters were required to meet minimum levels of income, property, and literacy. This centralization of political power through racial exclusion ensured a great concentration of wealth. However, it also led to internal contradictions in which different languages, cultures, and interests impeded the social cohesion needed to pursue a successful military campaign.

The Gran Chaco region was a distant backwater for Bolivia's elites, who were distracted by the vast mineral resources embedded deep in the Altiplano. Initially, business barons were riveted on the massive silver deposits of Potosí, but after those resources were depleted, their attentions turned to tin. The locus of activity was the huge Salvadora complex at Llallagua. The mine was only a few hundred kilometers north of Potosí. Llallagua was comparable in form, rising out of the high Andean sierra. Similar to what occurred with nitrates and rubber, the demand for tin soared at the turn of the twentieth century, with the proliferation of consumer staples. Tin has many commercial applications: its anticorrosive properties make it practical for packaging food and liquids and for coating iron to prevent rust; its malleability lends itself for soldering. No one took more advantage of the tin boom

---

[89] Nicola Foote and René Harder Horst, *Military Struggle and Identity Formation in Latin America: Race, Nation, and Community During the Liberal Period* (Gainesville: University Press of Florida, 2010).

than Simón Iturri Patiño, an astute entrepreneur of mixed blood who not only became one of the richest men of the world, but of all time. In 1905, as a young clerk at Casa Frick, a hardware store for miners in Oruro, he accepted the deed to a small mine as debt payment.[90] He lost his job for his imprudence, but the entrepreneurial Patiño parlayed the operation into the largest tin operation in the world. By World War II, the New York–based Patiño Mines & Enterprise Consolidated Inc. controlled almost the entire industry, owning smelters throughout the world. This allowed Patiño to become the main power broker in Bolivia, controlling both politicians and the judicial system. Royalties from the La Salvadora and Uncia mines represented three-fourths of the government's revenues, allowing him to control the state's apparatus and use it to suppress workers' unions and leftist movements.[91] Mining is a sector that lends itself to organization, due to its heavy dependence on labor. Patiño had the military disperse strikes and root out militant leaders. Like César Arana in the Putumayo, the Tin Baron became infamously rich through the subjugation of the indigenous population. As a result of the enormous wealth produced by the mining sector, the attention of the political oligarchy was riveted on the highlands, ignoring other parts of the country. This tunnel vision was a flaw that frequently plagued Bolivia—first in the Atacama, later in Acre, and now in the Chaco. However, La Paz's neglect of the region ended in 1926, when Standard Oil made a colossal find in Sanandita, which is situated in the eastern foothills of the Andes: oil.

The discovery of oil sent tremors through the country's political hierarchy because it was a threat to the political status quo. Until then, the country's economic and political wealth had been concentrated in the sierra. The financial resources and wealth created by the mining sector concentrated the country's political power in cities like La Paz, Oruro, and Potosí. However, the discovery of oil threatened to shift the locus of economic power to the lowland city Santa Cruz, and the vast stretches of the Chaco.

The Chaco is an arid scrubland just below the Amazon Basin. It forms a rough isosceles triangle outlined by three rivers: the western edge is marked by the shallow Parapetí River; the northern boundary is marked by the Paraguay River, as the waterway courses down from Mato Grosso; and the southern boundary is marked by the muddy Pilcomayo River. Asunción, the capital of Paraguay, sits at the apex of the triangle, and the Andes form the base. Brazil is to the north, and Argentina to the south.

The Chaco's ecosystem is complex. Most of the year, the region is dry, except during the two rainy seasons when it is inundated with heavy downpours. The vegetation is mainly scrub, thorny bushes, and dense forests of arid-land trees that

[90]   René Danilo Arze Aguirre, *Breve Historia de Bolivia* (Sucre: Universidad Andina Simón Bolívar, 1996).

[91]   John Henry Hewlett, *Like Moonlight on Snow: The Life of Simón Iturri Patiño* (New York: R. M. McBride & Company, 1947).

are not suitable for foraging. Many of the trees are of the Quebracho variety. The name literally means *axe breaker* in Spanish, which is a testament to their density and strength. The air is thick with dust and swarms of black flies. The only reliable source of potable water is from deep subterranean aquifers that are replenished during the rainy season. It is not hard to see why the Chaco is a veritable no-man's-land. Home to only a handful of nomadic tribes and a few rugged settlers, it was never a center of economic activity. Until the discovery of oil at Sanandita, no one thought it had any mineral wealth, which is why it was ignored by La Paz, which sat two thousand kilometers away. However, things changed when foreign geologists and wildcatters began to probe the empty wilderness.

The 1920s was the golden age of oil exploration. The automobile was in its ascendency, as the postwar recovery transformed itself into a consumer bonanza. Armed with credit for the first time, American households bought goods that had been previously out of reach. At the same time, manufacturers of automobiles and appliances, such as Ford and General Electric, moved into mass production arrangements that allowed them to drastically reduce prices. The proliferation of gasoline-powered vehicles pushed up the demand for hydrocarbons. Oil was no longer sought for its kerosene products, which were mainly used for lighting. Producers were keen on distilling it for its gasoline and diesel. Geologists improved their exploration techniques, which led to major finds in California and Texas, and began taking their processes abroad to secure more deposits. During the 1920s, they found mammoth oil fields in Iraq, Venezuela, and México. Standard Oil and Royal Dutch Shell were the technological leaders, and they were homing in on South America.

A year after Sanandita, Standard stuck oil again in Camiri, a little farther south. Given the prominent size of the fields, the company began to explore nearby regions, making additional finds in the province of Salta, Argentina. All eyes then shifted to the Chaco, as everyone believed that the scrubland contained the next Spindletop. It had many of the rugged features that were prevalent in other major oil-producing regions, such as Texas, California, and Iraq. Not to be left behind, Royal Dutch Shell, the Standard Oil's keen rival, tried to jump the gun by obtaining exploration and drilling rights from the Paraguayan government to the region. The problem was that no one was sure to whom the Chaco belonged.[92]

Like Bolivia, Paraguay had also ignored the Chaco. It was adjacent to the capital of Asunción, but the empty wasteland had no appeal. The only major role it had played in Paraguayan history was as an escape route for López Solano's troops as they fled the collapse of Humaitá during the War of the Triple Alliance. Technically, Bolivia had a strong legal claim to the region. Colonial documents and maps showed that it had been part of the Charcas Audiencia, but Paraguay's presence was stronger. Tribes of Guaraní roamed the scrubland, as well as colonies of German

---

[92] Julio José Chiavenato, *La Guerra del Petróleo* (Buenos Aires: Punto de Encuentro, 2007).

Mennonites who obtained their legal charters from the Paraguayan government. La Paz was also far removed. The lines of communication between the highlands and the Chaco were almost nonexistent. Given that possession trumped legal title under the precedent of *uti possidetis*, Paraguay's claim was stronger. Nevertheless, the two countries had long been distracted by other issues, and until then had not felt pressed to settle the territorial dispute.

Argentina made a weak attempt to annex the Chaco after the War of the Triple Alliance. Brazil, however, killed the initiative, wanting to keep a buffer between the two countries.[93] In 1887, Paraguay and Bolivia did make an effort to settle the dispute when they signed the Aceval-Tamayo treaty, which divided the Chaco in three parts: the western third was under Bolivia's domain; the eastern third belonged to Paraguay; and the middle was no-man's-land. The treaty was never ratified by the Paraguayan congress, but it was recognized as a protocol to keep the status quo. Each country was allowed to establish a series of small forts to stake out their territory. Given that the partition was informal, Royal Dutch Shell wanted to be certain that its land titles would be protected if it struck oil. Therefore, the company began pressing the Paraguayan military to expel the Bolivian garrisons.

Bolivia's political situation was complicated. In 1926, Hernando Siles Reyes had been elected president. A young reformer, his inclusive style was a break from the oppressive tactics used by his predecessors, including Bautista Saavedra. Siles founded the Nationalist Party and had a strong following among the young and intelligentsia. However, he was not opposed to using excessive force. In July 1927, an indigenous uprising broke out in the highlands between the cities of Potosí, Oruro, and Sucre. More than ten thousand peasants attacked farms and towns in protest of land expropriation. For decades, wealthy landowners had encroached on tribal lands in order to expand their agricultural production. Like feudal serfs, members of the indigenous community had been forced to pay tribute to the landowners. Frustrated by the indignation, they had finally risen up. Siles claimed to be firmly in support of the indigenous community, but he still sent troops to put down the rebellion. These forces, augmented by local militias, brutally rounded up the ringleaders. The president justified his tactics by saying that the movement had been infiltrated by Communists and anarchists, which was indeed true. The uprising was eventually subdued, but it drove an even deeper schism between members of the upper class and the indigenous population.[94] This would become a major detriment in the field of battle, when many soldiers refused to fight for a country that did not respect their civil liberties.

The possibility of finding oil in the Chaco stirred imaginations in Asunción. If such reserves existed, they could create vast fortunes and fill the government's

[93] Bruce W. Farcau, *The Chaco War: Bolivia and Paraguay, 1932–1935* (Westport, CT: Praeger, 1996).

[94] Robert J. Alexander and Eldon M. Parker, *A History of Organized Labor in Bolivia* (Westport, CT: Praeger Publishers, 2005).

threadbare coffers. Therefore, there was a great deal of enthusiasm to nail down its claim on the region. On December 5, 1928, Paraguayan troops, acting under pressure from Dutch Royal Shell, attacked the fort in Vanguardia. The defenders were caught unaware, and they were quickly overrun. In the process, six soldiers lost their lives before the enemy set fire to the rickety wooden structures. President Siles initially considered asking for international mediation, but instead he decided to retake the fort. Unfortunately, the military couldn't send reinforcements because the roads were impassable; it was the start of the rainy season. Therefore, he decided to retaliate by assaulting the Paraguayan fort of Boquerón, which was easier to access.

Seeing that the two countries were on the verge of war, the League of Nations intervened. It declared that Paraguay was an aggressor state. The two sides were ordered to move back to their original positions, and Asunción was forced to indemnify Bolivia for the cost of the damaged fortification.[95] The incident marked a small victory for President Siles. However, the onset of the Great Depression destabilized the economy, leading to widespread social unrest and his ouster in May 1930.

The social fault lines that lay just below the surface were becoming open fissures. Afraid of seeing the country descend into anarchy, the military, under the command of General Carlos Blanco, executed a coup d'état in June. With order restored, Blanco called for general elections the next year. Daniel Salamanca, a taciturn and irascible political hack, swept the field. One of his main objectives was to increase Bolivia's presence in the Chaco. Standard Oil, through its lobbyist Spruille Braden, was putting pressure on the political class to thwart Paraguay's territorial ambitions, but the company also wanted a port on the Paraguay River to export the oil that it was producing in Sanandita and Camiri. Last of all, it wanted to avert the possibility that the Bolivian government would nationalize the highly lucrative oil operations by keeping it distracted on a distant war.[96]

To engender public support, Salamanca claimed that the control of the Chaco would allow the nation to avenge the dishonor of the War of the Pacific by giving it the access to the sea that had been lost. He immediately ordered the construction of new forts in the Chaco to reinforce its claim. Troops and equipment were deployed into the scrubland. It was at this time that Bolivia's great logistical disadvantage became apparent. Not only was the region far removed from the highlands, but the roads to the Chaco were dirt tracks that transformed into impassible bogs during the rainy season.

Argentina also began playing a dominant role in the conflict. Ever since the War of the Triple Alliance, Buenos Aires had maintained a strong grip over the

---

[95] Margaret La Foy, *The Chaco Dispute and the League of Nations* (Bryn Mawr, PA: Bryn Mawr College, 1941).

[96] Chiavenato, *La Guerra Del Petróleo*.

Paraguayan economy and government. Argentines controlled huge swaths of land, as well as the largest companies, such as Milanovich Ltd., a shipping company that carried almost 80 percent of the country's trade, and Ferrocarril Central de Paraguay, the main train company. In all but name, Paraguay was a puppet state. Buenos Aires was also in deep collusion with Royal Dutch Shell. This was the so-called Decade of Infamy, when everything and everyone was for sale. British businesses, in particular, had enormous influence in Argentina. They owned meat-packing plants, railroads, and telephone companies. Royal Dutch Shell, for example, had major operations in the country, and it used its lobbying apparatus to promote its interests in the Chaco, and Argentina's president, Agustín Pedro Justo, one of most corrupt leaders in that country's infamous political history, was more than willing to comply. He and his pernicious foreign minister, Carlos Saavedra Lamas, would surreptitiously direct the conduct of the war. Argentine business owners and bankers made fortunes selling armaments to the belligerents at greatly inflated prices.

On paper, the two countries were not evenly matched. Bolivia's population was three times larger than Paraguay's, with more than 2.5 million inhabitants. Its economy was also triple the size of its neighbor, but it was going through a difficult period. The Global Depression had devastated the economy. Tin production had fallen by a third in 1931, dropping to thirty-one thousand metric tons from forty-five thousand tons the year before. The impact on the government's fiscal accounts was brutal, forcing it to implement draconian budget cuts. It slashed its work force in half, triggering a large increase in the unemployment rate. In 1932, with the government coffers running low, President Salamanca turned to Tin Baron Patiño for economic assistance. Patiño contributed £25,000 to modernize the Bolivian Air Force. Although Paraguay had also been hit by the global downturn, its economy was more insular, so the impact had not been as severe. Argentina was also surreptitiously providing assistance. Furthermore, Paraguay had an immense logistical advantage. Asunción was adjacent to the Chaco; it could mobilize resources faster and at less expense, an advantage that would help decide the outcome.

For four years, the two sides inched closer to war, with several border skirmishes as the armies jockeyed for position. International efforts to mediate the process made no headway, and diplomatic relations broke down. The conflict finally erupted in June 1932 at an unmarked rain gulley in the middle of the Chaco. The pond had been spotted by aerial reconnaissance, and Bolivian Major Óscar Moscoso was ordered to secure it. Given the arid nature of the region, controlling the centrally located pond would be advantageous. Indeed, much of the ensuing war would be fought for and around watering holes, springs, and wells.

Upon his arrival, Moscoso found that the small body of water was protected by a squad of Paraguayan soldiers. President Salamanca had sent explicit orders that the expeditionary force should peacefully take the lake, without any use of violence. Unfortunately, the major never received the order. He drove off the defenders, killing a corporal in the process. This incensed the Paraguayan military, and one month later, they counterattacked. Thus, the war was on.

President Salamanca initially considered downplaying the incident. His country was in no shape to embark on an expensive military adventure for what might still turn out to be just useless scrubland. The severity of the Global Depression was aggravating the existing social tensions, and he was keen on diverting the public's attention. Therefore, the Paraguayan counterattack was presented as an outright act of aggression. The Bolivian press incited the public through a series of alarmist articles that ignited a surge of nationalism. President Salamanca immediately hijacked the public outcry and ordered a full retaliatory strike. Not only was the military ordered to retake the pond, which had been named Chuquisaca, but it was sent to attack the forts of Corales, Toledo, and Boquerón.

The high command in La Paz was totally against the escalation. They felt that the Chaco units were ill trained and not properly armed. They wanted time to recruit more soldiers and obtain better equipment. However, President Salamanca did not want to call for a general mobilization. This would be a serious handicap throughout the war. Instead of marshaling the country's immense resources against a much smaller opponent, he prosecuted the war in dribs and drabs. As a result, Bolivia's superiority in size and population was never a decisive factor on the field of battle.

Bolivia did not have many factors in its favor. It had four thousand troops deployed in the Chaco, with supply lines that were badly stretched. There was a tense relationship between the executive and the military. President Salamanca had little confidence in Army Chief of Staff General Filiberto Osorio, considering him obstinate and argumentative. Moreover, international resentment against the country was on the rise. The attack on the three Paraguayan outposts was labeled as an act of aggression by the League of Nations, which placed an arms embargo on the Bolivia.

This highlighted the first of three handicaps that would dog the country. As in previous wars, logistics was a major problem. Landlocked, with a military front far removed from the main population centers, and now hobbled by an arms embargo, Bolivia fought with one arm firmly tied behind its back. Meanwhile, Paraguay, with its capital close to the front and assistance from a prosperous and generous neighbor, possessed tremendous advantages—advantages that would outweigh its inferiority in population and output.

Bolivia's second handicap was climatic. As was the case in two of the other Bolivian conflicts, the War of the Pacific and the Acre War, environmental issues would be critical. In the Altiplano, the home of most of the Bolivian fighters, the weather is cold weather, the land rocky, and water plentiful. In the thin air, there are few mosquitos. In the two earlier wars, soldiers from the highlands had been forced to fight in the torrential desert heat of the Atacama and the dense jungles of the Amazon. Now, they were being thrust into the arid scrubland of the Chaco, where water was scarce and poisonous snakes were plentiful. The days were oppressively hot and the nights uncomfortably cold. Swarms of mosquitos carried diseases like malaria and yellow fever. Of course, the Paraguayans had to deal with the same hardships, but they were more accustomed to them, having lived in the grasslands right across the river.

Bolivia's third handicap was its poor leadership. In 1932, on the eve of the conflict, Paraguay elected Eusebio Ayala as president. It was Ayala's second time in office, as he had governed a decade earlier. Ayala was competent, affable, and agreeable. He had a close relationship with the military, particularly with General José Félix Estigarribia, the head of the military. Cunning and shrewd, Estigarribia had an impeccable military pedigree. He was a graduate of Saint-Cyr, the prestigious French military academy, and he had also trained in Chile.[97] Ayala and Estigarribia would run the military campaign for the duration of the conflict, imbuing the leadership with a sense of direction and consistency. This was in contrast to the constant changes in direction that characterized the Bolivian operation.

The counterattack against Boquerón forced Asunción to call for a general mobilization. Young men reported to recruitment depots. Within a month, more than thirty-five thousand recruits were in basic training. Three months after the retaliatory attack, Paraguay launched an offensive to retake the fort. The Chaco was nothing more than a wasteland, but President Ayala claimed the war was an issue of national pride. In reality, he was under a great deal of pressure from Dutch Royal Shell and the Argentine government to secure the region. Bolivia took a similar approach. President Salamanca telegraphed Major Manuel Marzana, who commanded the outpost, to hold on at any cost. His force of four hundred men was up against an invasion force of four thousand soldiers. As General Estigarribia's division approached, they were detected by Bolivia's aerial reconnaissance. Thanks to Patiño's generosity, air supremacy would always be a tactical advantage for the Andean country, but it was never enough to change the outcome.

The airplanes strafed the advancing columns, but they could not stop them. On September 9, 1932, the enemy assault began. The Paraguayans thought the operation would be simple, since they outnumbered the defenders more than ten to one. Therefore, they launched several frontal attacks to overrun the fortification at Boquerón. However, the assaults were repelled by superior artillery fire and machine guns. This convinced General Estigarribia that he needed to surround the fortress and lay siege. Even though the two countries were fighting with twentieth-century weapons and technology, medieval siege tactics would remain a constant feature of the Chaco War. For almost two weeks, the encircled Bolivians held on, but their situation became tenuous. Munitions and water ran low, and a sense of desperation took hold. Massive reinforcements were still three months away, given the poor

[97] José Félix Estigarribia, *The Epic of the Chaco: Marshal Estigarribia's Memoirs of the Chaco War, 1932–1935* (Austin, TX: University of Texas Press, 1950).

travel conditions. The Bolivian high command decided to send a small company of reinforcements to help resupply the troops.

Led by Captain Victor Ustariz, a company of fifty-eight men marched toward Boquerón. The captain arrived under the cover of night on September 20, and attacked the enemy at dawn. Ustariz was unable to break through, but his action rallied the men inside the fort and motivated them to hold on. Furious, Estigarribia mobilized more soldiers, surrounding the beleaguered redoubt with a force of twelve thousand. A deadly cordon strangled Boquerón for almost a month. Desperation spread through the ranks. Men were forced to eat their horses and mules. The Bolivian Air Force tried to resupply the base, but many of the crates fell into enemy hands. Out of ammunition, water, and food, Marzana finally surrendered at the end of the month.

The fall of Boquerón was a major psychological blow to the Bolivian Army. Panic spread throughout the scattered outposts, and many men deserted. Emboldened, Estigarribia decided to embark on an offensive campaign to move the area of operation toward the Pilcomayo River, on the western edge of the Chaco. He attacked and took the outposts of Corrales, Toledo, and Arce. The initial part of the war had been a constant seesaw, whereby Paraguay and Bolivia exchanged a series of border forts. However, the conflict was moving into a more mobile phase, with the Paraguayan Army conquering territory that had previously been Bolivian. This forced La Paz to change tactics and adopt a more defensive posture. In reality, Paraguay lost a perfect opportunity to end the conflict because the Bolivian military was in a complete state of disarray. It was clear that La Paz needed to do something drastic or else lose the war. Therefore, President Salamanca decided to replace General Osorio with his close ally General José Leonardo Lanza. He, in turn, appointed Colonel Bernardino Bilbao Rioja to head the field operations.

Colonel Bilbao Rioja was a consummate tactician, and a pioneer of military aviation. He rallied his men, dug in, and set up a defensive line at road marker Kilometer 7. The move detained the Paraguayan advance. This allowed the retreating army to regroup. Lanza believed that the army needed to shorten its supply lines by establishing a string of large depots in Villa Monte, Ballivián, and Muñoz. The congress, however, was losing confidence in the president's ability to prosecute the war, and they wanted to make a more profound change.

Therefore, they decided to replace Lanza with General Hans Kundt, a German officer and veteran of the First World War. He was a well-known figure in Bolivia, having arrived as a young officer at the turn of the century. He had run a very successful training program before being recalled to Germany at the start of the Great War. Kundt was the embodiment of the Prussian military figure. He fought with bravery and distinction on the eastern front, earning several decorations. He was well loved by his men, but was not as capable as Estigarribia. Not only was the latter able to motivate and direct his troops, but his tactical skills were spotless. Nevertheless, the Bolivian congress had high hopes. They petitioned the Weimar

Republic to send Kundt back, and forced President Salamanca to surrender control over all military affairs.[98] The president was happy to comply, believing that since Kundt was a foreigner, he would be less likely to meddle in political matters, and focus only on the prosecution of the war. Indeed, the German leader's main goal was to end the conflict swiftly. He believed that the only way Bolivia could do so was by embarking on an offensive drive that would allow it to deploy its superiority in population and wealth.

The military resources that had been requisitioned during the siege of Boquerón were finally arriving in the theater of operations, giving Kundt the troops and munitions he needed to start his campaign. For the first half of 1933, he launched a series of attacks on the border forts that had been lost the year before. He took many of them, but his focus came to bear on the imposing citadel of Nanawa. Kundt thought that by taking the fortification, he could roll up the Paraguayan flank and march toward Asunción. He assembled an army of nine thousand troops and advanced. In wave after wave of frontal attacks, the general repeated the senseless carnage of World War I. The enemy was ensconced in trenches and fortified revetments. They were armed with machine guns and mortars that cut down the attacking soldiers. Despite their enormous sacrifice, the Bolivians were unable to take the fort. Two thousand men fell in combat, including many of the army's best officers and soldiers. Finally, they were forced to pull back. This marked the most southern advance by the Bolivian Army, and now Estigarribia was free to resume his offense.

The Bolivian Army was again in disarray. The problems of communication, organization, and motivation were clear. Any setback could easily degrade into a rout, given that many of the indigenous soldiers felt little or no affinity for their country or its cause. Moreover, they were fighting in an alien land that had little to do with theirs. There was no martial spirit in the ranks. The army suffered more reversals at Alihuatá and Campo Grande, but the most humiliating loss occurred in early December 1933, in Campo Vía. Estigarribia was able to stealthily encircle two divisions of Bolivian soldiers. A regiment of three thousand soldiers was able to break out and escape, but ten thousand men were taken prisoner, along with all of their equipment and provisions. This marked the single-largest defeat in Bolivian military history. A week after the disaster at Campo Vía, General Kundt resigned and returned to Cochabamba. After a year at the head of the army, he never saw the field of battle again.

The crushing defeat of Campo Vía and Kundt's resignation made it seem as if the war was over. In an act of humanitarian compassion, since it was the onset of the Christian Christmas holidays, President Ayala agreed to a cease-fire on December 19. Estigarribia welcomed the lull to rest his men, consolidate his position, and incorporate the treasure trove of munitions, fuel, and equipment that had been

---

[98] Hans Kundt and Raúl Tovar Villa, *Campaña del Chaco: El General Hans Kundt, Comandante en Jefe del Ejército in Bolivia* (La Paz: Editorial Don Bosco, 1961).

captured, but the cease-fire turned out to be a colossal mistake. Instead of using the truce to prepare a peace plan, the Bolivians used it to change their leadership, regroup, and resume the war.

Their first order of business was to appoint a new military commander. The baton was passed to General Enrique Peñaranda, the fourth and last leader of the conflict. Peñaranda had made a name for himself by leading the regiment that escaped from Campo Vía. However, he had relied heavily on two of his close lieutenants, Colonel Angel Rodriguez and David Toro. The former was a crack military strategist, the latter a Machiavellian genius. These two officers shaped many of the decisions during the last phase of the campaign. The second order of business was the regrouping of the Bolivian Army. In January 1934, the first of three hundred Chilean mercenary officers began to arrive and integrate themselves into frontline units. The troops also received new equipment to replace what had been lost, bringing in modern armaments. Last of all, a stream of fresh recruits began to augment the soldiers who had fallen in combat or been taken prisoner.

Many Paraguayan soldiers used the crease fire to visit their families. The high command had acquiesced to the furloughs, thinking that the conflict was practically over, but it soon became clear that the Bolivians were using the lull to prepare for a new offensive. There had been no diplomatic activity, and intelligence sources reported the movement of men and supplies to the front. As a result, leave passes were cancelled and the soldiers were forced to return to their units. On January 7, 1934, the truce expired and Estigarribia decided to resume his attack. However, he had lost his momentum. It was the onset of the rainy reason and the army could not move. Dirt roads turned into mud fields and progress was next to impossible. The Bolivians were also more motivated. Their ranks had been replenished by fresh recruits, and they were now operating closer to home. Therefore, they were able to gain better access to supplies and reinforcements.

As a result, they scored a series of small victories in the battles of La China, Campo Jurado, and Conchitas. At the Battle of Cañada Strongest, Peñaranda took a page out of Estigarribia's playbook by encircling two divisions. The units were attempting to outflank and take Ballivián, the army's bastion on the Pilcomayo River. The fortification had more than eighteen thousand troops and huge stores of ammunition, guns, and fuel. Destroying it would cripple the Paraguayan Army and destroy its capability to fight. On May 10, the plan went awry when the attackers were spotted by a Bolivian reconnaissance squad. The wily Colonel Rodriguez ordered his units to surround the approaching soldiers. A bloody melee ensued, where more than four hundred Paraguayans died. With no chance of escape, twelve hundred men surrendered. The capitulation resulted in a huge capture of guns, cannons, and trucks. It was the biggest Bolivian victory of the war, but dark days were not far ahead.

Despite the Paraguayan setback at Ballivián, Estigarribia had regained his momentum. He decided to shift the theater of operations farther north toward the

Paraguay River. He drove his men in a series of lightening attacks against the enemy at the desert camps of Picuiba and Carandayti. His objective was to outflank Ballivián, cutting off the bastion and choking it to death. He was under pressure to end the war quickly. The economic situation in Paraguay was becoming desperate; President Ayala had informed him that the country's resources were running out, and he could not reinforce him with additional equipment. At the same time, the Bolivians began to realize that the massive concentration of men and munitions was more of a liability than an asset. It anchored the army in one corner of the Chaco, reducing its ability to move freely through the region to take advantage of an opponent that was becoming weaker. Still, President Salamanca was afraid that Ballivián was too much of a political symbol to abandon. Soon, however, the country's leadership would be rattled by another disastrous defeat that would force it to take more aggressive action.

Halfway through the year, La Paz decided to make a push for the Paraguay River. The government remained under pressure from Standard Oil to secure a port so it could easily ship its oil. The military operation would be launched from the fort of Ingavi, but the Paraguayans learned of the plan and decided to thwart the attack. Instead of confronting the enemy at Ingavi, they decided to cut of its supply route. This involved taking a smaller fort, Cañada El Carmen.

Major Oscar Moscoso, the Bolivian officer who had led the first engagement of the war, was in charge of the fort. His forces had been greatly reduced in order to support some of the ongoing battles. He had been ordered to send reinforcements to help the beleaguered men at Picuiba and Carandaiti. He also sent three thousand men to reinforce Ballivián. Nevertheless, he still had two divisions at his disposal. Estigarribia decided he would drive a wedge between El Carmen and Ballivián, in order to prevent them from reinforcing each other. He then ordered his men to move up both sides of the fort and circle around, cutting it off from any hope of escape or rescue. El Carmen was in the middle of desert, with no access to water. On November 16, cut off from water for weeks and with little will to fight, it fell, with seven thousand men and all of its equipment, leaving Ballivián was totally exposed.

The news arrived in Ballivián in the midst of a rowdy party. Many politicians and members of the senior staff were inebriated. However, with the enemy at his flank, Peñaranda had no other choice but to order his men to torch the ammunition dumps and retreat toward Villa Montes, the last redoubt. The retreat was disorderly, and the enemy followed in hot pursuit. There were attempts to counterattack at Guachalla and Estrella, but the Bolivian soldiers' morale was shattered. The memories of the repressive methods used by the government to put down the insurrections were still fresh, and many deserted as the enemy approached. They crossed the Pilcomayo River and fled for their lives into Argentina.

The situation was so grim that President Salamanca decided to replace the high command once more. Ten days after the retreat from Ballivián, he flew to Villa Monte, without escorts or bodyguards. Peñaranda and the senior officers knew what was coming. Toro, who harbored presidential ambitions of his own, astutely devised a coup d'état to topple the leader. Senior officers surrounded the cottage where Salamanca was staying and forced him to resign. The reins of power were passed the next day to Vice President José Luis Tejada Sorzano.

The ringleaders blamed the deposed president for the fall of Ballivián. They argued that his refusal to disperse the troops and equipment to other outposts had made the fort extremely tempting to attack. They also said that his stinginess in mobilizing the country's resources was the reason why the war was going so poorly. Therefore, they rationalized, he had to go; they never doubted their own competence.

With the enemy in disarray, Estigarribia decided to press his advantage and bring an end to conflict. In the middle of January 1935, he advanced to the shore of the Parapetí River, the western boundary of the Chaco. This put him in firm control of the entire Chaco. Sadly, it was a Pyrrhic victory. The relentless advance into Bolivian territory had converted Paraguay into an aggressor country in the eyes of the League of Nations. Therefore, all arms sanction and embargos against Bolivia were reversed. Asunción reacted to the news by resigning its membership in the international organization.[99]

Salamanca's ouster allowed the high command to take off its gloves. On December 10, the government ordered a general mobilization, and a new army was prepared for battle. Troops and resources were moved to Villa Montes. Nestled in the lush forests that mark the foothills of the Andes, the soldiers were now in familiar territory. This was their land. They knew it. They loved it, and they were willing to die for it.

The Paraguayans were also in high spirits. Not only was the war going swimmingly well, a marvelous prize was within reach. The oil fields of Camiri were close on the horizon. Paraguay was bereft of oil, and it relied solely on Argentina for all of its energy needs. With the war grinding endlessly on, Buenos Aires was not interested in propagating it further. Therefore, it began reducing the supply of fuel in order to force the Paraguayans to the negotiating table. This made Asunción more eager to get its hands on Camiri. First, however, Estigarribia needed to destroy Villa Monte.

Colonel Bilbao Rioja, the heroic officer who had reversed the rout after the Battle of Boquerón by making a stand at Kilometer 7, was tasked with organizing the defense. Armed with refreshed and motivated troops, he was well prepared to repel the looming attack. Networks of interconnected and fortified trenches were dug around the perimeter. Reinforced bunkers were built to serve as barracks and command posts. Artillery crews staked out the entire outskirts of the fort in order to pour an endless barrage of shells on the oncoming enemy. On February 16,

---

[99] William R. Garner, *The Chaco Dispute: A Study of Prestige Diplomacy* (Washington, DC: Public Affairs Press, 1966).

1935, the Paraguayans attacked. In contrast to their previous operations, when they maneuvered deftly to envelope an outpost and lay siege, Estigarribia was forced to launch a frontal attack. Flanking maneuvers were easy in the empty plains of the Chaco, but they were much more difficult to coordinate and execute in the rugged Andean terrain. Wave upon wave of possessed soldiers charged against the well-emplaced defenders. The Paraguayans were desperate to destroy the fort and take possession of the towering oil derricks. Scores of soldiers were mercilessly cut down by machine guns and shredded to pieces by artillery shrapnel. The troops broke through the outer defenses, and almost penetrated the fort on several occasions, but the casualties were starting to mount. Paraguay was running out of men. Recruiters were conscripting fourteen-year-old boys and men over fifty to replenish the ranks. After a week of senseless carnage, the high command realized that the campaign was futile. Not only was Villa Monte impenetrable, Paraguay's supply lines were stretched and vulnerable to attack. The roles had reversed. The Bolivians were now closer to home, while the Paraguayans were far away. Nevertheless, Estigarribia noticed that the Bolivians were hunkered down in their foxholes. Therefore, he decided bypass the fort and advance toward the oil fields.

The Paraguayan thrust toward Camiri sent shock waves through La Paz. Suddenly, Standard Oil reversed its bellicose stance and argued that the war had to end. With the Chaco lost and its existing oil fields at risk, the company needed to end the conflict or face unacceptable losses. Paraguay was also willing to end the war. Its economy was shattered and population depleted. Even though it had the wind at its back, Asunción could no longer afford to fight. Last of all, the international community was putting pressure on the two nations to stop fighting. Two wars were raging through South America. Europe and Asia were being overrun by despots. Hence, it was time to end the carnage.[100] On June 14, 1935, the two sides agreed to a cease-fire.

Officers and soldiers came out of their trenches to hug each other and fraternize. The war represented a colossal cost that neither country could afford. Bolivia had lost fifty thousand men. Paraguay had lost thirty-five thousand, but given that its population was a third of Bolivia's, its losses had been proportionally greater. Paraguay gained most of the Chaco, but the fabled oil deposits were never found. For years, Paraguayan, British, and French prospectors drilled wells throughout the region, but they were all dry.[101] More than eighty-five thousand had lost their lives fighting for an empty patch of scrubland.

The Chaco War was the last major conflict between two South American nations. There would be border skirmishes in the Amazon, vestiges of the ongoing Rubber Wars, but the Chaco would be the last contested region on the continent. A

---

[100] Leslie B. Rout, *Politics of the Chaco Peace Conference, 1935–39* (Austin, TX: Institute of Latin American Studies, University of Texas Press, 1970).

[101] Farcau, *The Chaco War*.

series of international treaties finally defined the borders, and there were no more territorial uncertainties that could be exploited by international capitalists. The next war would be partially fought for maritime territory, but the main driver was the hearts and minds of domestic constituencies.

8 THE MALVINAS: WAR IN THE SOUTH ATLANTIC

THE MALVINAS: WAR IN THE SOUTH ATLANTIC

The low roar of the Atar 101 engine hummed in the background as Lieutenant Commander Roberto "Tito" Curilovic gingerly eased his Super Étendard to an altitude of ten meters. A convoy of three enemy ships had been spotted two hundred kilometers north of the Malvinas, providing a plump target. On the afternoon of May 25, 1982, Argentina's Independence Day, he took off from Río Grande naval air base, along with his wingman, Julio "Leo" Barrazza. At 4:30 p.m., their British-made Agave radar spotted the formation of ships on the distant horizon. Setting their computers in attack mode, the two airplanes launched their AM 39 Exocet missiles. Unbeknownst to the Argentine crew, one of the ships in the formation was the aircraft carrier HMS *Hermes*. Not only was the ship a key component of NATO's front line of defense, it was the task force's command ship. Sinking such a valuable asset would mark the end of the British adventure.

Alarms rang through the decks as the three ships' radars detected the incoming missiles. Swinging into the direction of the attack to provide the narrowest target and smallest radar cross section, the crew of one of the accompanying ships deployed its chaff canisters to interfere with the radar. The wind caught the cloud of aluminum strips and carried it away from the carrier, and in the direction of the SS *Atlantic Conveyor*, a heavily laden roll-on, roll-off container ship. The chaff expanded the container ship's radar image. The missile's control system was programed to lock onto the target with the largest cross section. Seconds before impact, the sea-skimming Exocets suddenly veered toward the merchant ship, which brimmed with fuel, munitions, and stores, detonating it in a blinding fireball. Sheer luck, rapid reaction, and a puff of wind narrowly averted the defeat of the British navy.

The Malvinas, also known as the Falklands, are a desolate outpost deep in the South Atlantic. The two main islands are East and West Falklands, each a hundred kilometers long, totaling an area of twelve thousand square kilometers. They are separated by a body of water called Falkland Sound. Sparsely inhabited, their main industries in 1982 were fishing and sheepherding. The archipelago had been colonized by a variety of nations, including France, the Netherlands, Spain, and Great Britain. After its war of independence, Argentina had also established a presence on the islands. However, it was ousted in 1833, when the British returned. From then on, they boosted their colonization efforts, establishing whaling and fishing industries. The advent of the steamship allowed the islands to become a strategic coaling station during the latter half of the nineteenth century.[102]

Things suddenly changed at the turn of the twentieth century, when the navy decided to use oil as its main source of fuel, thus minimizing the importance of coaling stations. The decline of the empire in the aftermath of World War I further reduced its importance. At the same time, the islands were seen as a symbol of European imperialism. Argentina laid claim to them, arguing that they had been part of the colonial viceroyalty. In 1953, President Juan Domingo Perón offered to buy the archipelago, but England refused. The islanders strongly rebuked the initiative, and the government acquiesced to their request. Two decades later, when Perón was back in office, the England offered to share the islands; he jumped at the deal, but when he died three weeks later, the offer was shelved.

The Malvinas was one of the last border disputes in South America. Most of the major differences had been settled through two hundred years of wars and negotiations. Four years earlier, a question about the boundaries in the Beagle Channel had almost led to war. The Argentine Navy moved into position and was hours from launching an attack against Chile, but mediation by the pope settled the matter. The competing claim on the islands was more of an afterthought than anything else. They were very far away. The capital of Port Stanley was more than twelve thousand kilometers from London and fifteen hundred kilometers from Buenos Aires. There had been rumors that there were large oil deposits close to the coastline, but nothing was ever discovered. In reality, the British colony was a painful drain on the government's coffers.

The 1970s were not kind to the United Kingdom. Struggling to emerge from the ravages of World War II and the collapse of its empire, the UK economy limped along. In the early 1980s, the country was mired in an unending recession. Stiff competition from Germany and Japan led to a decline in manufacturing. More than three million British citizens were unemployed, and bloody riots gripped the nation. Technological changes, particularly the ascendency of electric-powered trains, the advent of nuclear power, and the proliferation of gas turbines, reduced the demand for coal. This led to a sharp rise in labor unrest, especially among well-organized miners. Frustrated by the ongoing social and economic malaise, the electorate swung to the right in 1979, electing Margret Thatcher as prime minister. She immediately put in place a new set of policies to deregulate the economy, privatize state-owned companies, and relax labor laws.[103] Of course, the measures led to a violent backlash. The country was rocked by a series of crippling strikes and widespread social unrest. Thatcher's popularity plunged. With her back up against the wall, she was in dire need of some way to rally the nation and divert the public's attention away from its domestic affairs.

[102] Bonifacio del Carril, *The Malvinas/Falklands Case* (Buenos Aires: CIGA, 1982).

[103] Eric J. Evans, *Thatcher and Thatcherism* (London: Routledge, 1997).

The 1970s were also difficult for Argentina. The death of President Perón in 1974 destabilized the country. The presidency was passed to his wife, Isabel Martínez de Perón, who had served as his vice president. A former cabaret entertainer with just a fifth-grade education, she lacked the knowledge and skills necessary to run a country. For the next two years, she was heavily controlled by José López Rega, a fascist and astrologer who became her minister of social welfare despite his ties to the Argentine Anticommunist Alliance, an alleged death squad.

At the same time, a leftist insurgency was spreading throughout South America. With student and worker militancy on the rise, the military staged a coup in March 1976, and launched a brutal repression program. Tens of thousands disappeared, were murdered, or exiled. A series of oil shocks also hit the Argentine economy at the start of the decade, forcing it to rely heavily on external loans to balance its external accounts. Macroeconomic mismanagement led to a combination of high inflation and deep recession. Social unrest rose.

Like Margaret Thatcher, Argentina's military junta was desperate to take the public's attention away from the domestic front. It had already resorted to chicanery in the past, bribing the Peruvian football team so it would not advance to the finals of the World Cup. Now, it needed another publicity stunt. General Leopoldo Galtieri had recently toppled General Roberto Viola, and he needed to engender popular support. For this reason, he ordered a full invasion of the Malvinas and South Georgian Islands. Buenos Aires expected the United Kingdom to be too distracted by its own domestic problems to care. Moreover, the Argentines doubted there would be a counterattack, since that would be too costly for the economically strapped country. Last of all, they believed that the looming South Atlantic winter would dissuade the British Royal Navy from trying to retake the islands.

Thus it was that junta expected that its invasion would unleash a wellspring of nationalist fervor in Argentina, and without Argentina having to bear the cost of a military reprisal. Unbeknownst to them, the invasion was a godsend for Prime Minister Thatcher, who was also looking for a distraction.

The international environment during the 1970s was complex. The world was still mired in the depths of the Cold War. The United States and the Soviet Union had fought proxy wars in Africa and Southeast Asia. When Communist subversives infiltrated much of South America, Central America, and the Caribbean, leading to leftist uprisings, the United States had countered by setting up clandestine programs, such as Operation Condor, to foster military dictatorships that suppressed and dismantled communist movements. Argentina was one of the United States' closest allies in that process.[104] The 1970s was also a period of enormous capital flows. The oil shocks had left large money center banks flush with cash that needed to be reinvested. Ready and willing to take on new loans, Argentine military

[104] Cecilia Menjívar and Néstor Rodriguez, *When States Kill: Latin America, the U.S., and Technologies of Terror* (Austin: University of Texas Press, 2005).

leaders used the funds to modernize their equipment. They acquired state of the art planes and missiles, thus modernizing the national arsenal.

The commitments of the Cold War had forced Britain to dedicate enormous resources to its military. Its navy was much smaller than during World War II, but it still had a number of aircraft carriers, cruisers, and frigates. This equipment was an essential component of NATO's northern front, and it could not be placed at risk to protect far-flung colonies. Hence, both countries had the means and reasons to fight. They were each looking for a distraction, and a military conflict was just the thing. An incident a month before the actual invasion gave a precursor of what was to come. A group of Argentine metal workers, many of them disguised military personnel, had been hired on the South Georgia Islands to dismantle an old whaling station. They had suddenly proclaimed the island as Argentine territory and hoisted the national flag. The men were arrested and repatriated, but the crowds in Buenos Aires roared with approval. This feeler campaign convinced the generals to go ahead with a more audacious plan.

The invasion, code named Operation Blue, began on April 2, 1982. A squad of divers secured the beach at Port Stanley. This was followed by landings of amphibious vehicles. Unprepared for the assault, a company of sixty-nine Royal Marines put up a tepid defense, knowing it was futile to resist. They were too far away to wait for reinforcements, and they were too outnumbered to have any chance of survival.[105] Therefore, they surrendered. The next day, a smaller invasion force took the South Georgia Islands, removing all British presence from the South Atlantic.

The enterprise was initially supposed to be a short-lived affair. The junta wanted to demonstrate to the world that it could take the islands, but a mob of two hundred thousand people spontaneously poured into the streets of Buenos Aires to celebrate the victory. The outpouring of public support convinced the junta to replace the invasion force with an occupation force. People jammed the Plaza de Mayo in the center of Buenos Aires, praising the government. They sang songs proclaiming the rout against the British and warning the Chileans that they were next.[106] The Beagle incident left Argentina bitter taste, and there was a general sense of resentment between the two countries.

Fearing their neighbors to the east, the Chileans were more than ready to help the British. During the war, they passed on valuable human intelligence, radio intercepts, and telephone transmissions. They reported on ship movements. The Chilean intelligence post at Punta Arenas forwarded all aircraft traffic information to Santiago, where it was turned over to British military attachés, who relayed it to London. The information was good, but it was often outdated by the time it arrived at the fleet command post. British intelligence tried to reduce the relay time by

---

[105] Martin Middlebrook, *The Fight for the "Malvinas": The Argentine Forces in the Falklands War* (New York: Penguin, 1990).

[106] Martin Middlebrook, *The Argentine Fight for the Falklands* (South Yorkshire, England: Pen & Sword Military Classics, 2003).

secretly flying in radar and intelligence-gathering equipment to deploy along the border. The Chilean junta looked the other way, because they knew that unless the British defeated the Argentines, it was only a matter of time until they, too, came under attack.

That was why the British high command knew what was happening when an air bridge of Argentine transports began ferrying thirteen thousand conscripts and professional soldiers to replace the marines who had stormed the beaches. Ships carried heavy equipment, including tanks and artillery pieces. Field command was given to General Mario Menéndez, a veteran of the anti-insurgency operations. He concentrated the bulk of his forces on the western island, mainly around Port Stanley and the small airfield at Goose Green. The high command in Buenos Aires was sure that the British would not travel so far to rescue such a meaningless piece of real estate.

To their detriment, they did not fully comprehend the domestic situation in the United Kingdom, and Prime Minister Thatcher was anxious to show her resolve against powerful interest groups. She summoned her cabinet soon after the invasion and reviewed her options. Fortunately for all involved, one of them, a nuclear strike against Buenos Aires, was immediately shelved. The prime minister was determined to retake the islands, and she ordered the Royal Navy to prepare an invasion force. The admiralty appointed Rear Admiral Sandy Woodward to lead the flotilla. The admiral set the wheels in motion, preparing ships, troops, and equipment for deployment.

The armada set sail from Portsmouth, England, on April 19, slightly more than two weeks after the Argentines took Port Stanley. It was joined by nine warships that had been on a NATO exercise off the coast of Gibraltar. The task force of ninety-three ships stopped at Ascension Island, in the middle of the South Atlantic, to refuel and take on additional stores. The island is a giant volcanic rock that juts out of the ocean.

Among the additional stores were armaments, including AIM-9L Sidewinder missiles, the latest version of the American air-to-air missile, which had the capability of engaging enemy aircraft from any direction. The earlier version of the AIM-9 could only track aircraft in tail-chase engagements, in which the target's hot engines are facing the missile. However, since the AIM-9L had a cooled seeker head that allowed it to pick out the warmest parts in the sky, the new Sidewinder would represent an enormous advantage for British pilots, accounting for nineteen air-to-air kills.[107]

The US decision to support the British was made grudgingly. Efforts to defend colonial possessions were considered a thing of the past. Moreover, Britain was risking important NATO assets to recover a useless island. Nevertheless, President

[107] Brad Roberts, *The Military Implications of the Falkland/Malvinas Islands Conflict* (Washington, DC: Congressional Research Service, Library of Congress, 1982).

Ronald Regan had a strong affinity for Prime Minister Thatcher. They shared similar ideologies, and he admired her tenacity. Therefore, he ordered the Pentagon to pull out all the stops and supply the British with whatever equipment or intelligence they needed. A constant stream of airplanes flew from US bases to Ascension Island to bring the best technology to America's special friend. Satellites were redirected to orbit over the southern hemisphere to give London real-time intelligence on ship movements and intercepted communications. As a result, Britain was able to chip away at the advantage that the Argentines enjoyed in proximity.

The task force took a total of three weeks to reach the archipelago. It was divided into two components. The lead comprised two aircraft carriers and their support ships, and was tasked with securing air superiority over the theater of operations. The rear comprised the amphibious ships, which included requisitioned cruise ships, such as Cunard's *Queen Elizabeth 2* and P&O's SS *Canberra*. Along the way, Rear Admiral Woodhouse prepared the crews, conducting drills day and night. Marines honed their skills by shooting at floating targets and the pilots engaged in mock dogfights. Much of this was televised through the BBC, with the intent of demonstrating Britain's unwavering resolve.

In addition to HMS *Hermes*, the aircraft carrier HMS *Invincible* accompanied the flotilla. The two carriers carried a complement of twenty Sea Harriers, fighter jets designed and built by British Aerospace as vertical and/or short take-off and landing (V/STOL) aircraft. Not only would the Sea Harriers be able to operate on ships without the use of heavy catapults and arresting gear, but they were ideal for deployment from unprepared fields. This made them ideal for amphibious support, where runways were difficult to find.

As they made their way south, the sailors and soldiers longed for some progress on the diplomatic front. US ambassador to the United Nations Jean Kirkpatrick worked hard to avoid a war between two of America's closest allies. She could not see how these windswept islands could be worth fighting for. Behind the scenes, State Department Secretary Alexander Haig shuttled between the two countries trying to force them to the negotiating table. Peruvian President Fernando Belaúnde called Secretary Haig to offer his services, but there was little interest among the belligerents to negotiate. The wheels were in motion and the dogs of war were afoot.

The initial part of the voyage was pleasant, as the armada made its way through the tropics. Soon, however, the blue skies and turquoise waters gave way to the dark clouds and frosty chop of the South Atlantic. With winter looming, the crews prepared for action. It was time for Britain to show its fury. The first British operation was called Operation Paraquet, and it consisted of two components. It began with the establishment of a four-hundred-kilometer exclusive zone around the islands, which converted any vessels inside the area into armed combatants and thus liable for attack. This was done to limit the reinforcement and resupply of the deployed Argentine troops. The second part was the recapture of the South

Georgia Islands. The archipelago was far removed from the mainland, and it was defended by a small group of soldiers.

HMS *Antrim* was given the mission, and it brought along HMS *Plymouth*. A contingent of one hundred fifty SAS Special Forces was assigned to take the island. On April 25, the two ships delivered a thunderous artillery barrage into the surrounding hills to panic the defenders. The ploy worked. The Argentines capitulated without putting up a fight, but the victory almost turned into an enormous disaster when two helicopters ferrying a Special Air Service (SAS) team crashed in bad weather. Fortunately, there was no loss of life. The retaking of the Malvinas had started off well.

On May 1, the British task force crossed into the exclusion zone, but three enemy battle groups were converging at the same time. The aircraft carrier ARA *Veinticinco de Mayo* was approaching from the north, while a task force led by the cruiser ARA *General Belgrano* advanced from the south. Together, they would create a pincer attack on the British fleet. The nuclear-powered submarine HMS *Conqueror*, however, had been trailing the ARA *General Belgrano* for a few days. Although the World War II–era ship itself did not present a clear threat to the fleet, it was at the head of a pair of destroyers armed with Exocet missiles. Rear Admiral Woodward decided to make a show of force and ordered HMS *Conqueror* to engage ARA *General Belgrano*, but the cruiser had moved outside the exclusion zone. Needing clarification on how to proceed, the submarine's captain, Commander Chris Wreford-Brown sent a message London. The response was quick. The order to sink it came directly from Prime Minister Thatcher.[108] On the afternoon of May 2, HMS *Conqueror* fired a brace of three torpedoes. Two struck the ARA *General Belgrano*. One of them hit the bow and the other amidships, sinking it in less than forty-five minutes. About a third of the crew perished, unable to escape the icy water that rushed in, although some seven hundred were rescued. The show of force worked, and the Argentine Navy quickly backed away from the exclusion zone. The loss of the cruiser convinced Buenos Aires that its flagship was at risk. Therefore, it decided to redeploy the carrier's airplanes to land bases instead of risking such valuable assets. Hence, the next phase of the campaign moved aloft.

The arrival of the British fleet coincided with a British attack on Port Stanley Airport. Concerned that the Argentines would forward-deploy their jet bombers to the Malvinas, London decided to preemptively take out the airfield. That task was assigned to the Royal Air Force. An aging Vulcan bomber, along with a backup, was dispatched from Ascension Island to fly more than 12,600 kilometers so it could damage the runways with a string of thousand-pound bombs. The Vulcan had been designed during the late 1940s as a nuclear bomber, and it was completely obsolete. Indeed, that particular bomber was only three weeks away from being

108 Sandy Woodward, *One Hundred Days: The Memoirs of the Falklands Battle Group Commander* (Annapolis, MD: Naval Institute Press, 1997).

scrapped when it was tasked. However, it had one last mission to fly. The entire trip took twenty hours and required eleven tankers to complete. The bombers had not been aerially refueled for more than two decades, and they needed to be refitted for the new fuel ships. The daring operation, Operation Black Buck, left a crater in the middle of the runway that made the strip unusable for high-performance jet airplanes.[109] This forced the Argentines to base all of its air campaigns on the mainland, which limited their operational range.

The arrival of the British fleet off the coast of the Malvinas marked the start of the landing phase. Up to that point, the British had retaken the South Georgian Islands, sunk the ARA *General Belgrano*, and bombed Port Stanley Airport. The Argentines would soon have to go into action. Rear Admiral Woodward knew that the enemy airplanes would soon attack, so he ordered three of his Type 42 destroyers to take up picket positions at the far edge of his formation. The ships were armed with long-range radar and Sea Dart anti-air missiles. All three, HMS *Sheffield*, HMS *Glasgow*, and HMS *Coventry*, had been designed at the start of the Cold War. Their armaments were tailored to engage slow-moving, high-altitude Soviet bombers and cruise missiles, not fast-moving, low-altitude jets. They would soon realize how ill prepared they were.

HMS *Sheffield* was the first ship to feel the intensity of the Argentine fury. On May 4, Argentine patrol planes had detected the British destroyer earlier in the day, and the navy assigned two Super Éntendards from Río Grande airfield to take it out.[110] The French-made jets were loaded with Aérospatiale Exocets—seven-hundred-kilogram missiles that traveled at twice the speed of sound and had a range of seventy kilometers. The delivery tactics required the pilots to fly at very low altitudes to avoid detection. Once a target was acquired, the crews were ordered to advance to the launch window and fire the weapons, and then egress at a low altitude and return to base.

The Argentine pilots took off and proceeded to the target area. They worked hard to stay below the radar horizon, but were picked up by HMS *Coventry*. The destroyer went to battle stations, and warned HMS *Sheffield* of the incoming attack, but their message was never received. The HMS *Sheffield*'s crew was in a relaxed condition of readiness; there had been a long rash of false alarms, and the crew had decided to treat the incoming threat nonchalantly. The Argentine pilots maneuvered into range, fired their missiles, and escaped. HMS *Sheffield*'s radar system reported the incoming blips, but the officer of the watch disputed the information since no airplanes had been detected. Suddenly, a lookout spotted two incoming smoke plumes on the horizon. One of the missiles splashed into the water, but the other smacked the destroyer amidships. The warhead never detonated, but

---

[109] Andrew J. Brookes, *Vulcan Units of the Cold War* (Oxford: Osprey Publications, 2009).

[110] Paul Eddy, Magnus Linklater, and Peter Gillman, *War in the Falklands: The Full Story* (New York: Harper & Row, 1982).

twenty crew members died, twenty-four were injured, and the ship was lost. The missile's propellant spilled into the engine room and ignited. The impact disabled the water mains, which prevented the crew from combating the fire. Smoke and flames spread throughout the decks as damage control teams struggled to save the dying vessel. With casualties mounting, the commanding officer ordered his men to abandon ship. The hulk remained afloat for a few days, but rough seas made it founder. This marked the first combat loss for the British navy since World War II, with many more to come.

The next loss occurred a week later. On May 12, HMS *Glasgow*, another Type 42 destroyer, and HMS *Brilliant*, a Type 22 frigate, were on picket duty when they were attacked by a flight of A-4 Skyhawks, Douglas Aircraft Company jets designed during the 1950s as a carrier-based strike fighters. The Skyhawks had been workhorses during the Vietnam War. Although they were not as electronically sophisticated as the newer jets, they were highly maneuverable and effective. The Argentine bombers approached the two ships at low altitude and very fast. HMS *Brilliant* spotted the incoming threat and engaged its Sea Wolf missile system. The short-range battery swung into action, shooting down two Skyhawks. Soon another flight of bombers appeared on the horizon and pressed the attack. This time, however, the anti-air defensive system did not engage, and one of the warplanes dropped a bomb that pierced the hull of HMS *Glasgow*. The ordnance flew through the ship without exploding, but it left a gaping hole at the waterline, ruptured fuel lines, and disabled the two main engines. The ship did not sink, but it was out of commission and had to hobble back to Portsmouth.

The sinking of HMS *Sheffield* and the damaging of HMS *Glasgow* highlighted the extreme danger posed by the Argentine air force. At least four Exocets remained in Río Grande, and London was desperate to take them out. The SAS came up with Operation Mikado. It was loosely based on the Israeli raid on Entebbe, where a hundred commandos aboard a handful of Hercules C-130s managed to rescued 106 hostages. The idea behind Operation Mikado was that ninety British commandos would fly to Río Grande airfield and destroy the missiles, as well as any other military aircraft. In order to prepare for the mission, a stripped-down Sea King helicopter, loaded with an SAS reconnaissance team, departed on May 18 to set up an observation post on the outskirts of the base. On the way in, the helicopter flew into a dense fog and lost its way. Upon making landfall, the crew decided to fly to the Chilean border and unload the soldiers so they could proceed on foot.[111] They never made it to their destination, and they were eventually extracted by submarine. The Sea King helicopter was out of fuel and unable to return, so it flew toward the Chilean air base of Punta Arena; there, the crew destroyed their aircraft and escaped. They were eventually captured by a Chilean patrol, sent

---

[111] Alastair MacKenzie, *Special Force: The Untold Story of 22nd Special Air Service Regiment* (London: I. B. Tauris, 2011).

to Santiago, and repatriated. Although the Chilean junta lodged protests against London for the incursion into its air space, most people considered the protest to be a ruse, as it was clear that Santiago was aiding and abetting Argentina's enemy. However, the fighting was about to enter a more complicated phase and Britain needed all the help it could get.

The invasion force finally arrived on May 18. The formation of troop ships and ferries, carrying the amphibious landing force, was traveling at a slower speed. This allowed the advance portion of the fleet to clear the way. Sea Harriers pummeled Port Stanley Airport and readied the landing area. The amphibious operations began on May 21, with Major General Julian Thompson at the front. Commandos from the Royal Marines in the 3 Commando Brigade were the first off, hitting San Carlos beach. The Argentines were surprised by the location of the landing site; they had been waiting at Port Stanley, which was on the other side of the island. A series of feints kept the Argentines guessing, but they soon realized that the amphibious operation was taking place a hundred kilometers away. San Carlos had been chosen because the troops could get ashore there without having to deal with artillery threats and counterattacks. It was also inside Falkland Sound, which provided the ships with protection from the elements. However, the narrow stretch of water also reduced their ability to maneuver, thus making them more vulnerable in the case of aerial attack.

It did not take long for the bombers to arrive. The same day the landings started, HMS *Ardent* was attacked by a flight of Skyhawks. The frigate was shelling Goose Green when the bombers appeared. Commander Alan West immediately ordered his ship to take defensive maneuvers, but it was hit by a pair of MK-82 bombs. The ordnance exploded in the hangar deck, setting the ship on fire. Commander West was making way to rejoin the fleet and seek assistance when the HMS *Ardent* was beset by another flight of Skyhawks that riddled the ship with more bombs. The attack left the ship ablaze and unable to steer. With no other choice available, he ordered his crew to abandon ship.

All day, the fleet came under attack, as the landing ships disgorged their cargo. It turned out to be a brutal day for the Royal Navy. In addition to the sinking of HMS *Ardent*, four other warships were badly damaged. It was clear that the British were up against a formidable opponent.

The amphibious operation, unfortunately, moved glacially. This was made worse by the inclement weather, which slowed the loading of the boats. The paratroopers had no experience with beach landings, and there was a great deal of confusion when they hit the shore. The ships were in desperate need of air cover, but the low overcast grounded the Sea Harriers; given that the aircraft carriers were farther out to sea, they often faced tougher meteorological conditions.

The Argentines did not let up. Their airfields were not as adversely affected by the weather. Wave after wave of Skyhawks descended on the anchored fleet. With the transports lined up off the beach, it became known as "bomb alley," and during a five-hour period, more than sixty aircraft attacked the beachhead. Flying at rooftop level and at more than eight hundred kilometers per hour, the marauding jets were able to evade the ships' antiaircraft fire control systems, which could not lock onto the aircraft. The pilots hugged the island's rugged terrain to mask their approach. As the jets rose over the hills that overlooked the harbor, the pilots' windshields filled with the sight of the waiting ships. The Skyhawks swept across the water and drilled holes into the hapless ships. Many of the munitions failed to explode on impact because they were dropped from such low altitudes that they did not have time to arm. Still, the immense enthalpy of the hurtling projectile allowed it to rip through the ships, triggering fires, damaging equipment, and maiming crewmembers.

The failure of Operation Mikado meant that the British needed to have real-time information about incoming attacks in order to prepare their defenses. They deployed a pair of Nimrod surveillance planes out of a secret Chilean air base in the Pacific to monitor all movements in and out of Río Grande. The information helped, but it did not do much to counter the scale of the attacks. The Nimrod operations were in strict violation of Chile's neutrality, but Santiago did not care. Not only was Chile aiding the destruction of its enemy, but its assistance was seen by many as an act of gratitude for the important role Britain played in its various wars against Bolivia and Peru.

The next attack came on May 23, when HMS *Antelope*, a Type 21 frigate, was set upon by six Skyhawks. A bomb bounced short of the ship and pierced the hull without exploding. However, it detonated when a disposal team tried to defuse it, sinking the ship in the process. The navy decided that the best way to defend against the attacks was to place a gun line closer to shore. Walls of molten lead poured into the sky, splattering the water with shrapnel as the raiders approached, but the tactic had limited success. The British weapon systems were ineffective against the nimble jets. Therefore, they decided to use two decoys to lure them away from the disembarkations.

HMS *Coventry*, another Type 42 destroyer, and HMS *Broadsword*, a Type 22 frigate, were ordered to take up position at the northern edge of the sound on May 25. Argentine airplanes were swarming like hornets. It was Independence Day, and the junta needed a major victory. The prowling Skyhawks soon spotted the two ships. HMS *Broadsword* was armed with the Sea Wolf missile system, but its fire control systems failed to lock before the screaming jets released their bombs. One of them bounced off the surface of the ocean and destroyed the frigate's Lynx helicopter before plunging into the sea. The other tore into the destroyer, exploding below the main operations center and the forward engine room. Fires broke out and the ship began to list. Within twenty minutes, the captain ordered the crew to abandon ship. Explosions ripped through the decks before it capsized and sank. HMS *Coventry* was lost, but the landings were saved. Later that day, however, an Exocet would take out HMS *Atlantic Conveyor* and bring the operation to within an inch of defeat—had it sunk the aircraft carrier HMS *Hermes*.

With the beachheads established and supplies ashore, most of the troops set out for Port Stanley. Meanwhile, a battalion of paratroopers, 2 Para, under the command of Lieutenant Colonel "H" Jones, was sent to take Goose Green. The airfield was defended by a regiment of nine hundred men and threatened the invading force's right flank. Most of the Argentines were recent recruits, but they were highly motivated. They had dug into positions on the hills leading into the town. On the night of May 28, the paratroopers pounced, but the recruits put up a fierce firefight. The British did not expect to encounter so much resistance, and they failed to reach their objective by dawn. As the sun rose, the men had no place to hide and they came under withering machine gun fire. When Colonel Jones saw that the situation was becoming desperate, he called for a frontal attack against the main Argentine position. The colonel was known for his reckless bravery. He personally led the charge, but was killed immediately.

Command was passed to Major Chris Keeble, who called for close air support. His men were still pinned down when a pair of Sea Harriers swept in from the horizon and dropped a dozen cluster bombs on the Argentine position. The deadly ordnance is packed with hundreds of submunitions designed to spread across a very large area. This makes the weapon very effective against unprotected personnel. The cluster bombs spread terror in the Argentine ranks, and they began to pull back. After fifteen hours of fighting, Major Keeble sent a note to the defending commander saying that unless his men surrendered, he would order in more cluster-bomb attacks. The bombs had sown so much terror in the ranks that they decided to capitulate.[112] In the end, the Argentines reported fifty losses. The paratroopers lost seventeen. However, the engagement at Goose Green made it clear that the land campaign was going to be as difficult as the landing phase.

With the momentum moving against Argentina, Peru decided to wade in. The unmistakable assistance provided by the United States and Chile convinced the Peruvians that there was no such thing as neutrality in this conflict. Argentina had always been an ally against Chile, so it was time to return the favor. Therefore, in early June, President Belaúnde agreed to sell the Argentines a squadron of Mirage Vs, along with munitions, at knockdown prices. On June 3, a flight of ten fighters took off from their air base at La Joya, Peru, and proceeded to Tandil airfield in the province of Buenos Aires. The flight straddled the Chilean-Bolivian border, favoring the Bolivian side, until it entered Argentine airspace. The aircraft never saw battle, but their presence was seen as a great source of regional solidarity just in time for the final phase of the war, the defense of Port Stanley.

The battle plan against Port Stanley initially called for the use of helicopter transports to ferry the troops from San Carlos, but the sinking of the HMS *Atlantic Conveyor* had destroyed them. Therefore, there was no other option but to cross the island on foot. In order to expedite the process, a unit of Welsh Guards was

[112] Gregory Fremont-Barnes, *Battle Story: Goose Green 1982* (London: The History Press, 2013).

boarded on the RFA *Sir Galahad* and RFA *Sir Tristan*, headed for Bluff Cove to be held as reinforcements. However, the seas were rough and the ships took shelter in Fitzroy, a small harbor. Unprotected by any frigates or destroyers, they were easy targets. The landing officer pleaded with the ships' commander to disembark the troops so they could disperse, but he refused, saying that his destination was Bluff Cove. Up to now, the sky had been gray and overcast. However, when the clouds broke and the sun came out, Argentine air observers were given a clear view of the anchored transports. They immediately called in an airstrike. The commanding officer of the RFA *Sir Galahad* had decided to disembark his men when a squadron of Skyhawks appeared, hitting the munitions hold and lighting the ship on fire. Tragedy ensued, as more than forty men were incinerated. Many more were seriously burned. As a result, the main force attacking Port Stanley was left without reinforcements.

The commandos finally reached the outskirts of Port Stanley on June 11, and they prepared for the final assault. Major General Jeremy Moore relieved Major General Julian Thompson when the men arrived. He was supposed to have been in charge of the land campaign from the very beginning, but he had been detained and been unable to sail with the original task force. His arrival did not result in any changes to the battle plan, however, and the operation continued to grind ahead. By now, the British had amassed nine thousand men. The Argentine defense was concentrated in a ring of surrounding hills. The British attack would consist of two nocturnal assaults, when darkness would give the soldiers cover from machine gun fire and aerial bombardment. The first thrust would sweep into the south. The principle objective was to secure Mount Longdon, whose commanding heights allowed the Argentines to control the approaches to Port Stanley. The second thrust would sweep north to overrun Mount Tumbledown, which marked the entrance to the town.

The first part of the attack commenced at 11:00 p.m. on June 11, when 3 Para assaulted Mount Longdon. Tracers filled the air and flares lit the night as the paratroopers fought their way up the cragged mountainside. Night fighting is a particularly gruesome experience, even when assisted by night-vision goggles. The defenders rolled grenades down the hill, producing heavy casualties. As the attackers crowned the heights, General Menéndez called in an artillery strike, killing many of his own men. Still, the paratroopers fought on, and by dawn, Mount Longdon was in British hands. Unfortunately, the cost had been high. A total of fifty-four men died: twenty-three British and thirty-one Argentines. More than 167 were wounded.

The second part of the attack occurred two nights later on June 13, when the Second Battalion of the Scots Guards took Mount Tumbledown. General Menéndez understood that this was his last line of defense. Its loss would result in total defeat. Therefore, he deployed the elite Fifth Marine Regiment to protect the heights. More than seven hundred Argentine marines moved into position. In recent times, the Scots Guards, originally personal bodyguards to the monarch, had been known mainly for their ceremonial role. For example, they stand guard duty outside Buckingham Palace and accompany with the queen's retinue. Yet, they are a fighting force, and they fared well that frigid night as they made their way up the mount, taking cover behind the rocks strewn across the rugged terrain. A platoon of guardsmen flanked the defenders and set up a machine gun nest. The Argentines scattered for cover when the Scots Guard opened fire. Seeing the Argentine Marines in disarray, the Scots Guard made a frontal charge and took the redoubt. Many thought that the Battle of Mount Tumbledown was going to be the bloodiest battle, but just than thirty men died in the battle: the Argentines lost twenty, and the British lost ten.

The fall of the surrounding hills gave the British full command over the town. Helicopters lifted in artillery pieces, and the British began to pummel the approaches to the village. The constant hail of incoming shells destroyed Argentine morale. Recruits surrendered in droves. Sea Harriers added to the mayhem by making more cluster-bomb attacks. By now, the Argentine Naval Air Force had curtailed its attacks due to its significant losses. Finally, after three weeks of fierce fighting, Menéndez capitulated on June 14. The British had been outnumbered since the start of the war, but better coordination between land, sea, and air units, as well as strong leadership from commissioned officers and noncommissioned officers, allowed them to win. As in so many of the previous conflicts, the Malvinas War was a senseless loss of lives. The British casualties totaled 255 killed and 775 wounded; the Argentine casualties totaled 648 killed and 1,657 wounded. Three civilians died in the shelling. This time, the lives were not sacrificed for a commodity, but for the hearts and minds of two populations, to distract their attention from what was going on at home.

The use of war for domestic objectives is a risky proposition, with extreme payoffs and penalties. Clausewitz stressed that the outcomes of military engagements are hard to predict, calling it the "fog of war." For Prime Minister Margret Thatcher, the Malvinas turned out to be a huge success, despite Britain's massive disadvantage in prosecuting a campaign on the other side of the planet. It was the catalyst she needed to generate a wellspring of public support. Not only did it reverse her negative image, it propelled her to victory in the 1983 general elections. She remained in office until 1990, spearheading an ideological revolution that transformed the country and most of the world. Her unyielding doggedness and the legacy of her victory in the South Atlantic helped contribute to the collapse of the Soviet Union. The opposite happened to the Argentine dictators. The humiliating loss meant the death knell of the military junta. Within three days of the defeat, General Galtieri was ousted. Suppressed by years of repression, Argentina's democratic forces were resurrected.

The Malvinas was not a war between two South American states, but regional countries played important roles. Chile provided intelligence that became an integral part of the British campaign. Years later, Margret Thatcher assisted former Chilean dictator Augusto Pinochet after he was arrested in London, claiming that her country was deeply indebted to him for his cooperation during the operation. The help provided to Argentina by Peru was not as great, but it helped show a sense of regional solidarity.

In the end, the Malvinas was a bloody episode of modern warfare. In contrast to what is presented in the popular media, the Argentines fought very well. They took on one of the most sophisticated navies in the world, and came within seconds of defeating it. Its sailors, soldiers, and particularly airmen performed with distinction and bravery. Although no other South American country was directly involved, it was a hallmark example of what happens when Latins fight.

UNFINISHED BUSINESS

South America is not known for its belligerence, but its history has been as violent as other parts of the world. Since independence, the member countries fought a long succession of wars that separated South America into a patchwork of independent countries. The conflicts evolved from spear-carrying gauchos to trench warfare to low-flying cruise missiles. A vast cast of characters dominated the stage: selfless heroes like Paraguayan Major Pedro Duarte, who took on the brunt of the allied attack at the Battle of Yatay Creek during the War of the Triple Alliance, and Eduardo Abaroa, the Bolivian engineer who single-handedly defended the Topáter Bridge during the War of the Pacific; dashing leaders like General Manuel Bulnes, the Chilean military leader who thrived on unwinnable odds during the War of the Confederation, and Óscar Benavides, the indefatigable Peruvian major who was sent to oust the Colombians from the Putumayo during the Colombian-Peruvian War of 1932. There were also a fair number of cowards and buffoons, with Bolivian General Hilarión Daza topping that list; not only did his inept military skills convert his army into a rabble of drunks stumbling through the Atacama Desert, but he contributed enormously to the allied defeat. General Hans Kundt would not too far behind on that list. The Prussian general was great on the parade field, but disastrous on the battlefield. The wars highlighted the best and worst of the South American soldier, from the Brazilian mobs who populated much of the Acre War to the highly disciplined Argentine aviators who brought the British Royal Navy to the brink of defeat.

Many factors shaped the wars. They were influenced by institutional qualities and military leadership. In all of the conflicts, the organizational capabilities of the military were essential in determining the outcomes. The naval legacies left by the Portuguese court imbued Brazil with the maritime resources to decide the outcome of the Cisplatine and Platine Wars, the first confrontations to highlight the importance of the navy. The imperial fleet took control of the River Plate and choked off the commercial lifeblood of Buenos Aires. The professionalism of the Chilean officer corps allowed it to take on two larger adversaries during the War of the Confederation and the War of the Pacific, but the baseness of the conscript was a serious liability, particularly during the War of the Pacific. Given its vast coastline, it was not surprising that Chile would dedicate so many resources to its navy. This allowed it to establish command of the seas in both wars and win both contests. The institutional strengths of the Paraguayan Army allowed it to hold off the two largest countries in South America, but the sheer size of the opponents eventually overwhelmed it. Meanwhile, the proficiency of the Colombian high command convinced it to rearm before prosecuting a conflict in the middle of the Amazon.

Indeed, the quality of the officer corps is a key factor in any military conflict. The coordination of strategy and the execution of tactics depend totally on the training, skills, and commitment of the individuals tasked with implementation. It can make all of the difference between victory and defeat, despite the availability of equipment and soldiers. Bolivia and Peru illustrated this several times. In spite of their immense wealth and size, they were often hampered by the poor quality of their officer corps. Bolivia's military was top-heavy, with too many officers and not enough soldiers—a legacy of the Spanish Empire, when the officer corps was one of the few venues that creoles could use for upward social mobility. Middle class South American families competed to enroll their sons in officer training programs, while few individuals volunteered for the enlisted ranks. The flaw was in plain view during all three of the Bolivian conflicts: the War of the Confederation, the War of the Pacific, and the Chaco War. The military campaigns were also hampered by leadership problems back home. The instability of the Bolivian political system distracted the high command to the point that it was more interested in what was happening in La Paz rather than what was happening on the front. General Narciso Campero's decision to return home with the elite Fifth Division during the War of the Pacific was a deliberate tactical move to torpedo President Hilarión Daza. Likewise, President José Manuel Pando was more worried about leaving the politically unstable capital undefended than he was about keeping his army deployed to defend the lucrative rubber industry in Acre. Of course, the saddest incident was General Enrique Peñaranda's decision to overthrow President Daniel Salamanca in the midst of an outright retreat during the Chaco War. Unfortunately, Peru was not too far behind. Lima's decision not to assist Arica while it was under Chilean siege was mostly motivated by President Mariano Ignacio Prado's desire to squash the political prospects of Colonel Francisco Bolognesi, who was tasked with defending the port.

Societal conflicts were another institutional factor that affected the efficacy of the military. The War of the Confederation was as much a Peruvian civil war as it was a conflict between the alliance and Chile. The animosity cut two ways. The struggle was between northern and southern Peru, as well as between the indigenous and creole populations. A similar phenomenon occurred during the Chaco War, when many of the Quechua and Aymara recruits felt that there was no reason to fight for a country that had little regard for their basic civil liberties. This led to a high rate of desertion and capitulations in the Bolivian Army, even when the Bolivians had superiority in arms, munitions, and equipment. Of course, the opposite also occurred. Strong cultural bonds could create a common identity that allowed countries to take on superior adversaries. This happened during the War of the Triple Alliance. The campaign was really a genocidal war of extermination against the Guaraní, whose pride imbued the Paraguayan population with the strength to hold off an enormously superior force. It even allowed them to recruit Guaraní descendants from the enemy countries. Chile's strong sense of common identity also imbued its soldiers with the will to fight against a much larger foe. Senator Benjamín Vicuña Mackenna's ability to convert the loss of the *Esmeralda* into a victory and Commander Arturo Prat into a national martyr rallied the nation to fight an illegal war for the commercial gain of a handful of British merchants.

Climatic conditions were also important. Most people consider South America to be a tropical paradise, but its wars were fought in extreme settings. From the blazing heat of the Atacama Desert to the arid scrubland of the Chaco to the freezing conditions of the South Atlantic, South American soldiers and sailors were forced to endure the worst privations. Often, the oppressive environment was too much to endure. Bolivia's indigenous community fared poorly in the heat of the Atacama or the dampness of the Amazon or the bone-dry scrubland of the Chaco. The raw recruits from Northern Argentina had never encountered the cold of the Malvinas. Moreover, the immune systems of the Colombian police force sent to the Putumayo were not prepared for the tropical diseases that infest the Amazon.

Another important institutional quality that affected the wars was the military's ability to manage its logistics. All of the conflicts had important supply difficulties, due largely to the vast distances between key locations in South America. This ranged from the imperial Portuguese troops deployed in the Uruguayan pampas that were under constant attack from Artigas's gauchos to the warring garrisons in the Putumayo to the forward-deployed armada in the Malvinas. One of the biggest challenges in many of the South American wars was the ability to keep the troops fed and armed. The scarcity of water was often an obstacle, since many of the conflicts were fought in extremely arid regions. Therefore, logistics officers needed to make provisions for all water and forage.

However, the common denominator in almost all of the conflicts was boundary issues. The unexpected collapse of the Spanish Empire left unanswered questions about the lines of demarcation. Most of the disputes were settled amicably, but regions that contained valuable natural resources were often contested through wars. Many of these conflicts were abetted by foreign powers, particularly Great Britain. It played a central role in the development of the region, much more than any other nation. Even the United States played a smaller role, especially during the nineteenth century when it was in the midst of its gestation.

Conflict	Boundary Dispute	Contains Valuable Natural Resource	Foreign Instigator
Cisplatine-Platine	No	Yes	Yes
War of Confederation	No	No	No
War of Triple Alliance	No	Yes	Yes
War of the Pacific	Yes	Yes	Yes
Rubber Wars	Yes	Yes	Yes
Chaco War	Yes	Yes	Yes
Malvinas War	Yes	No	Yes

Many of the boundary conflicts were settled through the creation of buffer states. It is important to highlight that these buffer states were established by dividing regions in a way that would impede interactions between hostile countries, which brings us to one of the major conclusions of the book.

My main objective was to develop a deeper understanding of South America, to understand why the region had never coalesced into a single political entity. I wanted to understand the forces that prevented the separate countries from uniting. From a geographical standpoint, the South American wars help explain the formation of the political map: the four main viceroyalties of Brazil, Peru, Nueva Granada, and River Plate sit at the heart of the South American jigsaw puzzle. The modern states that are the legacies of these colonial units are now the four largest countries in South America. However, they are separated by four small countries—Uruguay, Paraguay, Bolivia, and Ecuador—that were created as buffers to impede contact. Just as isolators help insulate electrical currents, the buffer states were meant to reduce all interaction.

The creation of the buffer states was an expedient solution to a diplomatic problem, but they were designed with little consideration to the economic viability of these nations and the impact they would have on the continent. Many of the new nations lacked the natural resources or scale to be economically viable. Two of them were landlocked, making it difficult for them to trade with the international community. As a result, these buffer states became some of the most challenged and impoverished countries of South America. They also impeded the flow of the factors of production that are essential for economic integration, as the free movement of goods, capital, and labor fosters cooperation and integration.

The only way South America can advance to a higher level of political integration is by increasing trade and investment, which means that the buffer states are the key to the region's future. There needs to be a concerted plan to strengthen these nations by funneling to them the capital they need to construct new roads, railroads, and infrastructure. This will allow them to be converted from mere insulators to conduits of commerce and investment. Such cooperation will go a long way to erase the lingering grudges that crowd the region's psyche.

In the end, the South American wars were bloody affairs with countless episodes of atrocities and human rights violations. Many of the rivalries and hatreds that still permeate South American societies originated in these conflicts, but the wars were also important cauldrons that formed states and forged nations. As in other parts of the world, these conflicts could be used as catalysts to engender greater cooperation and integration. That is why we need to have a better understanding of the forces and ramifications of when Latins fight.

BIBLIOGRAPHY

ABECIA BALDIVIESO, Valentín. *La dramática historia del mar boliviano*. La Paz, Bolivia: Librería Editorial "Juventud," 1986.

ALEXANDER, Robert J. and ELDON M. Parker. *A History of Organized Labor in Bolivia*. Westport, CT: Praeger Publishers, 2005.

ALVAR LÓPEZ, Manuel. *Manual de dialectología hispánica: el español de América*. Barcelona: Ariel, 1996.

BANDEIRA, Moniz. *La Formación de los estados en la Cuenca del Plata: Argentina, Brasil, Uruguay, Paraguay*, 1st ed. Buenos Aires: Grupo Editorial Norma, 2006.

BARRETT, William E. *Woman on Horseback: The Biography of Francisco López and Eliza Lynch*. New York: Fredrick A. Stokes Company, 1938.

BENTO DA SILVA, Francisco and RODRIGUES DE ALBUQUERQUE, Gérson. "O Bolivian Syndicate e a questão do Acre," *História Viva*, January 3, 2004.

BETHELL, Leslie (Ed.), *Colonial Brazil*. Cambridge: Cambridge University Press, 1987.

BETHELL, Leslie. *Colonial Spanish America*. Cambridge: Cambridge University Press, 1987.

BETHELL, Leslie. *The Paraguayan War, 1864–1870*. London: Institute of Latin American Studies, 1996.

BONTINE CUNNINGHAME GRAHAM, Robert. *Retrato de un dictador: Francísco Solano López, 1865–1870*. Buenos Aires: Inter-Americana, 1943.

BOSCH, Beatriz. *Urquiza: gobernador de Entre Ríos, 1842–1852*, 2nd. ed. Paraná, Argentina: Editorial de Entre Ríos, 2001.

BREMER, Stuart. "Dangerous Dyads: Conditions Affecting the Likelihood of Interstate War, 1816–1965," *Journal of Conflict Resolution* 36, no. 2 (1992): 309–341.

BROOKES, Andrew J. *Vulcan Units of the Cold War*. Oxford: Osprey Publications, 2009.

BÚLNES, Gonzalo. *Historia de la Campaña del Perú en 1838*. Santiago de Chile: Imprenta de los Tiempos, 1878.

CARRIL, Bonifacio del. *The Malvinas/Falklands Case* Buenos Aires: CIGA, 1982.

CAVIERES, Eduardo and Crístobal Aljovín de Losada. *Chile-Perú, Perú-Chile en el Siglo XIX: La formación del estado, la economía y la sociedad*. Valparaíso, Chile: Ediciones Universitarias de Valparaíso, Pontificia Universidad Católica de Valparaíso, 2005.

CENTENO, Miguel Angel. *Blood and Debt: War and the Nation-State in Latin*

CENTENO, Miguel Angel. *Blood and Debt: War and the Nation-State in Latin America*. University Park, PA: Pennsylvania State University Press, 2002.

CHARLES, Daniel. *Master Mind: The Rise and Fall of Fritz Haber, a Nobel Laureate Who Launched the Age of Chemical Warfare*. New York: Ecco, 2005.

CHIAVENATO, Julio José. *La Guerra del Petróleo*. Buenos Aires: Punto de Encuentro, 2007.

CLEATON, Christin. *Spaniards, Caciques, and Indians: Spanish Imperial Policy and the Construction of Caste in New Spain, 1521–1570*. Saarbrücken, Germany: VDM Verlag, 2008.

CLUNY, Claude Michel. *Atacama: ensayo sobre la Guerra del Pacifico, 1879–1883*. México, DF: Fondo de Cultura Economica, 2008.

COLLIER, Richard. *The River that God Forgot: The Story of the Amazon Rubber Boom*. New York: Dutton, 1968.

DANILO ARZE AGUIRRE, René. *Breve Historia de Bolivia*. Sucre: Universidad Andina Simón Bolívar, 1996.

DE LA PEDRAJA, René. *Wars of Latin America, 1948–1982: The Rise of the Guerrillas*. Jefferson, NC: McFarland & Company, Inc., 2013.

DE LA PEDRAJA, René. *Wars of Latin America, 1982–2012: The Path to Peace*. Jefferson, NC: McFarland & Company, Inc., 2013.

DE LA PEDRAJA, René. *Wars of Latin America: 1899–1941*. Jefferson, NC: McFarland & Company, Inc., 2006.

DIEHL, Paul F., and GOERTZ, Gary. *War and Peace in International Rivalry*. Ann Arbor, MI: University of Michigan Press, 2000.

DONOSO ROJAS, Carlos and ROSENBLITT BERDICHESKY, Jaime. *Guerra, región, y nación: la Confederación Peru-Boliviana, 1836–1839*. Santiago de Chile: Ediciones de la Dirección de Bibliotecas, Archivos y Museos, 2009.

ECHÁVEZ-SOLANO, Nelsy and DWORKIN Y MÉNDEZ, Kenya C. (Eds.), *Spanish and Empire*. Nashville, TN: Vanderbilt University Press, 2007.

EDDY, Paul, LINKLATER, Magnus, and GILLMAN, Peter. *War in the Falklands: The Full Story*. New York: Harper & Row, 1982.

ENCINA, Francisco Antonio. *Portales: Introducción a la historia de la época de Diego Portales, 1830–1891*. Santiago, Chile: Nascimento, 1934.

ESTIGARRIBIA, José Félix. *The Epic of the Chaco: Marshal Estigarribia's Memoirs of the Chaco War, 1932–1935*. Austin, TX: University of Texas Press, 1950.

EVANS, Eric J. *Thatcher and Thatcherism*. London: Routledge, 1997.

FAGUNDES, Antonio Augusto. *Revolução Farroupilha: Cronologia do Decênio Heróico, 1835 à 1845*, 2nd ed. Porto Alegre, Brasil: Martins Livrerio, 2003.

FARCAU, Bruce W. *The Chaco War: Bolivia and Paraguay, 1932–1935*. Westport, CT: Praeger, 1996.

FELIÚ CRUZ, Guillermo. *Historiografía Colonial de Chile,* Santiago de Chile: Fondo Histórico y Bibliográfico. Santiago: José Toribio Medina, 1958.

FERGUSON, Niall. "Complexity and Collapse: Empires on the Edge of Chaos," Foreign Affairs, March/April 2010.

FLÓREZ, Luis. El español hablado en Colombia y su atlas lingüístico: presente y futuro de la lengua española. Madrid: OFINES, 1964.

FOOTE, Nicola and HARDER HORST, René. Military Struggle and Identity Formation in Latin America: Race, Nation, and Community During the Liberal Period. Gainesville: University Press of Florida, 2010.

FREMONT-BARNES, Gregory. Battle Story: Goose Green 1982. London: The History Press, 2013.

GALDÁMEZ LASTRA, Fabio. Historia militar de Chile: estudio crítico de la campaña de 1838-1839. Santiago de Chile: Trabajo Premiado En El Certámen Del Centenario, 1910.

GANSON, Barbara Anne. The Guaraní Under Spanish Rule in the Río de la Plata. Palo Alto, CA: Stanford University Press, 2003.

GARNER, William R. The Chaco Dispute: A Study of Prestige Diplomacy. Washington, DC: Public Affairs Press, 1966.

GAYLORD WARREN, Harris and WARREN, Katherine F. Paraguay and the Triple Alliance: The Postwar Decade, 1869-1878. Austin, TX: University of Texas at Austin, 1978.

GÓES, Marcus D. João: O Trópico Coroado. Río de Janeiro: Biblioteca do Exército Editora, 2008.

GRAHAM-YOOLL, Andrew. Imperial Skirmishes: War and Gunboat Diplomacy in Latin America. New York: Interlink Books, 1983.

GUERRA, João Paulo. Descolonização Portuguesa: O Regresso das Caravelas, 1st ed. Alfragide, Portugal: Oficina do Livro, 2012.

HARTLEY Jeffrey, William. Mitre and Urquiza: A Chapter in the Unification of the Argentine Republic. Madison, NJ: Library Publishers, 1952.

HENSEL, Paul R. and ALLISON Michael E. "The Colonial Legacy and Border Stability: Uti Possidetis and Territorial Claims in the Americas." Paper presented at the International Studies Association Meeting, Montreal, 2004.

HEWLETT, John Henry. Like Moonlight on Snow: The Life of Simón Iturri Patiño. New York: R. M. McBride & Company, 1947.

HOLLETT, David. More Precious than Gold: The Story of the Peruvian Guano Trade. Madison, NJ: Fairleigh Dickinson University Press, 2008.

JACKSON, Joe. The Thief at the End of the World: Rubber, Power, and the Seeds of Empire. New York: Viking, 2008.

KIPLE, Kenneth F. A Movable Feast: Ten Millennia of Food Globalization. Cambridge: Cambridge University Press, 2007.

KLOOSTER, Wim. Revolutions in the Atlantic World: A Comparative History. New York: New York University Press, 2009.

KOKOTOVIC, Misha. The Colonial Divide in Peruvian Narrative: Social Conflict and Transculturation. East Sussex, England: Sussex Academic Press, 2007.

KUNDT, Hans and TOVAR VILLA, Raúl. *Campaña del Chaco: el general Hans Kundt, Comandante en Jefe del Ejército en Bolivia*. La Paz: Editorial Don Bosco, 1961.

LA FOY, Margaret. *The Chaco Dispute and the League of Nations*. Bryn Mawr, PA: Bryn Mawr College, 1941.

LAGOS, Ovidio. *Arana, Rey del Caucho: terror y atrocidades en el alto Amazonas*. Buenos Aires: Emecé, 2005.

LEUCHARS, Christopher. *To the Bitter End: Paraguay and the War of the Triple Alliance*. Westport, CT: Greenwood Press, 2002.

LIMA, Oliveira. *Dom João VI No Brazil: 1808–1821*. Río de Janeiro: De Rodrigues & Co., 1908.

LYRA, Heitor. *História de Dom Pedro II, 1825–1891*. São Paulo: Companhia Editora Nacional, 1940.

MACK FARAGHER, John. *A Great and Noble Scheme: The Tragic Story of the Expulsion of the French Acadians from their American Homeland*. New York: W.W. Norton, 2005.

MACKENZIE, Alastair. *Special Force: The Untold Story of 22nd Special Air Service Regiment*. London: I. B. Tauris, 2011.

MACLEOD, Murdo J. and WASSERSTROM, Robert (Eds.). *Spaniards and Indians in Southeastern Mesoamerica: Essays on the History of Ethnic Relations*. Lincoln, NE: University of Nebraska Press, 1983.

MAESTRI, Mário. *Guerra no Papel: História e Historiografia da Guerra no Paraguai, 1864–1870*. Porto Alegre, Brazil: PPGH FGM Editora, 2013.

MARCHANT, Anyda. "Dom João's Botanical Garden," *Hispanic American Historical Review*. 41, no. 2 (1961), 259–274.

MARCO, Miguel Angél de. *La Guerra del Paraguay*, 1st ed. Buenos Aires: Planeta, 2003.

MARLEY, David F. *Wars of the Americas: A Chronology of Armed Conflict in the New World, 1492 to the Present*. Santa Barbara, CA: ABC-CLIO, 1998.

MATHEW, William M. *La firma inglesa Gibbs y el monopolio del guano en el Perú*. Lima: Banco Central de Reserva del Perú, 2009.

MENJÍVAR, Cecilia and RODRIGUEZ, Néstor. *When States Kill: Latin America, the U.S., and Technologies of Terror*. Austin: University of Texas Press, 2005.

MESQUITA, Otoni M. de. *La Belle Vitrine: Manaus Entre Dois Tempos 1890–1900*. Manaus: EDUA, 2009.

MIDDLEBROOK, Martin. *The Argentine Fight for the Falklands*. South Yorkshire, England: Pen & Sword Military Classics, 2003.

MIDDLEBROOK, Martin. *The Fight for the "Malvinas": The Argentine Forces in the Falklands War*. New York: Penguin, 1990.

MOLANO, Walter Thomas. *In the Land of Silver: 200 Years of Argentine Political-Economic Development*. North Charleston, SC: CreateSpace, 2012.

MONIZ BANDEIRA, Luiz Alberto "O Barão de Rothschild e a questão do Acre," *Revista Brasileira de Política Internacional* 43, no. 2 (2000).

MORITZ SCHWARCZ, Lília. *The Emperor's Beard: Dom Pedro II and the Tropical Monarchy of Brazil*, 1st American ed. New York: Hill and Wang, 2004.

OSCAR ACEVEDO, Edberto. *La intendencia del Paraguay en el Virreinato del Río de la Plata*. Buenos Aires: Ediciones Ciudad Argentina, 1996.

PAYRÓ, Roberto P. *El Río de la Plata: de colonias a naciones independientes: de Solís a Rosas, 1516–1852*. Buenos Aires: Alianza Editorial, 2006.

PINEDA CAMACHO, Roberto. *Holocausto en el Amazonas: una historia social de la Casa Arana*. Bogotá: Planeta Colombiana Editorial, 2000.

RAMÍREZ, Carlos María. *Artigas: debate entre "El Sud-América" de Buenos Aires y "La Razón" de Montevideo*. Montevideo: A. Barreiro y Ramos, 1884.

RAVEST MORA, Manuel. "La Casa Gibbs y el monopolio salitrero peruano: 1876–1878," *Historia* 41, no. 1 (2008): 63–77.

RELA, Walter. *Colonia del Sacramento: historia política, militar, diplomática 1678–1778*. Montevideo, Uruguay: Academia Uruguaya de Historia, 2006.

ROBERTS, Brad. *The Military Implications of the Falkland/Malvinas Islands Conflict*. Washington, DC: Congressional Research Service, Library of Congress, 1982.

ROBINS, Nicholas A. *Mercury, Mining, and Empire: The Human and Ecological Cost of Colonial Silver Mining in the Andes*. Bloomington, IN: Indiana University Press, 2011.

ROCA José Luis, *Ni con Lima ni con Buenos Aires: la formación de un Estado nacional en Charcas* (Lima: Instituto Francés de Estudios Andinos, 2007.

ROCCO, Fiammetta. *Quinine: Malaria and the Quest for a Cure that Changed the World*. New York: Harper Collins, 2003.

RODRÍGUEZ ALCALÁ, Guido and ALCÁZAR, José Eduardo. *Paraguay y Brasil: documentos sobre las relaciones binacionales, 1844–1864*. Asunción: Editorial Tiempo de Historia, 2007.

ROMERO, Javier. "The War of the Pacific," *Strategy and Tactics* 262, no. 5 (2013)

ROSS, Gordon. *Argentina and Uruguay*. New York: Macmillan, 1916.

ROUT, Leslie B. *Politics of the Chaco Peace Conference, 1935–39*. Austin, TX: Institute of Latin American Studies, University of Texas Press, 1970.

RUIZ MORENO, Isidoro J. *El Misterio De Pavón: las operaciones militares y sus consecuencias políticas*. Buenos Aires: Claridad, 2005.

SALAS-EDWARDS, Ricardo. *The Liquidation of the War on the Pacific: Nitrate and the War. A Fantastic Indemnity. The Government of Chili and the Creditors of Peru. The Question of Arica and Tacna. The Relations between Chili and Bolivia. What Chili Spends On Armament*. London: Dunlop & Co., Ltd., 1900.

SANTA CRUZ, Oscar de. *El general Andrés de Santa Cruz, Gran Mariscal de Zepita y el Gran Perú: documentos históricos*. La Paz, Bolivia: Escuela Tipográfica Salesiana, 1924.

SCHEINA, Robert L. *Latin America's Wars, Volume I: The Age of the Caudillo, 1791–1899*. Washington, DC: Brassey's Incorporated, 2003.

SCHEINA, Robert L. *Latin America's Wars, Volume II: The Age of the Professional Soldier, 1900–2001*. Washington, DC: Brassey's Incorporated, 2003.

SCHOFIELD SAEGER, James. *Francisco Solano López and the Ruination of Paraguay: Honor and Egocentrism*. Lanham, MD: Rowman & Littlefield, 2007.

SKIDMORE, Thomas E. Brazil: *Five Centuries of Change*, 2nd ed. Oxford: Oxford University Press, 2010.

TULLY, John. *The Devil's Milk: A Social History of Rubber*. New York: Monthly Review Press, 2011.

VALE, Brian. *Cochrane in the Pacific: Fortune and Freedom in Spanish America*. London: I. B. Tauris, 2008.

VAN VALEN, Gary. *Indigenous Agency in the Amazon: The Mojos in Liberal and Rubber-Boom*. Bolivia, 1842–1932. Tucson: University of Arizona Press, 2013.

WERLICH, David P. *Peru: A Short History*. Carbondale: Southern Illinois University Press, 1978.

WOODWARD, Sandy. *One Hundred Days: The Memoirs*

INDEX

2 Para, 172

Abaroa, 99, 100, 177

Abtao, 102

Aguirre, Atanasio, 70

Al-Andalus, 19

Almirante Cochrane, 98, 99, 102, 104, 105, 106

Alto Perú, 22, 24, 48

Amazonas, 76, 77, 126, 127, 129, 130

ammonium nitrate, 95

Ancash River, 61, 62, 63,

Anglo-Paraguayan Land Company, 91

Antofagasta, 97, 98, 99, 100, 101, 104, 105, 106, 118, 126, 127

APRA, 134

Aquidabán River, 67

Arana, Julio César, 129, 130, 131, 144

Arequipa, 48, 53, 57, 58

Arequipe, 112, 114

Arica, 48, 51, 64, 100, 102, 106, 107, 108, 109, 110, 111, 114, 115, 118, 178

Arteaga, Luis, 110

Artigas, José Gervasio, 33, 35, 40, 179

Ascension Island, 165, 166, 167

Atacama Desert, 13, 48, 54, 96, 97, 99, 100, 101, 105, 106, 108, 112, 115, 116, 119, 126, 134, 144, 149, 177, 179

Atar 161

Atlantic Conveyor, 161, 171, 172

Ayacucho, 47, 125, 126

Ayala, Eusebio, 150, 152, 154

Banco de Valparaíso, 97

Baquedano, Manuel, 111, 112, 113, 114, 115, 116, 117

Baron of Rio Branco, 128, 129

Barrazza, Julio "Leo", 161

Barroso, 76, 77, 88

Base Sur, 139

Battle of Angamos, 106

Battle of Campo Vía, 152, 153

Battle of Cañada de Gomez, 153

Battle of Caseros, 82

Battle of Cepeda, 35

Battle of Dolores, 110

Battle of Ilo, 111

Battle of Ituzaingó, 36

Battle of Matucana, 60

Battle of Miraflores, 116, 117

Battle of Moquegua, 111, 112

Battle of Pavón, 69, 74

Battle of Pisagua, 107, 108

Battle of Riachuelo, 77

Battle of River Buin, 61

Battle of Saraguro, 52

Battle of Socabaya, 53

Battle of Tacna, 113, 114

Battle of Tarqui, 130

Battle of Topáter Bridge, 99, 100,177

Battle of Yatay, 177

Battle of Yungay, 62, 63

Bay of Mejillones, 97

Belaúnde, Fernando, 166, 172

Belém, 126, 128

Belmont, 76

Benavides, Óscar, 131, 134, 177

Beresford, William Carr, 34

Berro, Bernardo, 70

Bilbao Rioja, Bernardino, 151, 155

Blanco Encalada, 55, 98, 99, 105, 106
Blanco, Carlos, 147
Blancos, 38, 39, 40, 41, 70, 72
Blasco Núñez Vela, 45
Bluff Cove, 173
Bolívar, Simón, 13, 23, 45, 47, 48, 52, 96, 130, 131, 144
Bolivian Syndicate of New York, 128, 129
Bolognesi, Francisco, 110, 114
Bonaparte, Joseph, 31
Bosch, 41
Bosch, Carl, 95
Bourbon Reforms, 22, 46, 49, 51
Braden, Spruille, 147
Braganza family, 9, 29, 30
Brown, William (Guillermo), 36
Bruguez, José María, 75
Buendía, Juan, 107, 108, 109, 110
Buenos Aires, 4, 23, 31, 32, 33, 35, 36, 37, 38, 39, 41, 47, 48, 51, 55, 56, 57, 67, 68, 69, 70, 71, 73, 74, 78, 81, 82, 85, 86, 87, 90, 91, 100, 104, 118, 129, 145, 147, 148, 155, 162, 163, 164, 165, 167, 172, 177
Bulnes, Manuel, 58, 59, 60, 61, 62, 63, 177
Bynnon, Jorge, 60, 61
Cabanagem, 39
cabichui, 81
Cabrera, Ladislao, 99
Cáceres, Andrés Avelino, 110, 116, 117
Callao, 54, 55, 56, 57, 58, 60, 61, 62, 102, 115, 116, 117
Callejón Huaylas, 61
Camiri, 145, 147, 155, 156
Campero, Narciso, 108, 111, 113, 178
Canberra, 166
Cápac, Lord Huayna, 135
Caquetá River, 129, 131, 133, 134
Caracol, 96, 99
Casa Frick, 144

Casa Gibbs, 97
Caste system, 21, 45, 47
Ceará, 125
Cenepa Basin, 138, 139
Cerro Corá, 67, 90
Chaco War, 7, 13, 143, 144, 146, 148, 150, 152, 156, 178, 179
Chacras, 137
Charcas, 46, 47, 48, 51, 145
Charles I, 45
Charles IV, 30, 32
Chiloé, 55
Cisplatine, 12, 32, 35, 36, 179
Cisplatine War, 7, 29, 30, 31, 32, 34, 36, 37, 38, 40, 41, 42, 68, 71, 92, 177
Cobija, 48, 53, 57, 64, 100
Colchagua Battalion, 62
Cold War, 163, 164, 168
Colónia do Sacramento, 32
Colonial organization, 22
Colorados, 38, 39, 40, 70, 72
Commander Condell, 103
Compañía de Salitres y Ferrocarriles de Antofagasta, 97, 98
Concordia, 77, 79
Cóndor Ridge, 138, 139
Confederation, 7 , 44, 12, 13, 14, 24, 33, 38, 39, 45, 46, 48, 50, 52, 53, 54, 55, 56, 57, 58, 59, 60, 61, 62, 63, 64, 69, 95, 96, 100, 116, 117, 177, 178, 179
Cordoba, 20, 33, 38
Correia da Câmara, José Antônio, 67, 90, 91
Corrientes, 73, 74, 75, 77, 78, 79, 81
Corumbá, 72
Count of Eu, 89, 90
Covadonga, 103, 104, 114, 116
Curilovic, Roberto "Tito", 161
Curuguaty, 90
Curupayty, 81, 83, 84, 85, 86, 118
Curuzu, 81, 83, 84
Dangerous Dyads, 11

Dávila, Juan, 101, 103
Daza, Hilarión, 98, 99, 102, 108, 109, 111, 177, 178
De la Mar, José, 52, 53
Decembrada, 89
Diehl, Paul, 11
Dom João, 29, 30, 31, 32, 33, 34
Dom Pedro, 34, 35, 36, 37, 40, 78, 79, 85, 89, 90, 91
Doña Carlota Joaquína, 32, 33
Dorrego, Manuel, 36
Dourados, 72
Duke of Caxias, 87, 88, 89, 90
Eastern Band, 32, 33, 34, 35, 36
Enduring Rivalries, 11
Entre Ríos, 33, 37, 38, 41, 71, 72, 78, 81, 91
Escala, Erasmo, 107, 108, 109
Esmeralda, 101, 102, 103, 104, 179
Estero Bellaco, 83
Estigarribia, Antonio de la Cruz, 77, 79, 80, 118
Exocet Missle, 161, 167, 168, 169, 171
Fall of Granada, 20, 23
Farroupilha Rebellion, 40, 41, 71, 78
Ferdinand VII, 30, 51, 89
Ferrocarril Central de Paraguay, 148
Flores, Venancio, 70, 71, 72, 73, 79, 80, 83, 84, 91
Fort Ballivián, 151
Fort Boquerón, 147, 149,151,152
Fort Carandayti, 154
Fort El Carmen, 154
Fort Muñoz, 151
Fort Picuiba, 154
Fort Vanguardia, 147
Fort Villa Monte, 151, 154, 155, 156
Francisco Burdett O'Connor, 53
Francisco Pizarro, 45
Freire, Ramón, 49, 50, 54, 55, 56
Frías, Tomás, 98
Galtieri, Leopoldo, 163, 174

Gálvez Rodríguez de Arias, Luis, 126, 127
Gamarra, Agustín, 52, 53, 54, 58, 59
General Belgrano, 67, 167, 168
Goertz, Gary, 11
Goodyear, Charles, 123
Goose Green, 165, 170, 172
Gran Colombia, 14, 51, 52, 135
Grau, Miguel, 103, 104, 105
Guano, 96, 97, 102
Guaraní, 40, 41, 42, 67, 73, 78, 79, 91, 143, 145, 178
Güepí River, 133
Guilarte, Eusebio, 62
Haber, Fritz, 95
Herrera, Ramón, 53
HMS Antelope, 171
HMS Ardent, 170
HMS Brilliant, 169
HMS Broadsword, 171
HMS Conqueror, 167
HMS Coventry, 168, 171
HMS Glasgow, 168, 169
HMS Hermes, 161, 166, 171
HMS Invincible, 166
HMS Sheffield, 168, 169
Huancavelica, 48
Huáscar, 102, 103, 105, 111, 112, 115, 135
Hullet & Co, 49, 55
Humaitá, 73, 76, 77, 81, 83, 86, 87, 88, 125, 145
Humala, Ollanta, 64
Independencia, 102, 103, 104
interregional conflicts, 11, 12, 13
Iquitos, 129, 130, 131, 132, 133 135, 136
Jesuits, 45, 46, 68
Jones, H., 172
José Félix Estigarribia, 150
Junot, General Jean-Andoche, 29
Junta of Seville, 31
Keeble, Chris, 172
Kew Botanical Gardens, 124

Klooster, Wim, 12
Kundt, Hans, 151, 152, 177
Lanús, Anacarsis, 82
Lanza, José Leonardo, 151
Leticia, 130, 131, 132, 133, 134
Lezama, José Gregorio de, 82
Liberating Crusade, 70
Lima, 31, 46, 47, 49, 50, 51, 52, 53, 54,
    55, 58, 59, 60, 62, 63, 87, 96, 97, 100,
    101, 106, 108, 113, 114, 115, 116, 117,
    130, 131, 132, 133, 134, 135, 136, 138,
    139,149, 178, 179
Llallagua Mine, 143
López, Eliza Lynch, 69, 90, 91
Luque, 88, 90
Magallanes, 102, 105
Manaus, 126, 127, 129, 133
Mapuche, 55
Marañón River, 135, 136, 137, 138
Margret Thatcher, 162, 163, 165, 166,
    166, 167, 174, 175
Markham, Clements, 123
Marquês de Olinda, 71, 75, 76, 77
Marques Lisboa, Joaquim, 70
Marquis of Tamandaré, 70, 81, 82, 85
Marzana, Manuel, 150, 151
Mato Grosso, 32, 72, 81, 84, 125, 129,
    144
Mena Barreto, João Manuel, 90
Mendoza Leiva, Abelardo, 134
Menéndez, Mario, 165, 173, 174
Meza, Pedro Ignacio, 75, 76, 77
Miranda, Francisco, 45
Mitre, Bartolomé, 69, 70, 71, 73, 74, 79,
    81, 82, 83, 84, 85, 86, 87, 91, 118
Mollendo, 112
Monteagudo, Bernardo de, 47
Montero, Lizardo, 110, 111, 113
Montevideo, 31, 33, 35, 38, 39, 40, 41,
    71, 72, 91, 139
Moscoso, Oscar, 148, 154
Mount Longdon, 173

Mount Tumbledown, 173, 174
Napo River, 129, 132, 135, 136
Nimrod, 171
Norberto, Gentil Tristan, 127
Norte Chico Mountains, 96
North Group, 136, 137
O'Connor, Francisco Burdett, 53, 61
O'Higgins, Bernardo, 45, 49, 50, 99,
    102
Olaya Herrera, Enrique, 132, 133
Operation Condor, 163
Operation Mikado, 169, 171
Orbegoso, Luis José de, 53, 58, 59
Oruro, 109, 144, 146
Osorio, Filiberto, 149, 151
Pan de Azúcar, 61, 62, 63
Pando, José Manuel, 127, 128, 129, 178
Paposo River, 97
Paquisha Outpost Skirmish, 138, 139
Paraguayan patriotic army, 67
Paraná River, 39, 73, 74, 75, 76,77, 84
Parapetí River, 144, 155
Paso de los Libres, 77, 79
Paso de Patria, 81, 82,
Paso Pucu, 83
Patiño Mines & Enterprise Consoli-
    dated Inc., 144
Patiño, Simón Iturri, 144
Paunero, Wenceslao, 79, 86
Paysandú, 70, 71, 72, 73, 78
Paz, Marcos, 86, 87
Pedro Álvares Cabral, 29
Pedro II, 37, 39, 40, 78, 79, 85, 89, 90,
    91
Pedro Silva, 62
Peñaranda, Enrique, 153, 154, 178
Pérez, Candelaria, 62
Perón, Juan Domingo, 162, 163
Peruvian Amazon Company, 129, 130
Phillip II, 46
Phillipp Braun, Otto, 53
Piérola, Nicolás de, 111, 114, 115, 116

Pilcomayo River, 144, 151, 153, 154

Pinochet, Augusto, 175

Pinto, Aníbal, 99, 115

Pinzón, Luis Hernández, 95

Plácido de Castro, José, 128

Platine, 12, 29, 30, 31, 32, 34, 36, 37, 38, 40, 41, 42, 70, 71, 92, 177, 179

Ponsonby, John, 36

Port of Mollendo, 112

Port Stanley, 162, 164, 165, 167, 168, 170, 172, 173

Portales, Diego, 45, 50, 55, 56, 57

Potosí, 22, 37, 46, 48, 51, 67, 97, 143, 144, 146

Prado, Mariano Ignacio, 102,10, 111, 178

Praieira Revolt, 40

Prat, Agustín Arturo, 102, 103, 104, 179

Prieto, José Joaquín, 50, 58

Province of El Oro, 137

Puerto Acre, 126, 127

Puerto Bolívar, 137

Punta Arena, 169

Punta Arenas, 164

Putumayo, River Basin, 129, 130, 131, 132, 133, 134

Queen Elizabeth 166

Regional trade, 24, 54

religious and social order, 21, 22

Restoration Movement, 54, 55, 57, 59

RFA Sir Galahad, 173

Rímac, 105

Río de Janeiro Protocol of 1942, 137

Río de la Plata, 22, 23, 32, 37, 68, 78

Río Grande do Sul, 32, 40, 41, 71, 78

Ríograndense Republic, 40

Riva Agüero–Benavente Treaty, 100

Rivadavia, Bernardino, 36

River Plate, 32, 33, 35, 36, 37, 38, 46, 47, 48, 57, 67, 68, 177, 180

Rivera, Fructuoso, 39

Robles, Wenceslao, 74, 77, 80

Roca, Julio Argentino, 118

Rodríguez de Francia, José Gaspar, 68

Rodriguez, Angel, 153

Rojas, José Antonio de, 45

Rosario, 38

Rosas, Juan Manuel de, 37, 38, 39, 40, 41, 42, 55, 56

Royal Dutch Shell, 145, 146, 148

Royal Geographical Society, 123

Rubber Wars, 12, 123, 124, 125, 126, 129, 130, 132, 134, 136, 138, 139, 140, 156, 179

Salamanca, Daniel, 147, 148, 149, 150, 151, 152, 154, 155, 178

Salaverry, Felipe Santiago, 53, 57, 58

Salitre, 95

Salomón-Lozano Treaty, 131, 132, 134

San Carlos Beach, 170

San Fernando, 87, 88

San Lorenzo Island, 54

San Martin, Jose, 47, 51

Sanandita Oil Field, 144, 145, 147

Sánchez Cerro, Luis Miguel, 132, 133, 134

Santa Catarina, 32

Santa Cruz, 48, 51, 52, 53, 55, 56, 57, 60, 61, 62, 63, 144

Santa Fe, 33

São Borja, 77, 78

Scots Guards, 173, 174

Sea Harriers, 166, 170, 172, 174

Sidewinder Missile, 165

Siles Reyes, Hernando, 146

Simpson, Robert, 58

Skyhawks, 169, 170, 171, 173

Solano López, Francisco, 67, 68, 69, 70, 71, 73, 74, 75, 78, 80, 81, 82, 83, 84, 85, 87, 88, 89, 90, 91, 118

South Georgia Islands, 163, 164, 168

Special Air Service, 167, 169

Standard Oil, 144, 145, 147, 154, 156

Sucre, Marshall Antonio José de, 47, 47, 51

Super Éntendards, 4, 168
Super Étendard, 161
Tarapacá, 96, 101, 107, 109, 110, 111, 114, 115, 116, 118, 119, 133
Tejada Sorzano, José Luis, 155
Thatcher, Margaret, 162, 163, 165, 166, 167, 174, 175
The Devil's Paradise, 130
Theatro da Paz, 126
Third Republic of Acre, 128
Thompson, Julian, 170, 173
Tiwinza, 139
Treaty of Ayacucho, 125, 126
Treaty of Paucarpata, 57
Treaty of Tordesillas, 29, 125
Truth, 130
Tuyutí, 83, 84, 85, 86, 87, 88
Union, 105, 111
United Restoration Army, 58
Urquiza, 37, 38, 40, 41, 69,70, 71, 72, 73, 78, 82, 91, 92
Urquiza, Justo José de, 37, 40
Uruguaiana, 77, 78, 79, 80, 81, 82, 84, 118
USS Lackawanna, 115, 117
Uti possidetis juris, 23, 24, 47, 48, 125, 146
Valenzuela, Jerónimo, 62, 90

Varela, Felipe, 86
Vásquez Cobo, Alfredo, 133
Veinticinco de Mayo, 167
Vergara, José Francisco, 107, 110
Viceroyalties, 11, 22, 23, 29, 47, 180
Villa Montes, 154, 155
Villalba, Tómas, 72
Volta da Empresa, 128
Vulcan Bomber, 167
War of the Confederation, 11, 12, 13, 14, 24, 38, 39, 45, 58, 62, 63, 64, 95, 100, 107, 116, 117, 177, 178
War of the Pacific, 11, 13, 24, 95, 98, 100, 105, 114, 118, 119, 125, 126, 127, 147, 149, 177, 178, 179
War of the Triple Alliance, 11, 13, 40, 42, 67, 69, 78, 84, 89, 91, 92, 102, 104, 118, 119, 125, 127, 145, 146, 147, 177,178
Wickham, Henry, 123
Williams, Juan, 101, 102
Woodward, Sandy, 165, 167, 168
Wreford-Brown, Chris, 167
Yberá, 76
Ybicui, 90
Zamudio, Anselmo, 116
Zepita Battalion, 110

CPSIA information can be obtained
at www.ICGtesting.com
Printed in the USA
BVOW09*0056121116
467657BV00001B/1/P